I will confess that up until a few years ago I was a meat eat

or a mushroom burger topped with melted Swiss cheese on a grilled sesame bun or marinated grilled chicken, not to mention pork tenderloin coated in a garlic-Dijon mustard crust. But then, my eating habits began to slowly transform when a new family moved into the 1920's house that sits on ten acres directly across the street from where I live. Little by little, I watched the family convert the property into a farm and each week new animals began to appear--horses, a cow, a bull, goats, sheep, chickens, rabbits, dogs, and turkeys. In the evenings as my family and I sat down to dinner, from our bay window, we could see the chickens scurrying in the yard, the horses grazing in the fields, and we could hear the cow and bull loudly mooing. And then it hit me! How could I watch and enjoy those beautiful creatures day in and day out, especially at dinnertime while supping on a meal consisting of beef, pork, poultry or lamb?

My conscience grew heavy with guilt and I asked myself how could I possibly eat the very animals I enjoyed watching romping and grazing in the fields directly across the road from my home? At first, I decided I would omit all beef from my diet and then I subsequently decided to give up all meat. In the beginning, my decision to stop eating meat was quite difficult because I thought that my food choices would be limited, but my compassion for the animals helped me to stay true to my decision. I began experimenting in the kitchen to see how many meatless main courses I could create and that is how the idea for this cookbook was conceived...I would create 365 meatless meals, one for every evening of the year!

I have since learned that there are varying degrees of vegetarians. There are those folks who not only do not eat meat, but they also have eliminated all seafood and dairy products from their diets. There are some people who go so far as to not even eating honey because it is produced by bees! There are others who just omit red meat from their diets. As for me, I have eliminated all meats from my diet but I do eat sea food. For those of you who have decided to eliminate all meats from your diet or for those of you who may have decided to cut back on your meat intake, I hope you will enjoy experimenting with my 365 meatless recipes. Remember, no recipe is written in stone. As I have written before in my previous cookbook, *Italian Family Classics, Four Generations of Italian Recipes,* think of your kitchen as a laboratory. Experiment. Practice. Experiment again, and keep going until you personalize that recipe calling it your own.

Enjoy!

Maryann Perillo Karimi

THE MONTHS AT A GLANCE

January 1—Lasagna

2—Lentil Soup

3—Grilled Vegetable Panini

4—Steamed Mussels

5—Tomato Bisque Soup with Grilled Cheese Sandwiches

6—Spinach & Parsley Omelet

7—Beer Battered Fish & Chips

8—Baked Zucchini Casserole

9—Linguine with Italian Tuna, Garlic, & Oil

10—Broccoli & Cheese Twice Baked Potatoes

11—Cream of Asparagus Soup

12—Domates Yemistes Me Rizi/Baked Stuffed Tomatoes (Greek)

13—Fish Nuggets

14—Olive & Swiss Panini

15—Khoresh Bademjan/Eggplant Stew (Persian)

16—Carrot Soup

17—Fried Tilapia with Turmeric

18—Salad with Wild Rice

19—Mushroom Zucchini "Pasta"

20—Nacho Dinner

21—Baked Salmon Fish Sticks & Dipping Sauce

22—Meatless "Meat"ball Sandwiches

23—Sautéed' Winter Greens

24—Moroccan Soup

25—Chick Pea Chili

26—Wild Rice Cakes

27—Orecchiette with Mushrooms & Radicchio

28—Shepherd's Pie

29—Garlicky Shrimp & Fennel

30—Black Beans & Saffron Rice

31—Egg-Drop Noodle Soup

February 1—Braised Swordfish with Dates (North African)

2—White Pizza with Arugula

3—Sautéed' Mushrooms & Gorgonzola

4—Black-Eyed Peas & Collards

5—Israeli Couscous with Sun-Dried Tomatoes

6—Stir-Fried Chinese Noodles

7—Upside-Down Dinner: Baked French Toast with Pear & Gruyere

8—Grilled Red Snapper with Roasted Red Pepper Tapenade

9—Orzo & Pea Salad

10—Minestrone Soup

11—Italian Mac & Cheese

12—Vegetarian Stuffed Peppers

13—Asian Glazed Tilapia

14—Fondue Night

15—Zucchini Parmigiana

16—Penne with Mushroom Sauce

17—Pizza Night

18—Black Bean Veggie Burgers

19—Shrimp Oreganato & Linguine

20—Potato & Onion Frittata

21—Chili

22—Kew-New-Jew (Lentil & Butternut Squash Soup (Persian)

23—Portobello Mushroom Parmigiana

24—Salmon Burgers

25—Linguine with Garlic & Oil

26—Risotto with Butternut Squash

27—Cheese Soufflé'

28—Lobster Fra Diavolo

March 1—Asian Scallops

2—Zucchini Pizza

3—Manhattan Clam Chowder

4—Pasta e' Fagioli (Pasta & Cannellini Beans)

5—Portobello Mushroom Burgers

6—Broccoli & Cheese Crepes

7—Grilled Swordfish with Lemon Basil Pesto

8—Italian Vegetable Soup

9—Tuna Melt Panini

10—Seared Scallops

11—Italian Baked Fish in Packets

12—Pasta e' Lentica (Pasta & Lentils)

13—Matzoh Ball Soup (Jewish)

14—Near Eastern Curried Butternut Squash & Rice (Indian)

15—Eggplant Nuggets

16—Cream of Peanut Soup

17—Steamed Cabbage

18—Shrimp Stir-Fry with Sesame Seeds

19—Italian Pasta Salad with Tuna

20—Broccoli Quiche

21—Baked Fish with Walnut, Currant, & Herb Stuffing (Middle Eastern)

22—Curried Lentils & Rice (Indian)

23—Potato Leek Soup

24—Omlet-e Khorma/Date Omelet (Persian)

25—Moussaka (Greek)

26—Baked Eggs, Italian Style

27—Irish Vegetable Soup

28—Seafood Fra Diavolo

29—Spicy Mexican Corn Chowder

30—Aromatic Gypsy Soup

31—Ricotta Gnocchi in Sage Sauce

April 1—Greek Pizza

2—Mushroom Bourguignon

3—Eggplant Parmigiana with Spaghetti

4—West African Yam Soup

5—Beer-Battered Coconut Shrimp

6—Paella Valenciana (Spain)

7—Ash-e-Reshteh/Legume & Noodle Soup (Persian)

8—Escarole & Bean Soup

9—Eggplant Rollatini

10—Mediterranean Goat Cheese Tart

11—Quick & Easy Linguine & Clam Sauce

12—15 Bean Soup

13—Asparagus Frittata

14—Grilled Tuna Steaks with Salsa

15—Spanokopita/Spinach Pie (Greek)

16—Shrimp Creole

17—Spicy Shrimp Stew

18—Broccoli & Cheese Frittata

19—Broiled Red Snapper with Orange Sauce

20—Tortellini Soup

21—Arabian Eggplant Salad

22—Spinach & Cheese Stuffed Shells in a Cream Sauce

23—Lentil Spinach Soup

24—Salmon Teriyaki

25—Roasted Pears with Bleu Cheese

26—Taco Pizza

27—Hearty Vegetable Soup

28—Roasted Beet & Goat Cheese Ravioli

29—Baked Haddock with Oven Roasted Potatoes

30—Calzone

May 1—Baked Ziti

2—Dolmeh-Ye-Barg-E Mo/Stuffed Grape Leaves (Persian)

3—Striped Bass with Couscous & Roasted Brussel Sprouts

4—Fettuccine Alfredo

5—Mock Crab Cakes

6—Shrimp Tortillas with Mango Salsa

7—Pizza Margherita with Basil Pesto

8—Swiss Chard Wraps

9—Linguine with Butter, Cheese, & Baby Spinach

10—Shrimp Fried Rice

11—Eshkeneh/Egg Drop Soup (Persian)

12—Felafel Pitas (Middle Eastern)

13—Kuku Sabzi/Green Vegetable Omelet (Persian)

14—Rockfish alla Marinara

15—Sunny Side Up Eggs Over Sautéed Vegetables

16—Avocado Tacos (California-Mexican)

17—Pasta Primavera

18—Red Snapper En Papillote

19—Baked Zucchini, Tomato, & Squash Casserole

20—Shrimp & Orzo

21—Chickpea Salad Sandwiches (Middle Eastern)

22—Mirza Ghasemi (Persian)

23—Oriental Shrimp Wraps

24—Brown Rice Casserole

25—Pasta with Sun-Dried Tomatoes

26—Greek Lentil Casserole

27—Spinach & Bean Casserole

28—Tex-Mex Rancheros

29—Easy Lobster Salad

30—Rotelle with Cherry Tomatoes Pomodoro

31—Grilled Shrimp Kabobs & Rice

June 1—Gazapacho

2—Perciatelli with Crab Sauce

3—Shrimp Roll Ups

4—Grilled Goat Cheese & Heirloom Tomato Sandwiches

5—Simply Linguine

6—Tex-Mex Corn & Beans with Tostitos

7—Grilled Salmon Pitas with Cucumber Yoghurt Dill Sauce

8—Grilled Vegetable Kabobs

9—Quinoa & Corn Salad

10—Baked Tomato Tapas

11—Cucumber "Spaghetti" & Scallions

12—Shrimp Salad

13—Parmesan Baby Spinach & Asparagus Quinoa

14—Avocado & Grapefruit Salad

15—Moroccan Lentil Casserole

16—Summer Farmers' Market Salad

17—Fusilli with Cherry Tomatoes & Fresh Baby Spinach

18—Baked Polenta & Vegetable Casserole

19—Cold Cucumber Soup

20—Cobb Salad Stuffed Pitas

21—Mediterranean Grilled Eggplant & Tomato Vinaigrette

22—Baked Tilapia with Champagne Mustard

23—Apple & Cheddar Panini with Fig Jam

24—Egg Salad and Caramelized Onion Sandwiches

25—Spaghetti & Calamari Sauce

26—Spanish Omelet with Manchego Cheese & Olives

27—Beer Batter Fried Shrimp

28—Seared Grouper with a Vegetable Medley

29—Lemon, Orzo, & Shrimp Soup

30—Grilled Mediterranean Vegetable Sandwiches

July 1—Fruit & Spinach Salad

2—Sun-Dried Tomato, Mozzarella, & Basil Panini

3—Hummus Platter

4—Baked Beans & "Hot Dogs"

5—Joey's Pasta

6—Tuna Salad

7—Crab Quiche

8—Giambotta/Sautéed Summer Vegetables (Italian)

9—Farfalle (Bowties) & Broccoli Pesto

10—Yellow Squash Casserole

11—Grilled Cod & Salad

12—Crab & Lobster Stuffed Shells

13—Greek Salad

14—Chilled Zucchini Soup

15—Tomato & Cheese Pie

16—Grilled Polynesian Swordfish with Pineapple Mango Salsa

17—Seafood Salad

18—Roasted Vegetable Tapas

19—Huevos Rancheros Salad

20—Marinated Vegetable Salad

21—Upside Down Dinner/Whole Wheat Blueberry Pancakes

22—Swiss Chard & Herb Omelet

23—Grilled Pizza Blanca

24—Heirloom Tomato Salad with Bleu Cheese & Wild Rice

25—Mushroom, Spinach, & Cheese Strata

26—Italian Tuna Salad

27—Crab Cakes

28—Caprese Panini

29—Curried Shrimp with Snow Peas

30—Ab Dough Khiar/Yoghurt Salad (Persian)

31—Roasted Red Asian Peppers Stuffed with Goat Cheese

August 1—Wild Rice Salad

2—Panzanella Salad

3—Summer Seafood Stew

4—Chilled Strawberry Soup

5—Baked Spaghetti Squash with Fontina

6—Sandwich Night

7—Garides Me Saltsa/Shrimp in Tomato & Feta Sauce (Greek)

8—Roasted Vegetable Frittata

9—Cool Watermelon Salad

10—Tomato & Cheese Tart

11—Halibut & Summer Vegetables En Papillote

12—Tuna Casserole with a "Twist"

13—Tri-Color Couscous with Apricots & Pine Nuts

14—Oatmeal & Spinach

15—Stuffed Flounder Roll-Ups

16—Felafel #2 (Middle Eastern)

17—Muenster & Apple Open-Faced Sandwiches

18—Beer Steamed Clams

19—Tomato & Fruit Salad

20—Greek Salad Wraps

21—Grilled Swordfish with Sun-Dried Tomatoes & Olive Tapenade

22—Kidney Beans in Tomato Sauce with Saffron on Rice (Middle Eastern)

23—Couscous with Green Peas & Parmesan

24—Grilled Tuna Steaks with Anchovies, Olives, & Capers Tapenade

25—Mozzarella Omelet with Parsley & Tomato Sauce

26—Beet, Cheddar, & Apple Tarts

27—Shrimp & Collards Pilau (Cajun)

28—Penne with Swiss Chard & Eggplant

29—Lemon & Herb Crusted Bass

30—Grilled Cheese Sandwiches with Sun-Dried Tomatoes Tapenade

31—Spicy Hot Fruit Kabobs

September 1—Shrimp Teriyaki

2—Fish Tacos with Corn Salsa

3—Roasted Vegetables

4—Beet Soup

5—Lemon Shrimp En Papillote

6—Baked Tomatoes & Cheese

7—Steamed Wild Rice with Toasted Hazelnut Butter

8—Tex-Mex Corn Casserole

9—Mixed Greens with Asian Pears, Apples, Pecans, and Herbed Pita

10—Mushroom & Pappardelle Soup

11—Kuku Bademjan/Eggplant Omelet (Persian)

12—Lentil & Onion Soup with Brown Basmati Rice

13—Cod in Tomato Broth

14—Boiled Ricotta & Spinach Balls

15—Broccoli Soup

16—Egg-Fried Rice

17—Channa Masala (Indian)

18—Mushroom Lasagna

19—Shrimp Fettuccine

20—Pecan & Dill Crusted Salmon

21—Eggplant Pizzas

22—Jambalaya (Creole)

23—Khoresh-E Kadu/Zucchini Stew (Persian)

24—Sweet & Spicy Indian Seafood Stew

25—Wild Rice with Roasted Butternut Squash

26—Eggplant, Mushroom, & Rice Casserole

27—Greek Lentil Soup

28—Mushroom Omelet

29—Potato & Egg Heroes

30—Cream of Mushroom & Barley Soup

October 1—Pumpkin Lasagna

2—Stuffed Eggplant

3—Spicy Hot Tex-Mex Rice & Beans

4—Italian Swiss Chard Soup

5—Stir-Fry with Spicy Peanut Sauce

6—Portobello "Steaks" with Cauliflower Puree'

7—Salmon & Squash En Papillote

8—Pepper & Egg Heroes

9—Easy No-Cook Dinner Night

10—Pasta E' Pesilli/Pasta & Peas

11—Quinoa with Peas & Green Onions

12—Lemon Tilapia Picata

13—Kuku-Ye Gol-E Kalam/Cauliflower Omelet (Persian)

14—Collard Greens & Brown Rice Pilaf

15—Mediterranean Vegetable Bake

16—Gefilte Fish (Jewish)

17—Harira (Moroccan Ramadan Soup)

18—String Bean, Zucchini, & Eggplant Stew (Mediterranean)

19—Roasted Pumpkin & Black Bean Chili

20—Korma (Indian)

21—Smoked Bluefish-Apple Hash

22—Mexican Flatbread Pizza

23—Baked Farfalle with Vegetables

24—Baked Flounder with Tomato Basil Marinade

25—Kale Soup

26—Baked Eggs with Acine Pepe in Tomato Sauce

27—Cassoulet

28—Eggplant Stir Fry

29—Creamy Shrimp & Wild Rice Soup

30—Stuffed Trout

31—Pumpkin Soup

November 1—Huevos Rancheros

2—Grilled Shrimp in a Balsamic Molasses Sauce

3—Squash Frittata

4—Split Pea Soup

5—Autumn Salad with Roasted Vegetables

6—Mussel Bisque Provencal

7—Collard Greens—Spicy Hot

8—Baked Stuffed Yellow Squash Boats

9—Asian Spicy Salmon

10—New England Clam Chowder

11—Vegetable Pot Pie

12—Oatmeal, Cheese, & Eggs

13—Vegetable Gratin

14—Spinach & Bean Quesadillas

15—Spaghetti with Lemon & Toasted Pecans

16—Zucchini Caprese Panini

17—Blackened Catfish Sandwiches

18—Near Easter Curry (Indian)

19—Goat Cheese & Sun-Dried Tomato Pizza

20—Bean Casserole (Tex-Mex)

21—Carrot-Fennel Soup

22—Penne with Lemon Ricotta

23—Mash Piyazu/Bean & Onion Porridge (Persian)

24—Seared Scallops with Lemony Baby Spinach

25—Black-Eyed Peas, Nectarines, & Mandarin Salad

26—Baked Stuffed Shells

27—Spicy Okra & Basmati Rice (Indian)

28—Salmon Loaf

29—Crunchy Asian Shrimp Slaw in Cabbage Cups

30—Creamy Corn Chowder

December 1—Mung Bean Soup

2—Sautéed Kale with Pine Nuts & Dried Cranberries

3—Baked Italian Stuffed Squash Boats

4—Quinoa Salad with Shrimp

5—Whole Wheat Linguine, Tomatoes, & Clams

6—Rockfish with Parsley-Onion Salad

7—Baked Brie En Croute

8—Roasted Vegetable & Ricotta Pizza

9—Savory Shrimp, Spinach, & Onion Turnovers

10—Spicy Flounder with Bell Pepper & Rosemary

11—Creamy Mushroom Soup

12—Baked Pasta with Spinach & Butternut Squash

13—Oatmeal for Dinner with Mushrooms & Asparagus

14—Deep Fried Calamari & Shrimp

15—Pasta Putanesca

16—Grilled Trout with Sautéed Red & White Grapes

17—Shrimp & Grits

18—Kuku Sibzamini/Potato Pancakes (Persian)

19—Fish Souvlaki Pitas with Dill Sauce (Greek)

20—Mexican Stuffed Shells

21—Roasted Vegetable & Garbanzo Beans with Couscous

22—Cannelloni with Alfredo Sauce

23—No-Fuss Veggie Pockets

24—Shrimp Scampi

25—Homemade Manicotti/Cheese-Filled Crepes

26—Spicy Israeli Couscous with Butternut Squash & Pistachios

27—Chip Crusted Fish Fillets

28—Peperonata on Rosemary Focaccia

29—Israeli Couscous with Eggplant & Plum Tomatoes (Middle Eastern)

30—Fish Kabobs & Roasted Tomato Salad

31—Salmon with Dilled Rice

<u>Ingredients:</u>

Tomato Sauce:

¼ cup extra virgin olive oil	1½ tbs. dried oregano
2 med. onions, chopped	10-12 fresh basil leaves, julienned
6 garlic cloves, finely chopped	1½ tsp. sugar
2-35 oz. cans crushed tomatoes	½ cup grated Parmigiano-Reggiano cheese
35 oz. water	Salt & pepper

Lasagna:

2-1 lb. boxes of lasagna, prepared according to pkg. directions cooked until al dente.

2 tbs. olive oil

3 lbs. ricotta cheese

1½ lbs. freshly grated mozzarella

1 cup freshly grated Parmigiano-Reggiano cheese

<u>Directions:</u>

You must first prepare the sauce because you will need it when layering the lasagna. In a 5 or 6 quart saucepan, heat the olive oil over medium heat. Add in the onion and garlic and cook until golden. Next, add in the tomatoes, water (add in the water a little at a time until the desired consistency has been reached), oregano, basil, sugar, grated cheese, salt and pepper. Stir; cover. Reduce heat to low-medium and simmer for about one hour.

Once the sauce has cooked, fill a 12 quart pot three-fourths of the way with salted water. Add in the olive oil and bring to a boil. Once the water has reached its boiling point, add in the lasagna, one at a time. Gently stir and cook for about 8-10 minutes or until al dente. Do not overcook! Drain and rinse under cold water to cool so you can handle the pasta when layering.

Next, using a deep lasagna pan, ladle in 2-3 cups of tomato sauce and sprinkle with some grated cheese, making sure that the entire bottom of the pan is layered with tomato sauce. Take the lasagna noodles one at a time and run your hand along the noodle to remove any excess water. Begin lining the bottom of your pan with the pasta (I always line the bottom of the pan with 2 layers of the pasta to act as a good support when serving portions). Once lined with the pasta, spoon on tomato sauce entirely covering the first layer of the pasta. Then spoon on ricotta and entirely spread it over the first layer. Sprinkle generous amounts of mozzarella and grated cheese and top with another layer of the lasagna noodles, using only 1 layer this time.

Continue this process until all the pasta has been used. Once you have placed the final layer of the pasta on top, just spoon on tomato sauce, and sprinkle with mozzarella and grated cheese. Do not put ricotta on top layer. Place the pan in a pre-heated 350 degree oven for approximately 45 minutes until lasagna is bubbling, the cheese has melted, and the top layer starts turning crispy.

JANUARY 2 **LENTIL SOUP**

Ingredients:

¼ cup extra virgin olive oil

1-16 oz. pkg. lentils, washed & drained

6 lg. garlic cloves, finely chopped

1½ tbs. oregano

3 lg. carrots, peeled, washed, and sliced

12 cups water

2 lg. celery stalks, washed, and sliced

Salt & pepper, to taste

1 lg. or 2 med. onions, peeled and sliced

½ cup pasta such as elbows, ditalini, or farfalle

Directions:

In a 5 qt. saucepan, heat olive oil over medium heat and add in the garlic. Sauté until golden. Next add in the carrots, celery, onions, and 2 cups of water. Cover and simmer for 10 minutes. Then add in the lentils, remainder of the water, oregano, salt, and pepper. Stir then cover and continue to let simmer on low heat for 1 1/2 hours. *****NOTE:** Pasta may be added to this soup. If pasta is desired, after having cooked the soup for 1 1/4 hours, add in 1/2 cup of desired pasta and cook until pasta is al dente. Serve while hot.

JANUARY 3 **GRILLED VEGETABLE PANINI**

Ingredients:

Olive oil

2 lg. red peppers, quartered

1 med. - lg. eggplant, cut into ½" thick slices

Salt & pepper

2 zucchini, cut lengthwise into ½" thick slices

1-8 oz. pkg. thin sliced provolone

1 lg. red onion, cut into ½" thick slices

4 ciabatta rolls, halved

<u>Directions:</u>

Heat a grill pan over medium-high heat. Brush the olive oil onto the eggplant, zucchini, onion slices, and peppers. Sprinkle with salt and pepper then place vegetables on grill pan in batches until fork tender and grill marks appear. This should only take about 3-4 minutes on each side.

When all the vegetables have been grilled, slice the ciabatta rolls in half and arrange the vegetables on the bottom half of each roll. Place a slice of cheese on top of the vegetables and then top each with the remaining halves of the rolls forming a complete sandwich. Place sandwiches, 2 at a time, into a hot Panini press for about 8 minutes or until the bread is crispy and cheese has melted.

JANUARY 4 **STEAMED MUSSELS**

<u>Ingredients:</u>

3½-4 lbs. mussels

2 tbs. olive oil

½ cup shallots, chopped

6 med. garlic cloves, minced

1½ cups dry white wine, such as Sauvignon Blanc

½ cup organic vegetable stock

Italian bread or French baguette diagonally

     sliced and grilled

½ cup organic vegetable stock

1-14.5 oz. can diced tomatoes

1 tsp. dried oregano

1 tsp. fresh thyme leaves

Salt & pepper

½ cup chopped fresh parsley

<u>Directions:</u>

When buying mussels, be sure to use them within 24 hours because they are live animals. Rinse well under cold water. Discard any that are chipped, cracked, or open. Pull off beards and soak in a bowl of water so that they will expel any sand or grit. Then rinse and set aside in refrigerator.

In a Dutch oven, heat oil over medium-high heat. Add in shallots and garlic. Sauté for 2 minutes. Next, add in the wine, vegetable stock, tomatoes, oregano, thyme, salt and pepper. Stir and bring mixture to a boil. Add in the mussels, leaving heat on high and cover. After 2 minutes, remove lid and give mussels a quick toss. Cover the pot again and let cook for another 5-6 minutes. When done, the mussels should all be wide-opened. Toss any mussels that remain closed. Add in the parsley; toss with a spoon. Serve in individual bowls with grilled bread on the side.

JANUARY 5 **TOMATO BISQUE SOUP WITH GRILLED CHEESE SANDWICHES**

Ingredients for Soup:

6 tbs. butter	4 cups vegetable stock
½ cup onion, diced	2 tbs. butter
2 garlic cloves, minced	2 tbs. flour
1½ tsp. dill weed	2 tsp. salt
1 tsp. oregano	½ tsp. black pepper
1 tsp. basil	1¼ cups heavy cream
5 cups canned crushed tomatoes	2/3 cup half & half
6 oz. tomato paste	

Directions for Soup:

In a large Dutch oven, melt 4 tablespoons of butter over low-medium heat and sauté onions, garlic, and herbs until onions are soft. Add tomatoes, tomato paste, and vegetable stock and let simmer. Meanwhile in a small saucepan, melt the remaining 2 tbs. butter over medium heat, then add the flour. Whisk constantly to form a roux (paste mixture). Once finished, add to tomato mixture, along with salt and pepper. Increase heat, bring to a boil, then lower heat and let simmer for about 30-40 minutes. During the last 15 minutes, uncover and add in the cream and half and half. Serve with grilled cheese sandwiches.

Ingredients for Sandwiches:

8 slices thick white bread

8 thick slices cheddar cheese (you may substitute Swiss or any other cheese of choice)

Butter

Directions for Sandwiches:

Pre-heat a skillet or griddle pan over medium high heat. Generously butter one side of each bread slice. Place buttered side down. Place two slices of cheese on top of each bread slice and top with second slice of bread. Spread butter on top of second bread slice. Place sandwiches in a skillet or on griddle pan and place a heavy grill press on top or any heavy plate will do. When underside is golden, flip over, and brown the other side. Grill until cheese has melted. Serve hot with soup.

JANUARY 6 **SPINACH AND PARSLEY OMELET**

Ingredients:

2 tbs. extra virgin olive oil

1 sm. bunch green onions, using all of the white
                & 1/2 of the green parts

1-16 oz. bag fresh baby spinach

1 bunch Italian flat leaf parsley, chopped

6 eggs, beaten

Salt & pepper, to taste

1 cup crumpled feta cheese

Directions:

Heat the oil in a non-stick skillet over medium heat. Add in the onions and sauté until white parts are translucent. Stir frequently. Add in the spinach, cover and, when spinach has wilted, add in the parsley, salt, and pepper to the eggs. Mix well. Once the spinach has wilted, remove cover and slowly pour egg mixture over the spinach and onions. Let cook on low heat without disturbing until it begins to set. Before eggs completely set, sprinkle on the crumbled cheese and cover for 2 minutes. Divide into 4 quarters and serve.

JANUARY 7 **BEER BATTERED FISH AND CHIPS**

Ingredients:

Chips:

Oil

4 large baking potatoes, leaving skin on, cut into thick wedges, pat dry

Salt

Fish:

1-12 oz. bottle of beer

2 cups all-purpose flour

1 tsp. kosher salt

½ tsp. black pepper

½ tsp. garlic powder

1½ lbs. cod fillets, cut into wide strips

Directions:

Chips:

Heat the oil to 375 degrees in a large saucepan or Dutch oven. Carefully place potatoes in the hot oil and fry until golden on all sides. Remove with a slotted spoon or kitchen spider and place on a baking sheet lined with paper towels. Generously sprinkle with salt and place baking sheet in a pre-heated 225 degree oven to keep warm while fish is frying.

Fish:

In a large bowl whisk together beer, 1½ cups of flour, salt, pepper, and garlic powder. Pat fish dry and coat the fish in the beer batter. Then dredge in the remaining ½ cup of flour. Fry fish until deep golden on both sides. Be sure to turn often so one side will not overcook. Transfer to a paper lined baking sheet and keep warm in oven with fries until all the fish has been fried.

JANUARY 8 **BAKED ZUCCHINI CASSEROLE**

Ingredients:

3 cups zucchini, diced with skin on

1 med. onion, chopped

1 cup biscuit mix

4 eggs, beaten

½ cup canola oil

½ cup grated Parmesan cheese

½ tsp. thyme

1 tsp. parsley flakes

½ tsp. salt

¼ tsp. black pepper

½ cup grated Gruyere cheese

Directions:

In a large bowl, mix all ingredients together with the exception of the Gruyere cheese. Blend well. Pour mixture into a buttered 9" x 12" glass baking dish. Bake in a pre-heated 350 degree oven for about 30-40 minutes until golden. Remove from oven and immediately sprinkle with the Gruyere cheese. Serves 6-8.

JANUARY 9 **LINGUINE WITH ITALIAN TUNA, GARLIC & OIL**

Ingredients:

1 lb. linguine pasta

1 cup extra virgin olive oil

8 garlic cloves, sliced

½ tsp. crushed red pepper flakes

½ tsp. freshly ground black pepper

2-6 oz. cans Italian tuna packed in olive oil

1/3 cup fresh Italian parsley, chopped

Directions:

Cook linguine according to directions on package until al dente. While the pasta is cooking, heat the oil in a large skillet over medium heat. Add in the garlic, red pepper, and black pepper. Cook until garlic is lightly golden, then add in the tuna (including the oil). Drain the pasta and add directly to the skillet with the garlic and tuna. Toss well. Sprinkle with parsley and serve immediately.

JANUARY 10 **BROCCOLI & CHEESE TWICE BAKED POTATOES**

Ingredients:

4 lg. Russet potatoes	Salt & pepper, to taste
1½ cups chopped broccoli florets	1 cup shredded extra sharp cheddar
½ cup light cream	2 tbs. finely chopped chives

Directions:

Bake potatoes in a 375 degree pre-heated oven for 1 hour. In the meantime, in a medium saucepan, steam broccoli until tender, but firm. Drain and set aside.

Cut off a thin slice from the top of each potato and scoop out the centers leaving a ¼" shell. Place the scooped out potatoes in a bowl and place shells on a baking sheet. Mash the potatoes; add the cream, salt, pepper, 2/3 cup of cheese, and chives. Stir. Divide broccoli florets into each of the 4 potatoes then spoon in the mashed potatoes. Sprinkle on the remaining cheese and bake in oven for about 10-12 minutes, until heated through and cheese on top has melted.

JANUARY 11 **CREAM OF ASPARAGUS SOUP**

Ingredients:

3 tbs. olive oil	1 potato, peeled & diced
1 lg. onion, finely chopped	1½ fresh asparagus, cut into ½" pieces
2 garlic cloves, minced	¾ cup half and half
2 celery stalks, finely chopped	1½ tsp. kosher salt
3 tbs. flour	½ tsp. freshly ground black pepper
6 cups water	

Directions:

Heat oil over medium heat in a saucepot. Add in the onion, garlic, and celery. Cook until translucent and tender. Stir in the flour and mix well. Add in the water, potato, asparagus, and bring to a boil. Then reduce heat and let simmer for about 20-25 minutes.

Transfer the soup to a blender and puree in batches. Return puree to the pot then stir in the half and half, salt, and pepper. Heat and serve immediately.

JANUARY 12 DOMATES YEMISTES ME RIZI/BAKED STUFFED TOMATOES (GREEK)

Ingredients:

1 cup par-boiled long-grained Basmati rice

6 lg. beefsteak tomatoes, firm yet ripe

2 tsp. salt

6 tbs. olive oil

½ cup onions, finely chopped

¾ cup canned crushed tomatoes

¼ cup water

½ cup flat leaf parsley, finely chopped

2 tbs. fresh mint, finely chopped

3 lg. garlic cloves, minced

¼ tsp. dried Greek oregano

Freshly ground black pepper

¼ cup water

Directions:

Par-boil rice as instructed on package directions. Drain and set aside.

Slice off the tops of each tomato (about ¼") and set aside. Using a teaspoon, hollow out each tomato by removing the inner pulp. Discard as many seeds as you can but retain the pulp and transfer to a bowl. Sprinkle 1 teaspoon salt inside each tomato, then turn them upside down on paper towels to drain.

In the meantime, heat the oil in a 10" or 12" skillet, over moderate heat. Add onions and sauté until translucent. Stir in the rice, tomato pulp, ½ cup crushed tomatoes, parsley, mint, garlic, oregano, 1 tsp. salt, and pepper. Cook together until liquid evaporates and mixture is thick. Transfer tomatoes to a baking dish, cut side up, and fill each one with stuffing (be sure to pack stuffing in firmly because it does shrink while baking). Cover each tomato with reserved tops. Combine ¼ cup crushed tomatoes with ¼ cup water and pour around the tomatoes. Bake tomatoes in a pre-heated 350 degree oven for 20-25 minutes, basting occasionally. Serve warm.

JANUARY 13 **FISH NUGGETS**

Ingredients:

1 qt. canola oil heated to 350 degrees   ½ cup flour

1 large egg, beaten   ½ tsp. garlic powder

1 cup milk   ½ tsp. onion powder

½ tsp. black pepper   2 lbs. cod or halibut, cut into 1" cubes

½ cup corn meal   Coarse salt

Directions:

Pre-heat oil in a deep pot. In a medium bowl, whisk the egg, milk, and pepper together. In another bowl or even large zip-lock bag, combine the corn meal, flour, garlic powder, and onion powder. Dip the fish cubes into the egg/milk mixture, drain, then coat well in flour mixture. Place a few nuggets at a time in the hot oil and fry until golden brown on all sides. Remove from oil and place on platter lined with paper towels. Sprinkle with salt. Serve while hot accompanied by various sauces such as tartar, honey-mustard, cocktail sauce, ketchup, honey, salsa, or your own favorite dipping sauce.

JANUARY 14 **OLIVE & SWISS PANINI**

Ingredients:

8 thick slices of olive bread   4 lg. thick tomato slices

8 slices Swiss cheese   2 tbs. olive oil

½ cup olive tapenade

Directions:

Arrange bread slices on a clean hard surface. Place 1 slice of cheese on each slice of bread. Next, spread the olive tapenade over 4 of the bread slices. Place the tomato slices over the tapenade and close with the cheese and bread. Brush the outsides of each of the 4 sandwiches with the olive oil and cook in a pre-heated Panini maker until golden on both sides and cheese has melted. ***NOTE:** A grill pan and press can be substituted for the Panini press.

JANUARY 15 **KHORESH BADEMJAN/EGGPLANT STEW (PERSIAN)**

Ingredients:

6 Asian eggplants, peeled and sliced in half lengthwise	½ tsp. black pepper
Olive oil	1 tsp. turmeric
1 lg. onion, halved and thinly sliced	4 lg. tomatoes, sliced
1 tbs. lemon juice	1 tbs. dill weed
2½ cups water	2 cups steamed rice
2 tbs. tomato paste	Plain yoghurt
1 tsp. salt	

Directions:

Heat the oil in a medium frying pan over medium-high heat and brown eggplants on both sides. Transfer to a platter lined with paper towels to drain any excess oil. In a medium saucepot, heat oil over medium heat, add onions and sauté until golden and translucent. Next add in the lemon juice, water, tomato paste, salt, pepper, and turmeric. Stir well. Add the eggplants to the pot with the onions. Place tomato slices on top of the eggplant slices. Sprinkle the dill weed over the mixture. Cover and simmer on medium-low heat for 40 minutes. Serve over steamed rice. Accompany with a few tablespoons of plain yoghurt on the side.

JANUARY 16 **CARROT SOUP**

Ingredients:

1 tbs. olive oil	2 tsp. fresh ginger
1½ cups carrots, diced	1/3 cup white wine
1 large onion, diced	4 cups unsalted vegetable stock
2 garlic cloves, chopped	Salt & pepper
1 tbs. orange zest	Chopped chives

Directions:

Heat oil in a medium saucepot over medium heat. Add in the carrots, onions, and garlic, and sauté until carrots are soft. Next add in the orange zest and ginger. Cook for another 2-3 minutes. Add in the wine and stock; increase heat and bring mixture to a boil, then reduce heat and let simmer for about 10-15 minutes. Remove from heat and let cool then process in a blender until smooth. Season with salt and pepper. Serve in individual bowls. Sprinkle with chives.

JANUARY 17 **FRIED TILAPIA WITH TURMERIC**

Ingredients:

4-4 oz. pieces of tilapia	Italian-style bread crumbs
1 large egg, beaten	1 tsp. turmeric
¼ cup milk	Canola oil for frying

Directions:

Pat dry the tilapia with paper towels and set aside. In a shallow bowl, whisk egg and milk together. Heat the oil in a non-stick skillet over medium-high heat. Spread breadcrumbs out onto a piece of wax paper. Add turmeric to the breadcrumbs and blend together. Dip the tilapia into the egg mixture, then evenly coat both sides with breadcrumbs. Place in skillet. Fry until a rich golden brown on each side. May be accompanied with a salad, fries, or any side of your choice.

JANUARY 18 **SALAD WITH WILD RICE**

Ingredients:

1 cup baby spinach, washed & drained	½ cup finely chopped celery
1 cup red cabbage, thinly shredded	½ cup cooked wild rice
1 cup arugula, washed & drained	½ cup toasted almond slivers
½ cup thinly sliced green onions, green & white parts	Tarragon vinaigrette (recipe below)
1 sm. red onion, halved & thinly sliced	½ cup plain croutons
1 cup canned petite peas	

Directions:

In a large bowl, add the first 8 ingredients and toss well. Sprinkle the almonds on top and give one quick toss. Drizzle on the vinaigrette and refrigerate for 1 hour. Remove from refrigerator; add croutons on top. Serve immediately.

Tarragon Vinaigrette: In a small bowl, mix together ½ cup olive oil and ¼ cup balsamic vinegar from Modena. Whisk in 1½ tablespoons chopped fresh tarragon, 1 teaspoon Mediterranean Sea salt and ½ teaspoon freshly ground black pepper.

JANUARY 19 **MUSHROOM ZUCCHINI "PASTA"**

Ingredients:

1 cup shitake mushrooms, sliced very thinly

¼ tsp. crushed red pepper

1/3 cup extra virgin olive oil

¼ cup freshly grated parmesan

2 tbs. fresh lemon juice

2 med. zucchini, cut into thin strips

¼ cup green onion (white parts only), finely chopped

3 tbs. fresh basil, julienned

1 tsp. Mediterranean Sea salt

1/3 cup toasted pine nuts

½ cup freshly ground black pepper

1/3 cup parmesan cheese

Directions:

Slice mushrooms very thinly. Set aside. In a large bowl, whisk together the oil, lemon juice, onion, salt, black pepper, red pepper and cheese. Toss in the mushrooms, stir, and set aside. Cut the zucchini into very thin strips. Add to mushroom mixture. Next, add in the basil and pine nuts. Mix well. Sprinkle with remaining cheese. Serve with sliced Italian bread.

JANUARY 20 **NACHO DINNER**

Ingredients:

Cooking spray

1 tsp. dried basil

1 medium green bell pepper, chopped

¼ cup chopped fresh cilantro

1 large onion, chopped

6 oz. baked corn tortilla chips

1 chipotle chili in adobo sauce, chopped

2 cups shredded Romaine lettuce

1-15 oz. can pinto beans, rinsed and drained

1 cup diced, peeled avocado

1-15 oz. can black beans, rinsed and drained

¾ cup thinly sliced red onions

1-14 oz. can diced tomatoes

¾ cup Four Cheese Mexican

1 tsp. garlic powder

6 tbs. sour cream

1 tsp. dried oregano

Directions:

Coat a large non-stick frying pan with cooking spray oil and set over medium heat. Add in the bell pepper and onion. Allow to cook for 5 minutes. Add in the chipotle chili, some adobe sauce, beans and tomatoes to the pan. Cover and simmer for 5 minutes on reduced heat. Remove from heat, and then stir in the cilantro. Using 6 dinner plates, arrange 1 1/3 cups chips on each of the plates. Add 1 cup mixture to each, then 1/3 cup shredded lettuce, 2½ tablespoons avocado, 2 tablespoons onion, 2 tablespoons cheese, and 1 tablespoon sour cream. Enjoy!

JANUARY 21 **BAKED SALMON FISH STICKS AND DIPPING SAUCE**

Ingredients:

Fish Sticks:

1-18 oz. center cut salmon fillet	¼ tsp. black pepper
2 lg. eggs, beaten	Seasoned bread crumbs
½ tsp. sea salt	Spray oil

Ingredients:

Dipping Sauce:

½ cup mayonnaise	Pepper
1 tsp. freshly squeezed lemon juice	1 tbs. fresh chives, chopped
¼ tsp. salt	

Directions:

Fish Sticks:

Cut the fish in half to make 2 fillets, then slice each half into ½" strips. Dip each strip into beaten egg, then generously coat with bread crumbs. Place strips on baking sheet that has been sprayed with oil and place in a pre-heated 400 degree oven for about 20-25 minutes until golden brown.

Dipping Sauce:

Combine all ingredients in a small bowl. Refrigerate while fish sticks are in the oven then serve.

JANUARY 22 **MEATLESS "MEAT"BALL SANDWICHES**

Ingredients:

1 lb. stale country-style white bread (crusts removed)

1½ cups milk

3 large eggs

½ cup freshly grated Parmigiano-Reggiano cheese

2 tbs. dried parsley

1 tbs. dried thyme

2 garlic cloves, minced

Salt & pepper

1 cup olive oil

4 long Italian rolls

3 cups of tomato sauce

2 cups shredded mozzarella

Directions:

In a large bowl, combine the bread and milk and set aside until the bread is completely soaked then squeeze dry. Crumble the bread and place in a food processor or blender. Quick pulse until crumbs form (approximate yield: 4 cups).

In a large bowl, combine the crumbs, eggs, cheese, parsley, thyme, garlic, salt, and pepper. Form into balls that measure about 2 inches in diameter. Set prepared balls aside on a platter for 20 minutes.

Heat oil in a non-stick skillet over medium-high heat. Add in the "meat"balls and brown on all sides. Place on a platter lined with paper towels to drain any excess oil.

Slice each loaf lengthwise. Place 3 "meat"balls on each. Ladle sauce over the "meat"balls, sprinkle with mozzarella and bake in a pre-heated 375 degree oven until bread has crisped and cheese has melted. Serve immediately.

JANUARY 23 **SAUTEED' WINTER GREENS**

Ingredients:

2 tbs. olive oil

1 lg. onion, diced

5 garlic cloves, minced

1 lb. broccoli rabe, remove tough stems

½ lb. kale, rough chopped

½ lb. Swiss chard, rough chop

1 lb. collard greens, rough chopped

2 tbs. pine nuts, toasted

1-15 oz. can Italian stewed tomatoes

½ tsp. crushed red pepper flakes

1/3 cup shaved Parmesan

Directions:

In a large skillet, heat oil over medium-low heat. Add garlic and onion and sauté until onion is translucent. Increase heat to medium and add the four greens. Stir and cook until wilted. In the meantime, lightly toast the pine nuts in a small skillet over low heat without using any oil.

Once the greens are wilted, stir in the tomatoes, sauté for about 5-7 minutes. Season with the pepper, give a quick toss and transfer to a serving bowl. Sprinkle with pine nuts and shaved cheese. Serve with warm crusty bread slices.

JANUARY 24 **MOROCCAN SOUP**

Ingredients:

2 tbs. olive oil	2 med. zucchini, cut into ¼"pieces
2 onions, chopped	½ cup uncooked couscous
½ tbs. ground cumin	1-15.5 oz. can garbanzo beans, drained
½ tbs. ground ginger	¼ cup chopped cilantro
¾ tsp. paprika	Sea salt
¼ tsp. cayenne pepper	Freshly ground black pepper
32 oz. low sodium organic	
vegetable stock	

Directions:

Heat the oil in a 5 qt. sauce pot over medium heat. Add onion, cumin, ginger, paprika, and cayenne pepper to the sauce pot. Mix well. Cook for 2-3 minutes then add stock and bring to a boil. Add the zucchini, couscous, and chick peas; stir and cover. Bring to a boil once again then lower heat and let simmer for 5 minutes. Add in the cilantro, salt, and pepper, stir and serve. May be accompanied with flat Arabian bread and plain yoghurt.

JANUARY 25 **CHICK PEA CHILI**

Ingredients:

2 tbs. olive oil	1 tsp. crushed red pepper flakes
1 lg. onion, diced	¼ tsp. turmeric

5 garlic cloves, minced

4 cups butternut squash, peeled & cubed

1 tbs. tomato paste

1½ tsp. ground cumin

1 tsp. salt

20 oz. pkg. vegetable stock

28 oz. can crushed tomatoes

1 cup frozen peas

2-15 oz. cans chick peas, drained

¼ cup fresh cilantro, chopped

Directions:

Heat oil in a large skillet over medium-high heat. Add in the onions and sauté until translucent. Next add in the garlic and squash. Sauté for 6 minutes. Then add in the paste, cumin, salt, pepper, and turmeric. Cook for 2 minutes on medium-low heat.

In the meantime, in a large sauce pan, heat vegetable stock over medium-high heat. Add in the tomatoes, peas, chick peas, then transfer and combine the squash mixture to the sauce pan with the vegetable stock. Cover and simmer on medium-low heat for 45 minutes. Garnish with cilantro. Serve hot.

JANUARY 26 **WILD RICE CAKES**

Ingredients:

¾ cup wild rice

¾ cup brown Basmati rice

3 lg. eggs

1/3 cup bread crumbs

¾ cup finely chopped green onions

½ tsp. black pepper

Directions:

In a medium saucepan, bring 3 cups salted water to a boil over high heat. Add both the wild rice and Basmati rice, stir, and reduce heat to low. Cover and cook for about 45-50 minutes until rice is tender and water has been absorbed. Remove from heat and let rice cool.

In a medium bowl, beat eggs; add in rice, cheese, bread crumbs, onions, and black pepper. Mix well.

Heat 1 tablespoon of oil in a 12" non-stick skillet over medium heat. Moisten hands and scoop up a ¼ cup portion of rice mixture. Form a ball and flatten into a patty. Place in heated skillet and cook until browned then flip over and brown other side. Place 4 in pan at the same time. Repeat the process until all the mixture has been fried, adding oil as needed.

Accompany with sliced pears or apples.

JANUARY 27 **ORECCHIETTE WITH MUSHROOMS AND RADICCHIO**

Ingredients:

3 tbs. olive oil, divided

10 oz. sliced cremini mushrooms

6 slices stale Italian bread, coarsely chopped

4 medium leeks (white & light green parts), sliced

2 tbs. butter

1 head radicchio, cored and shredded

4 garlic cloves, minced

1 tbs. dried oregano

1 tsp. sea salt

½ tsp. black pepper

1 lb. orecchiette, cooked

¼ cup reserved pasta water

½ cup mascarpone cheese

1/3 cup grated Parmesan

Directions:

In a large skillet over medium-high heat, heat 2 tbs. olive oil. Add in the mushrooms and cook until tender. Using a slotted spoon, transfer mushrooms to a large bowl when done.

Add bread to same pan and cook until lightly golden. Transfer bread to same bowl as mushrooms.

Add remaining olive oil to the pan, heat, and add leeks, along with the butter. Sauté until soft and tender. Next, add the radicchio, garlic, oregano, salt, and pepper to the pan. Sauté for another 5-7 minutes, stirring constantly. Transfer to the same bowl.

Add the pasta to the large bowl along with the reserved water. Mix well. Serve in individual bowls. Garnish each with a tablespoon of mascarpone cheese and sprinkle with Parmesan.

JANUARY 28 **SHEPHERD'S PIE**

Ingredients:

4 lg. russet potatoes, peeled & thinly sliced

6 parsnips, peeled & thinly sliced

1 cup half & half

4 tbs. olive oil, divided

Sea salt, to taste

Freshly ground black pepper, to taste

3 garlic cloves, minced

2 lg. carrots, diced

2 celery stalks, diced

8 oz. cremini mushrooms, sliced

1 tsp. fresh rosemary, chopped

¼ tsp. dried thyme

1½ cups brown lentils

1 cup vegetable stock

1 lg. onion, diced

Directions:

Place potatoes and parsnips in a large sauce pan with salted water. Bring to a boil then simmer until vegetables are soft. Drain well. Return to sauce pan and mash. Add half and half, 2 tablespoons olive oil, season with salt and pepper. Set aside.

Put lentils in a medium sauce pan and cover with water. Bring to a boil, and simmer until lentils are soft. Drain and set aside.

Heat the remaining oil in a large skillet over medium heat. Add in the onion and garlic and cook until onions are translucent. Add carrots, celery, and mushrooms. Cook until tender. Add in the lentils, rosemary, thyme and half of the stock. Mixture needs to be moist but not watery. If more liquid is needed, add additional stock a little at a time. Season with salt and pepper.

Place vegetable mixture in a large, deep casserole dish. Evenly spoon mashed potatoes over the vegetables. Bake in a pre-heated 350 degree oven until potatoes begin to brown. Serve hot.

JANUARY 29 **GARLICKY SHRIMP AND FENNEL**

Ingredients:

3 lbs. extra-large shrimp, peeled & deveined

1 tsp. sea salt

3 tbs. extra virgin olive oil

½ tsp. crushed red pepper

1 cup thinly sliced fennel bulb

2 tbs. butter, room temperature

½ cup shallots, thinly sliced

1/3 cup fennel fronds

7 garlic cloves, minced

2 cups cooked couscous

1 lemon, zested and juiced

Directions:

Heat the oil in a large heavy skillet over medium heat. Add in sliced fennel, shallots, and garlic. Sauté until tender. Add in lemon zest and juice, salt, and pepper. Stir. Cook together for 30 seconds. Next add in the butter. Once butter has melted, add in the shrimp and mix well. Cook until shrimp has turned pink, about 3 minutes. Do not overcook.

Place couscous on a large platter and spoon shrimp mixture on top along with all the juices. Sprinkle fennel fronds evenly on top. Serve immediately.

JANUARY 30 **BLACK BEANS AND SAFFRON RICE**

Ingredients:

2 tbs. canola oil	½ tsp. ground turmeric
1½ cups chopped yellow onion	Salt & pepper, to taste
1 orange bell pepper, diced	2-15 oz. cans black beans, drained
1 jalapeno pepper, minced	2 cups cooked rice
3 garlic cloves, minced	¼ tsp. crushed saffron
3 cups diced tomatoes, including juice	¼ cup fresh cilantro, chopped

Directions:

Heat the oil in a heavy skillet over medium heat. Toss in the onion, bell pepper, jalapeno, and garlic. Sauté until the vegetables are tender but not overly soft. Add in the tomatoes along with the juice, beans, turmeric, salt, and pepper. Reduce heat to low and simmer.

In the meantime, mix in the saffron with the rice and place on a large serving platter. Spoon the vegetable mixture over top of rice. Sprinkle with cilantro. Serve immediately.

JANUARY 31 **EGG-DROP NOODLE SOUP**

Ingredients:

9 oz. ramen noodles	3 med. carrots, peeled, thinly sliced
84 oz. low sodium vegetable broth	6 sm. green onions, thinly sliced, divided
1 tsp. ground ginger	3 lg. eggs, beaten
2 garlic cloves, minced	1 tbs. sesame oil
1 tbs. low sodium soy sauce	

Directions:

Bring about 64 oz. water to a boil in a medium pot over medium-high heat. Add in the noodles and cook for 3 minutes. Then drain and set aside.

In a 5 qt. pot over medium-high heat, bring stock, ginger, garlic, and soy sauce to a boil. Reduce heat and let simmer. Add in the carrots and most of green onions (leaving about 2 tbs. for garnish), and cook until carrots are tender but not soft. Whisk the eggs and oil together and slowly pour egg mixture into the broth. Allow to firm then stir continuously to break up the eggs. Add in the noodles and cook to blend all ingredients for 1 minute. Serve in 6 individual soup bowls and garnish with remaining green onions.

FEBRUARY 1 **BRAISED SWORDFISH WITH DATES (NORTH AFRICAN)**

Ingredients:

2½ lbs. swordfish, cut into 2" chunks	½ tsp. ground coriander
Salt & pepper	½ tsp. crushed red pepper
2 tbs. butter, divided	1 tsp. ground turmeric
2 tbs. olive oil, divided	1 cinnamon stick
4 cups chopped onion	2 cups vegetable stock
1 tsp. minced fresh ginger	½ cup pitted dates, chopped
1/3 cup pitted green olives, chopped	3 tbs. fresh lemon juice
2 tbs. flour	¼ cup fresh cilantro
¾ tsp. ground cumin	2 cups garlic couscous, cooked

Directions:

Sprinkle sword fish with salt and pepper. Heat 1 tablespoon of butter and 1 tablespoon of oil in a large Dutch oven over medium-high heat. Add sword fish to pan a little at a time. Seer on each side and remove from pan. Do the same with the next batch.

Add remaining butter and oil to Dutch oven then add in the onions and ginger. Sauté until translucent. Add in olives then stir in the next 6 ingredients, stirring constantly. After 1 minute, stir in the stock and bring to a boil. Return swordfish to pot, cover and reduce heat. Cook for 5-6 minutes. Add in the dates and lemon juice and let simmer for 2 minutes. Garnish with cilantro. Serve over couscous.

FEBRUARY 2 **WHITE PIZZA WITH ARUGULA**

Ingredients:

1 lg. prepared & cooked pizza crust	4 tsp. olive oil
1 cup ricotta cheese, room temperature	1 tbs. fresh lemon juice
½ cup shaved Parmigiano-Reggiano cheese, divided	½ tsp. lemon zest

6 oz. baby arugula, washed & drained   Salt & pepper

1 sm. red onion, thinly sliced

Directions:

Pre-heat oven to 400 degrees.

Place prepared pizza crust on a parchment lined pizza tray. Place in oven for 5 minutes to heat. At the end of the 5 minutes, remove from oven. Quickly spread the ricotta on top of the pizza crust but leave a 1" border. Sprinkle ½ of the shaved cheese on top and return to oven for 4 minutes.

While pizza is in the oven, whisk together the oil, lemon juice, and zest. Place arugula and onions in a bowl and pour oil and lemon dressing on top. Toss well. Remove pizza from oven and top with arugula mixture and serve.

FEBRUARY 3 SAUTEED' MUSHROOMS AND GORGONZOLA

Ingredients:

1½ tbs. extra virgin olive oil   Salt & pepper

1-8 oz. pkg. sliced cremini mushrooms   3½ cups half & half

2 cups thinly sliced onion   2/3 cup quick cooking polenta

1 tsp. minced garlic   3 oz. gorgonzola, crumbled

1 tsp. thyme

Directions:

Heat oil in a non-stick skillet over medium-high heat. Add mushrooms and sauté for 5 minutes or until tender. Add in onion and garlic and sauté for 5 minutes. Next, add in thyme, salt, and pepper then stir, cover, and reduce heat to low to keep warm.

In a medium saucepan over medium-high heat, bring the half and half to a boil. Stir in the polenta and reduce heat to medium. Cook for 5 minutes, stirring frequently, so that no clots will form and until mixture has thickened. Turn off heat and stir in the gorgonzola. Season with black pepper. Divide polenta among 4 plates. Top with mushroom mixture and serve.

FEBRUARY 4 **BLACK-EYED PEAS AND COLLARDS**

Ingredients:

1 tbs. olive oil	32 oz. no-sodium vegetable stock
1 lg. onion, chopped	Salt & pepper
4 lg. garlic cloves, minced	12 oz. fresh collards, lg. chopped
¼ tsp. crushed red pepper flakes	15 oz. can black-eyed peas
1-15 oz. can diced tomatoes	4 tbs. grated Parmesan

Directions:

In a Dutch oven, heat oil over medium-high heat. Add in onion, garlic, and crushed red pepper. Stirring frequently, cook until golden. Add in the tomatoes. Cook for 2 minutes. Next, add in the stock, salt, pepper, and collards. Mix well. Cover then reduce heat to medium-low and simmer for 1½ hours, stirring occasionally. Add in the beans and continue to cook for 20 more minutes. Ladle into individual soup bowls for serving. Sprinkle 1 tablespoon cheese over each bowl before serving.

FEBRUARY 5 **ISRAELI COUSCOUS WITH SUN-DRIED TOMATOES**

Ingredients:

3 garlic cloves, minced	2½ cups vegetable stock
½ cup small chopped sun-dried tomatoes + 2 tbs. of oil from jar	2 tsp. olive oil
1 tbs. dried oregano	½ tsp. salt
¼ tsp. crushed red pepper flakes	2 cups Israeli couscous
½ cup cubed mozzarella	8 basil leaves, julienned

Directions:

In a large bowl, combine the garlic tomatoes, oil from the tomato jar, oregano, red pepper flakes, and mozzarella. Combine well and set aside.

In a medium saucepan, bring the stock, oil, and salt to a boil. Add in the couscous, stir, cover, remove from heat, and set aside for 5 minutes. At the end of 5 minutes, remove lid from sauce pan, fluff couscous with a fork and add to bowl with the tomato mixture. Sprinkle with basil leaves on top and serve either hot or room temperature.

FEBRUARY 6 **STIR-FRIED CHINESE NOODLES**

Ingredients:

12 oz. Chinese egg noodles (fresh or frozen, but thawed)

2 tbs. canola oil

2 cups sliced cremini mushrooms

6 lg. garlic cloves, minced

4 green onions, diagonally sliced

1/3 cup low-sodium soy sauce

2 tbs. brown sugar

2 tbs. fresh lime juice

1½ tbs. dark sesame oil

1½ tbs. ketchup

1 tbs. chili paste

2 cups baby spinach

Directions:

Cook noodles according to package directions but without the salt. Drain and set aside. Heat the oil in a large heavy skillet or wok over medium high heat. Toss in the mushrooms, stirring occasionally and cook for 4 minutes. Next add in the garlic and green onions. Stir often. Whisk together the soy sauce through chili paste and add to pan. Increase heat bringing to a boil. Add noodles; toss well. Add in the spinach that has been washed and drained. Turn off the heat. Toss until spinach wilts, about 1 minute. Serve immediately.

FEBRUARY 7 **UPSIDE DOWN DINNER: BAKED FRENCH TOAST WITH PEAR AND GRUYERE**

Ingredients:

4 cups Anjou pears, peeled & sliced

2 tsp. melted butter

6 tbs. sugar, divided

Cooking spray

12 slices cinnamon swirl bread, cut in half diagonally

1 cup shredded Gruyere

1½ cups milk

4 eggs, beaten

1 tsp. ground cinnamon

1½ tbs. turbinado sugar

½ cup maple syrup

Directions:

In a large bowl, toss together the pears, butter, and 1 tbs. of the sugar.

Coat an 11" X 7" ceramic baking dish with cooking spray. Arrange half of the bread in the dish; spoon pear mixture over bread; sprinkle with cheese. Arrange remaining bread on top.

Whisk together the remaining sugar, milk, eggs, and cinnamon then pour over the bread mixture. Cover and chill for 8-10 hours.

Pre-heat oven to 350 degrees. Uncover dish, sprinkle with turbinado sugar and bake for 1 hour. Remove from oven and let stand for several minutes. Then drizzle with syrup and serve hot.

***NOTE: THIS DISH CAN BE PREPARED IN THE MORNING AND BAKED IN THE EVENING.*

FEBRUARY 8 **GRILLED RED SNAPPER WITH ROASTED RED PEPPER TAPENADE**

Ingredients:

Red Snapper:

4-6 oz. red snapper fillets

Olive oil for brushing

Salt and pepper, to taste

Tapenade:

1 lg. red bell pepper, roasted	1 tbs. fresh lemon juice
1 tbs. dried oregano	1 tsp. olive oil
1/3 cup freshly grated parmesan	Salt & pepper, to taste
¼ cup capers, rinsed and drained	Lemon wedges
4 garlic cloves	

Directions:

Red Snapper:

Pre-heat grill. Place the fillets on a platter and pat dry with a paper towel. Brush both sides of each fish with olive oil and season with salt and pepper. Set aside. Place on grill once grill is hot and cook for 2 minutes on each side or until desired doneness.

Tapenade:

Place pepper on outdoor grill or on cooktop if you have a gas range. Rotate pepper until all sides have blackened. Then transfer to sink and remove all blackened skin. Rinse under cold water and remove stem and seeds then pat dry. Place pepper in blender or food processor along with the remaining ingredients and pulse until a paste has formed. Spread tapenade on top of each fillet and serve with lemon wedges.

FEBRUARY 9 **ORZO AND PEA SALAD**

Ingredients:

½ cup freshly squeezed lemon juice

2 tbs. extra virgin olive oil infused with garlic

1 tbs. Dijon mustard

½ tsp. sea salt

½ tsp. freshly ground black pepper

¼ cup scallions (green onions), finely chopped

8 oz. orzo pasta, cooked according to pkg. directions

1½ cups cooked frozen peas

1 cup snow peas, blanched & chopped

1 cup fresh herbs—parsley, chives, & mint

½ cup toasted pine nuts

2 tsp. lemon zest

Fresh chopped dill weed, for garnish

Directions:

In a small bowl, whisk together the first 6 ingredients. Cover and refrigerate for 15 minutes.

In a large bowl, combine the remaining 6 ingredients. Toss together with the dressing. Garnish with the dill weed and serve.

FEBRUARY 10 **MINESTRONE SOUP**

Ingredients:

3 tbs. olive oil

1 lg. onion, diced

2 garlic cloves, chopped

1 lg. potato, peeled & diced

2 celery stalks, diced

2 lg. carrots, diced

2 cups frozen lima beans

2 cups frozen peas

1-19 oz. can cannellini beans

1 can diced tomatoes

1 bunch fresh Italian parsley, chopped

Salt & freshly ground black pepper, to taste

¾ cup grated Parmigiano-Reggiano cheese, divided

8 oz. ditalini pasta

Directions:

Heat olive oil in a 6 qt. saucepot over medium heat and add the onion and garlic. Sauté until golden. Add in the potato, celery, and carrots and sauté for 2-3 minutes. Then add in the lima beans, peas, cannellini beans, tomatoes, parsley, salt, and pepper and fill the remainder of the pot with water. Increase heat to high to bring to a boil, then lower heat to medium-low and simmer for 1½ hours. Add in the pasta, and cook until al dente. Next, add in the ½ cup of cheese and stir. Serve immediately into individual bowls. Sprinkle with additional cheese on top of each serving. Croutons or crusty Italian bread may be served with each portion, if desired.

FEBRUARY 11 **ITALIAN MAC AND CHEESE**

Ingredients:

1 lb. cavatappi (corkscrew pasta)	12 oz. Fontina cheese
6 tbs. butter	8 oz. grated mozzarella, firmly packed
½ cup flour	1/3 cup freshly grated Parmesan
4 cups milk	¼ cup Italian bread crumbs
1 tbs. + ½ tsp. fresh Italian parsley, finely chopped	

Directions:

Prepare the pasta according to directions on package to al dente. While the pasta is cooking, melt butter in a 5 qt. saucepan on low-medium heat, then add in the flour and whisk together. When blended, increase heat to medium, then slowly add in the milk and continue to whisk. Next add in the pepper and ½ teaspoon of parsley. When the sauce has thickened, add in the Fontina and mozzarella cheeses. Stir well until both have melted.

Once the pasta has cooked, drain well and add to cheese sauce. Then transfer to a buttered 9" X 13" glass baking dish; sprinkle with Parmesan cheese and bread crumbs. Place baking dish on top of a jelly sheet to avoid spills in oven and bake in pre-heated 350 degree oven for about 25-30 minutes until top turns golden and sauce is bubbling. Garnish with remaining parsley and serve hot.

FEBRUARY 12 **VEGETARIAN STUFFED PEPPERS**

Ingredients:

Tomato Sauce:

2 tbs. extra virgin olive oil	5 fresh basil leaves, julienned
1 med. onion, chopped	Salt & freshly ground black pepper
1-35 oz. can crushed tomatoes	1 tsp. sugar
16 oz. of water	¼ cup freshly grated Parmigiano-Reggiano

1 tbs. dried oregano

Stuffed Peppers:

4 large peppers for stuffing—	½ tsp. dried thyme
1 ea. red, yellow, orange, & green	1 tbs. dried parsley
¼ cup extra virgin olive oil	¼ tsp. crushed red pepper
1 med. red pepper, seeds removed, diced	Salt, to taste
1 med. onion, chopped	1 cup cooked orzo
1-4 oz. can mushrooms, drained & chopped	2/3 cup grated Pecorino-Romano, divided
½ pint grape tomatoes, sliced	

Directions:

Tomato Sauce:

Heat the oil in a 4 qt. saucepan over medium heat. Add onions and garlic. Sauté for 2-3 minutes then add in the tomatoes and the rest of the ingredients. Increase heat and bring mixture to a boil. Then lower heat, cover, and let simmer on low for 45 minutes to 1 hour stirring occasionally. If sauce should start to evaporate, just add a little more water.

Stuffed Peppers:

Rinse the 4 large peppers to be used for stuffing. Slice off the tops and remove stems. Set the tops aside. Remove the seeds. Place the peppers upright in a large pot or Dutch oven and fill 1/3 of the pot with water. Place the tops of the peppers in pot as well. Cover pot and bring to a boil. Cook the peppers until par-boiled (tender but still firm). Remove the peppers from the pot and rinse under cold water to stop the cooking process. Drain. Using a 9" X 9" baking dish, ladle 1½ cups tomato sauce into the dish. Place peppers into the pan and set aside.

In the meantime, heat ¼ cup oil in a frying pan over medium heat. Add in the chopped red pepper and onion. Sauté for 3-5 minutes. Next, add in the mushrooms and sauté for 2 minutes. Then add in the tomatoes, oregano, thyme, parsley, crushed red pepper, and salt, to taste. Stir mixture and sauté for an additional 5 minutes. Add in the cooked orzo, stir, and then mix in 1/3 cup of the grated cheese. Remove from heat.

Stuff the peppers to the very top with the orzo mixture; place pepper tops on each stuffed pepper and place in a pre-heated 350 degree oven for 30 minutes. Remove pan from oven and spoon the remaining tomato sauce on top of each pepper. Grate additional cheese on top of each and place pan back into the oven for an additional 10-15 minutes or until tops of peppers become slightly crispy.

FEBRUARY 13 **ASIAN GLAZED TILAPIA**

Ingredients:

2 tbs. soy sauce	1 tbs. sesame seeds
2 tbs. honey	4 tilapia fillets
1 tsp. ground ginger powder	1 lime, quartered
½ tsp. crushed red pepper flakes	Sesame oil for frying

Directions:

In a small bowl, whisk together the first five ingredients. Brush over fillets. Heat a large non-stick frying pan over medium heat. Add the fillets and cook for about 3-5 minutes on each side. Serve with lime wedges. May be accompanied by a salad, rice, or any side of your choosing.

FEBRUARY 14 *VALENTINE'S DAY* FONDUE NIGHT

Ingredients for Main Course:

Cheese Fondue:

1 cup white wine such as Sauvignon Blanc	Broccoli florets
10 oz. imported Swiss cheese, grated	Cauliflower florets
10 oz. Gruyere cheese, grated	Red peppers, cut into 1" pieces
2½ tbs. all-purpose flour	Baby carrots
Rye or Pumpernickel bread	Grape tomatoes
1 baguette cut into large but bite-sized cubes	Apple wedges

Directions:

Cheese Fondue:

In a fondue pot or a 4 qt. sauce pot, simmer the wine over medium-low heat. While stirring, gradually add in both cheeses. Once both have melted, slowly stir in the flour.

Prepare an array of bite-sized foods for dipping onto a large platter along with wooden skewers or fondue forks.

<u>Ingredients for Dessert:</u>

Easy Chocolate Fondue:

1 cup whipping cream

16 oz. good quality chocolate, milk, dark, or semi-sweet broken into pieces

2 tsp. orange liqueur or hazelnut liqueur (optional)

Strawberries	Mandarin orange slices
Sliced bananas	Pound cake cubes
Pears, large diced	

<u>Directions:</u>

Easy Chocolate Fondue:

In a small pot, over low heat, heat the cream until warm then add in the chocolate pieces. Do not allow to boil. Stir well. If adding in a liqueur, stir in at this time.

Prepare an assortment of bite-sized foods for dipping on a large platter along with wooden skewers or fondue forks.

FEBRUARY 15 **ZUCCHINI PARMIGIANA**

<u>Ingredients:</u>

Marinara Sauce:

3 tbs. extra virgin olive oil	5 fresh basil leaves
4 garlic cloves, finely chopped	Salt & pepper
1-35 oz. can crushed tomatoes	¼ tsp. crushed red pepper
1½ tbs. dried oregano	1 tsp. sugar

Zucchini:

Olive oil

6 medium zucchini, peeled & sliced round to 1" thick	Italian seasoned breadcrumbs
	1 lb. shredded mozzarella
2 large eggs, beaten	1 cup grated Parmesan cheese

Salt and pepper

Directions:

Marinara Sauce:

Heat the oil in a 3 qt. sauce pan over medium heat. Add in the garlic and cook until slightly golden. Next add in the tomatoes and remaining ingredients. Stir, then cover and simmer on low heat for 30 minutes.

Zucchini:

Peel zucchini and slice round to 1" thick. Next, beat 2 eggs in a bowl and add in salt and pepper. Then generously pour breadcrumbs onto a shallow plate or onto a sheet of wax paper.

Heat the oil in a 10" skillet on medium-high heat. In an assembly line manner, dip the zucchini slices one at a time into the eggs (draining off the excess) then coat with breadcrumbs and fry until golden on each side. As the zucchini brown on each side, place onto a plate lined with paper towels to absorb any excess oil. When all of the zucchini have been fried, spoon 2 cups of the marinara sauce into a 9" X 12" baking pan and spread it around the entire bottom of the pan. Begin placing the zucchini into the pan. Once one layer has been put down, spoon sauce over top of each slice, then sprinkle with mozzarella and grated cheese. Repeat this layering process until all of the zucchini have been used. Top with sauce, mozzarella and grated cheese and bake in a pre-heated 350 degree oven for approximately 30 minutes until cheese melts and top turns a light brown.

FEBRUARY 16 **PENNE WITH MUSHROOM SAUCE**

For those of you who were once meat eaters and have decided to eliminate meat from your diet but still get that occasional meat craving, try substituting Portobello mushroom in your dishes. They add a "meaty" robust flavor and are a good alternate or replacement, especially for beef.

Ingredients:

¼ cup extra virgin olive oil

1 med. onion, chopped

4 med. garlic cloves, finely minced

1-10 oz. pkg. Baby Bella mushrooms, halved

1-35 oz. can crushed tomatoes

16 oz. of water

1 tbs. dried oregano

6-8 fresh basil leaves, julienned

1 tsp. sugar

½ cup grated Parmesan, divided

1 tsp. salt

1 tsp. black pepper

¼ tsp. crushed red pepper

16 oz. box penne, cooked to al dente

Directions:

In a medium sauce pan, heat oil over medium heat. Add onions and garlic. Sauté for 2-3 minutes and add in the mushrooms. Stir and let simmer until mushrooms are tender. Lower heat and carefully add in the tomatoes. Contents may splatter when coming into contact with the hot oil. Add in remaining ingredients, with the exception of ¼ cup grated cheese and the pasta; increase heat and bring to a boil. Then lower heat, cover, and let simmer on low for 45 minutes to 1 hour, stirring occasionally. If sauce should evaporate, just add a little more water.

Remember to taste the sauce to check if the seasonings are to your liking and, if not, simply add more salt and pepper, if needed.

When sauce is almost done, prepare the penne according to directions on package. Remove from heat, drain and transfer to a large platter. Spoon the mushroom sauce on top. Generously sprinkle with remaining cheese and serve immediately.

FEBRUARY 17 **PIZZA NIGHT**

Ingredients:

Pizza Sauce:

1 tbs. olive oil	5 or 6 fresh whole basil leaves
1 ½ tsp. minced garlic	1 tsp. dried oregano
1-35 oz. can crushed tomatoes	Salt & pepper, to taste

Dough (yields 2 extra-large pizzas):

2 ¼ cups water heated to 125 degrees	1 tbs. salt
2 ½ tbs. active-dry yeast	2 tbs. olive oil, plus extra to grease bowl
1 tbs. sugar	6½-7 cups bread flour or all-purpose flour

Pizza:

For the actual pizza itself you will need grated Parmesan cheese, shredded mozzarella, and any toppings of your choice such as mushrooms, peppers, onions, anchovies, just to name a few.

Directions:

Pizza Sauce:

Heat the oil in a medium sauce pan over medium heat. Add in the garlic and cook until golden. Next, add in the remaining ingredients and simmer on medium-low heat 30 minutes, stirring occasionally.

Dough:

In a small pot, heat water over medium-low heat. Do not overheat because it will burn the yeast. Meanwhile, in a large mixer fitted with a dough hook attachment add yeast to mixing bowl. Pour in the water and allow mixture to ferment for 1 minute. Next, add in the sugar, salt, oil, and 4 cups of flour. Turn mixture on to lowest speed. When all of the ingredients have blended (mixture should look like pancake batter), add 2 ½ cups of flour. Knead in mixer for 4-5 minutes. Dough will thicken and form around hook. If dough begins to stick to bowl, add the remaining flour a little at a time then knead for an additional 1-2 minutes.

Remove dough from bowl and place on a hard clean surface that has been lightly dusted with flour. Knead by hand for 1 or 2 minutes to make sure that all of the air bubbles are out of the dough. Place in a large bowl that has been lightly greased with olive oil. Roll dough around in oil so that it is greased on all sides. Cover bowl tightly with clear plastic wrap and set bowl in a warm place. Let rise until double in bulk (about 30-45 minutes). Remove dough from bowl and place on a lightly floured hard surface once again. Knead by hand until all air bubbles are out. Divide dough into 2 equal halves. Knead each one forming a ball and set on a lightly floured surface. Cover and let rise to double in bulk. When the 2 dough balls have risen, turn oven on to 450 degrees. The oven must be very hot before you put in the pizza.

While oven is warming, roll out dough 1 at a time on a floured surface. Each one should measure about 16" in diameter [***NOTE: If smaller pizzas are desired, after the first rising, divide the dough into 3 round balls, instead of 2]. Place pizza on a large pizza tray that has been sprayed lightly with spray oil. Next, brush olive oil onto the top of the dough then, using a ladle, spread the pizza sauce over the dough, but leave about a 1" border with no sauce so that a nice crust will form while baking. Next, sprinkle oregano, garlic powder, salt, pepper, grated Parmesan cheese, and generous amounts of shredded mozzarella on top. Then add any topping of your choice such as sliced mushrooms, diced green peppers, diced onions, just to name a few. Bake for about 20-25 minutes or until pizza is a rich golden color and cheese has melted. Remove from oven and let sit for a few minutes before serving.

FEBRUARY 18 **BLACK BEAN VEGGIE BURGERS**

Ingredients:

1-16 oz. can black beans, drained & rinsed	1 tbs. chili powder
½ green bell pepper	1 tsp. hot sauce
½ yellow onion	½ cup bread crumbs
3 garlic cloves, skin removed	Salt & pepper, to taste
1 egg	4 hamburger buns

Directions:

Pre-heat oven to 375 degrees. Line a jelly roll pan with non-stick aluminum foil and set aside. In a medium bowl, mash the beans with a fork forming a thick paste. Next, add the bell pepper, onion, and garlic into a food processor and finely chop. Then, add in the beans, egg, chili powder, hot sauce, bread crumbs, salt, and pepper, and pulse until mixture holds together. Form into 4 patties, place on foil-lined pan and bake about 10 minutes on each side. Place on buns and serve with lettuce, tomatoes, and ketchup.

FEBRUARY 19 SHRIMP OREGANATO AND LINGUINE

Ingredients:

1 lb. linguine

1/3 cup extra virgin olive oil

6 garlic cloves, minced

2-14.5 oz. cans Italian stewed tomatoes

2 lbs. large raw shrimp, peeled and deveined*

1 tbs. dried oregano

Salt, to taste

½ tsp. crushed red pepper flakes

Parsley sprigs, for garnish

Directions:

Prepare pasta according to directions on package to al dente. Drain.

While pasta is cooking, heat the oil in a 12" skillet over medium heat. Add in the garlic and sauté until golden. Do not overcook. Add in the tomatoes, oregano, salt, and pepper. Stir and let simmer for 2 minutes. Next, add in the shrimp. If using raw shrimp, simmer in sauce for 3 minutes or until shrimp has turned pink on both sides. *If using cooked shrimp that has previously been frozen, just add in and stir. Let simmer for 1-2 minutes. Serve immediately over pasta. Garnish with parsley.

FEBRUARY 20 POTATO AND ONION FRITTATA

Ingredients:

¼ cup extra virgin olive oil

4 large potatoes, peeled and cut into ¼" slices

2 medium onions, sliced

10 large eggs, whisked

Salt & freshly ground black pepper

¼ cup dried French tarragon

1 tsp. garlic powder

Directions:

Peel potatoes. Wash, cut and pat dry. Peel onions and slice. In a large 10" or 12" non-stick skillet that is oven proof, heat oil over medium heat. Once the oil has been heated, add the potatoes and onions to the pan. Stir occasionally so that the potatoes and onions do not burn and cook until potatoes are fork tender.

In the meantime, whisk the eggs and add the remaining ingredients to the eggs. Check pan to see if more oil is needed, and if so, add more oil. Then reduce heat and evenly pour the egg mixture over the potatoes and onions. Continue to cook on stove top for 5 minutes then place in a pre-heated 350 degree oven until eggs are set and not runny. Remove from oven, cut into wedges and serve with a light salad on the side and sliced French baguette.

FEBRUARY 21 **CHILI**

Ingredients:

1 tbs. olive oil	8 oz. canned black beans, drained
3 garlic cloves, minced	8 oz. can dark red kidney beans, drained
1 med. onion, chopped	8 oz. can pinto beans, drained
1 celery stalk, chopped	8 oz. can corn, drained
½ cup diced carrots	1 tsp. cumin
½ cup chopped green bell pepper	2 tsp. dried oregano
1/3 cup chopped red pepper	1 tsp. garlic powder
1 tbs. chili powder	1 tsp. crushed red pepper flakes *
¾ cup sliced Baby Bella mushrooms	Salt, to taste
2-14 oz. cans diced tomatoes with liquid	Shredded cheddar cheese

***NOTE: If you like spicier chili, just add more pepper or 1 chopped jalapeno pepper.

Directions:

Heat the oil in a large Dutch oven over medium heat. Add in the garlic, onion, celery and carrots. Sauté until tender. Next add in the peppers and chili powder. Cook for about 5 minutes. Add in the remaining ingredients, except for the cheese and stir. Cover; bring to a boil. Then lower heat to medium-low and let simmer for 30 minutes, stirring occasionally. Serve hot in individual bowls and top with cheese. Corn bread or tortilla chips may accompany this dish.

FEBRUARY 22 **KEW-NEW-JEW (LENTIL AND BUTTERNUT SQUASH SOUP) PERSIAN**

This recipe was given to me by Ahang Zafari, a native of the city of Nahavan in the province of Hamedan, Iran. It was passed down to her by her father, Mr. Parviz Zafari who loves to cook. Ms. Zafari currently lives in Connecticut with her husband and children. I wish to express my sincere thanks to both her and her kind dad for sharing this delicious recipe with me!

Ingredients:

3 tbs. olive oil

1 lg. onion, diced

8 garlic cloves, finely chopped

1 lb. butternut squash, cubed

1 lb. pkg. lentils, washed & drained

12 cups water

Directions:

Heat the oil in a 5 qt. saucepan over medium heat. Toss in the onion and garlic and sauté until onions are translucent. Next, add in the butternut squash and cook on low-medium heat until squash is very soft, stirring frequently. When very soft, gently mash with back of spoon, but leave some small chunks for texture. Add in the lentils, water, salt, and pepper and continue to cook until liquid boils down, lentils are tender, and a thick porridge-like soup is formed. Stir often to avoid it sticking to the bottom of the pot. Serve in individual bowls with sliced warm bread.

FEBRUAY 23 **PORTOBELLO MUSHROOM PARMIGIANA**

Ingredients:

Marinara Sauce:

3 tbs. extra virgin olive oil

4 garlic cloves, finely chopped

1-35 oz. can crushed tomatoes

1½ tbs. dried oregano

5 fresh basil leaves

Salt & pepper, to taste

¼ tsp. crushed red pepper

1 tsp. sugar

Portobello Parmigiana:

8 lg. Portobello mushrooms

2-3 tbs. extra virgin olive oil

Salt and freshly ground black pepper

½ cup grated Parmigiano-Reggiano

1¼ cups shredded mozzarella

Directions:

Marinara Sauce:

Heat the oil in a 3 qt. saucepan over medium heat. Add in the garlic and cook until lightly golden. Next, add in the tomatoes and remaining ingredients. Stir then cover and simmer on low heat for 30 minutes.

Portobello Parmigiana:

Lightly drizzle some olive oil into a 9" X 12" glass baking dish and evenly spread oil over bottom of dish. Using a brush, lightly brush oil onto each cap and place mushrooms, cap side down, into baking dish. Then lightly drizzle oil into undersides of each mushroom; sprinkle with salt and pepper and place baking dish into a pre-heated 350 degree oven for 10-15 minutes or until slightly tender. Remove baking dish from oven and transfer mushrooms to a plate. Evenly ladle some marinara sauce into the glass baking dish and return mushrooms back to the dish, cap side down. Spoon remaining sauce evenly into each mushroom cap, sprinkle with grated cheese, and then sprinkle each with the mozzarella. Bake in a pre-heated 350 degree oven until cheese has melted and begins to turn golden, about 15 minutes.

***SERVING SUGGESTION: Serve 2 caps per person and you may serve pasta with marinara sauce as a side dish.

FEBRUARY 24 **SALMON BURGERS**

Ingredients:

2 tsp. freshly chopped parsley	1 cup plain breadcrumbs
2 scallions, chopped	Kosher salt & black pepper
2 eggs	2-6½ oz. cans boneless pink salmon, drained
1 tbs. mayonnaise	2 tbs. extra virgin olive oil
1 tbs. freshly squeezed lemon juice	4 hamburger rolls with sesame seeds, halved
Pinch of cayenne pepper	Tartar sauce & arugula, for topping

Directions:

In a medium bowl combine the first 9 ingredients, but only 2 tablespoons of the bread crumbs. Line a baking sheet with parchment paper and brush with oil. Sprinkle remaining bread crumbs on a plate. Divide the salmon mixture into 4 patties that are ¾" thick. Next press both sides of each burger down onto the plate with the bread crumbs and place on parchment lined tray. Loosely cover with plastic wrap and refrigerate for 45 minutes to 1 hour. Pre-heat oven to 425 degrees. Remove pan from refrigerator and place in heated oven. When burgers are browned on one side, flip over to brown the other side. Transfer to individual plates with buns and place burger on bottom of each bun. Top with tartar sauce and baby arugula, then cover with top halves of buns. Serve with crab chips.

FEBRUARY 25 **LINGUINE WITH GARLIC AND OIL**

Ingredients:

1 lb. linguine	½ tsp. crushed red pepper flakes
1 cup extra virgin olive oil	¼ cup fresh Italian parsley, chopped
8 garlic cloves, sliced	1 cup grated Parmigiano-Reggiano cheese

Directions:

Cook linguine according to directions on package until al dente. In the meantime, heat the oil in a small saucepan over medium-low heat. Add in the garlic and red pepper flakes and sauté until garlic is lightly golden. Stir constantly and do not let the garlic burn or become dark brown because it will become very bitter. Remove from heat and set aside.

Drain the pasta but reserve 1 cup of the pasta water. Return the pasta to the saucepan, add ½ cup of the reserved water and the garlic and oil mixture. Turn heat on to medium and gently toss the pasta. If dry, add the remaining ½ cup of pasta water. Toss well. Transfer pasta onto a large serving platter and sprinkle with parsley and cheese. Serve immediately.

FEBRUARY 26 **RISOTTO WITH BUTTERNUT SQUASH**

Ingredients:

6 cups butternut squash,	5 tbs. butter
diced into 1" cubes	½ cup minced shallots
Olive oil	1½ cups Arborio rice
Mediterranean sea salt	½ cup Sauvignon Blanc
Freshly ground black pepper	¼ tsp. saffron powder
48 oz. no-sodium vegetable stock	1 cup freshly grated Parmesan cheese

Directions:

Place squash on a sheet pan. Drizzle with olive oil and sprinkle with salt and pepper. Toss. Place in a pre-heated 400 degree oven and roast until very tender (approximately 30 minutes). Be sure to toss after 10 or 15 minutes.

In the meantime, heat the vegetable stock in a 3 qt. saucepan over low heat.

In a large Dutch oven, melt butter over medium-low heat then add in the shallots and sauté until translucent. Add rice and stir, then add in the wine. Allow to cook for 2-3 minutes. Ladle in 2 ladles of stock, add saffron, 1 teaspoon salt and ½ teaspoon pepper. Stirring frequently, let simmer until all liquid has been absorbed. Continue to ladle in 2 more ladles of stock, stir often and as liquid becomes absorbed, add in more stock. Once the rice is tender and al dente, turn off the heat, then add in the roasted squash and grated cheese. Combine well. Serve hot.

FEBRUARY 27 **CHEESE SOUFFLE'**

Ingredients:

½ cup unsalted butter	1 tsp. freshly ground black pepper
½ cup all-purpose flour	8 egg yolks, room temperature
2 cups milk	8 egg whites, room temperature
1 tsp. salt	4 cups cheese (2 cups each shredded Gruyere & white cheddar)

Directions:

In a medium saucepan, melt butter over medium-low heat; stir in flour and begin to whisk until a paste forms. Add in the milk, salt, and pepper, and whisk together over medium heat until mixture become thick and starts to bubble. Lower heat to very low and slowly stir in cheese until it has completely melted. Remove from heat and let sit for a brief time.

In a large bowl, beat the egg yolks and gradually add the cheese sauce to the egg yolks, stirring constantly. Make sure cheese sauce is not too hot because eggs will scramble when combining the two.

Using an electric stand mixer fitted with a whisk attachment beat the egg whites on high speed until stiff peaks have formed. Gently fold in ½ of the stiff egg whites into the cheese sauce and combine. Do the same with the remaining egg whites. Pour into a large soufflé dish or individual ramekins.

Bake in a pre-heated 350 degree oven for about 35-40 minutes or until a knife inserted in center comes out clean. Serve immediately.

Ingredients:

1-2 lb. lobster, par-boiled	1 tbs. oregano
Salt	½ cup dry white wine
Water	1 tsp. salt
2 tbs. extra virgin olive oil	1 tbs. crushed red pepper flakes*
4 garlic cloves, minced	1 lb. spaghetti or linguine, to al dente
1-35 oz. can San Marzano whole tomatoes	

***Note:** Additional crushed red pepper may be added if a spicier flavor is desired.

Directions:

In a deep stock pot, bring 4 cups salted water to a boil. Add in the lobster and par-boil for 5½ minutes.

In the meantime, in a deep skillet, heat oil over medium heat, add in the garlic, and sauté until lightly golden. Add in the tomatoes and gently crush.   Next add in the oregano, wine, salt and pepper flakes. Allow to simmer for 30 minutes.

Remove the lobster from the pot, crack open the shell and remove meat. Add large chunks to the sauce and continue to cook for 20 more minutes. Drain pasta and spoon sauce over pasta.

MARCH 1 **ASIAN SCALLOPS**

Ingredients:

16 lg. scallops	1½ tsp. ginger powder
5 tbs. low-sodium soy sauce	Sesame oil for frying
3 tbs. Worcestshire sauce	1 tbs. honey
3 garlic cloves, minced	1 tbs. sesame seeds

Directions:

In a bowl, whisk together the soy sauce, Worcestshire sauce, garlic, and ginger. Add in the scallops. Toss gently. Cover bowl with plastic wrap and refrigerate for 2-3 hours.

Heat a non-stick skillet on medium-high heat. Add in the oil and swirl around pan to coat bottom. When oil begins to sizzle, add in the scallops and sear for 2-3 minutes until a crust forms, then turn over and repeat. Transfer to a plate. Heat the marinade in the same pan. Add honey and stir. Pour marinade over scallops, sprinkle with sesame seeds and serve. May be accompanied with rice.

MARCH 2 **ZUCCHINI PIZZA**

Ingredients:

1 prepared pizza dough

Olive oil

1 tbs. garlic powder

1 tsp. dried oregano

½ cup grated Parmesan cheese

1 lg. zucchini, sliced

12 oz. shredded mozzarella

1 lg. beefsteak tomato, thinly sliced

Directions:

Roll out dough to fit a 12" pizza tray that has been sprayed with non-stick spray oil. Brush olive oil on dough. Sprinkle with garlic powder, oregano, and Parmesan cheese. Lay on the zucchini slices. Sprinkle on the mozzarella and place the tomato slices on top. Bake in a pre-heated 425 degree oven for about 20-25 minutes until dough has turned golden and cheese has melted and is bubbling.

MARCH 3 **MANHATTAN CLAM CHOWDER**

Ingredients:

1 dozen quahogs or cherrystone clams

4 cups water

3 tbs. butter

1 lg. onion, diced

6 cloves garlic, minced

2 celery stalks, diced

2 carrots, peeled and diced

2 potatoes, peeled & diced

1-35 oz. can whole tomatoes, pureed

1 tsp. oregano

1 tbs. dried parsley

½ tsp. thyme

Sea salt

Freshly ground black pepper

<u>Directions:</u>

Scrub the clam shells and rinse. Discard any that are cracked or opened. In a large pot or Dutch oven, add in the clams along with the water. Bring to a boil over medium-high heat, cover pot, reduce heat to medium, and allow clams to steam for about 8-10 minutes, until they are all opened. Remove clams from pot and discard any that have not opened. DO NOT DISCARD THE WATER. Then remove clams from shell and roughly chop. Set aside. Strain water and set aside as well.

Next, using the same pot, melt butter over medium flame. Add the onions, garlic, celery, carrots, and potatoes. Stirring occasionally, allow vegetables to sauté for 6-8 minutes. Then add in the tomatoes, clam broth, and remaining ingredients. Stir all ingredients, reduce heat to low, cover and let simmer for 30-40 minutes. Serve hot.

MARCH 4 **PASTA E' FAGIOLI (PASTA AND CANNELLINI BEANS)**

<u>Ingredients:</u>

3 tbs. extra virgin olive oil	¼ cup grated Parmigiano-Reggiano cheese
4 lg. garlic cloves, minced	¼ tsp. crushed red pepper flakes
1-35 oz. can crushed tomatoes & 16 oz. water	1 tsp. salt
1-19 oz. can cannellini beans, drained & rinsed	1 tsp. sugar
2 tbs. dried oregano	1 lb. ditali pasta, cooked to al dente

<u>Directions:</u>

In a medium sauce pan on medium-low heat, heat olive oil and add garlic. Sauté until both are lightly golden.   Next, add in the tomatoes and water, then stir. Add in the beans, oregano, ¼ cup cheese, pepper, salt, and sugar. Stir. Cover and bring to a gentle boil then reduce heat and let simmer for 45 minutes.

Once sauce is done, prepare pasta as suggested on package directions. Be careful not to overcook the pasta. Drain and pour into a large bowl. Pour all of the sauce into the bowl with the pasta and stir well. Generously sprinkle with grated cheese and serve in individual bowls. Sprinkle with additional cheese before serving.

MARCH 5 **PORTOBELLO MUSHROOM BURGERS**

Ingredients:

4 lg. Portobello mushroom caps	Sea salt
¼ cup balsamic vinegar from Modena	Freshly ground black pepper
2 tbs. garlic infused olive oil	4 slices provolone cheese
1 tsp. fresh thyme leaves	4 hamburger rolls with sesame seeds
1 tbs. minced garlic	Lettuce, tomatoes, & ketchup (toppings)

Directions:

Place mushrooms in a shallow glass baking dish, smooth side up. In a small bowl, mix together the vinegar, oil, thyme, garlic, salt, and pepper. Pour the marinade over the mushrooms and marinate for 15 minutes. Turn mushrooms over in dish every 5 minutes.

In the meantime, place each half of the hamburger rolls on a baking sheet and into a pre-heated 350 degree oven for about 5-6 minutes until lightly toasted.

Brush a grill pan with olive oil and pre-heat over medium heat. When pan is hot, place mushrooms on the grill pan and grill for about 6-8 minutes on each side. Brush each side with remaining marinade while grilling. About 1 minute before removing mushrooms from grill pan, top with provolone. Place on bottom halves of toasted buns and top with lettuce, tomatoes, and ketchup. Cover with top halves of buns. This dish may be accompanied with fries or chips.

MARCH 6 **BROCCOLI AND CHEESE CREPES**

Ingredients:

2 eggs	Canola oil
1½ cups water	1 pkg. fresh broccoli florets
1 cup flour	1½ cups grated cheddar cheese
¼ tsp. salt	

Directions:

In a large bowl, using a hand mixer, combine eggs, water, flour and salt. Set aside for 10 minutes to allow air bubbles to dissipate so that the batter will be smooth.

Heat a 6" non-stick pan over medium-low heat. Using a brush, coat the inside of the pan with oil. Using a small ladle, pour approximately 1 oz. of the batter in the center of the pan and swirl around to coat the entire bottom of the pan. Cook for no more than 30 seconds, then flip crepe over and cook the other side for about 10-12 seconds. Slide the crepe out of the pan and onto a large platter. Repeat process but do not place hot crepes on top of one another. Separate each layer with wax paper and let cool. Set aside.

Using a 4 qt. pot, add broccoli and ½ cup water. Cover and steam broccoli over medium-high heat. Arrange crepes on baking sheets. As soon as broccoli has steamed, drain and put about 7 or 8 florets on one half of each crepe. Sprinkle cheese on the broccoli, fold empty half of crepe over then sprinkle with additional cheese over the outside of each crepe. Place on a baking sheet that has been lined with parchment paper and place in a pre-heated 350 degree oven for 5-7 minutes to allow cheese to melt. Serve hot.

MARCH 7 **GRILLED SWORDFISH WITH LEMON BASIL PESTO**

Ingredients:

4 cups fresh lemon basil	½ cup extra virgin olive oil
4 cloves garlic	1 cup grated Parmesan cheese
½ cup toasted pine nuts	4-6 oz. swordfish steaks
1 lemon, zested and juiced	Olive oil
½ tsp. salt	Salt
½ tsp. freshly ground black pepper	Black pepper

Directions:

Using a food processor, blend the first 6 ingredients. When pine nuts are finely chopped, slowly add in the oil while processor is running. Once mixture is creamy, add in the cheese.

Place a grill pan over medium-high heat. Brush both sides of the fish with olive oil and season with salt and pepper. Grill the fish for about 5-6 minutes on each side allowing grill marks to show. Place the fish on individual dinner plates, top with the lemon basil pesto, and serve.

MARCH 8 **ITALIAN VEGETABLE SOUP**

Ingredients:

3 carrots, peeled, washed, & sliced	1-14.5 oz. can Italian stewed tomatoes
2 lg. celery stalks, washed & sliced	½ cup grated Parmigiano-Reggiano, divided
1 lg. onion, peeled & sliced	Salt & pepper, to taste

1 tsp. garlic powder   ¾ cup acine pepe pasta

2-32 oz. containers of organic vegetable stock

Directions:

In a 6 qt. saucepan over medium heat, add the carrots, celery, onion, garlic powder and 2 cups of vegetable stock. Cover and simmer until vegetables start to become slightly tender (about 8-10 minutes). Add in the remaining ingredients through the salt and pepper, but only ¼ cup of cheese. Cover. Let simmer on medium-low heat for about 1½ hours, then add in the pasta, stir, and simmer until pasta has cooked. Serve in individual bowls. Sprinkle each bowl with additional cheese before serving.

MARCH 9 TUNA MELT PANINI

Ingredients:

2-6 oz. cans tuna packed in olive oil, drained   2 tsp. fresh parsley, chopped

Approximately 6 tbs. mayonnaise   4-3 oz. slices provolone cheese

1 celery stalk, finely chopped   2 cups arugula

1 small red onion, finely chopped   4 ciabatta rolls

Directions:

In a medium bowl, empty the tuna and with a fork, gently flake. Mix together the tuna, mayonnaise, celery, onion, and parsley and evenly divide amongst the 4 bottom halves of the rolls. Place a slice of provolone on top of each and top with arugula. Then place the top halves of the rolls on each of the sandwiches. Cook in a Panini press on medium-low heat until bread is toasted and cheese has melted (approximately 6-8 minutes).

MARCH 10 SEARED SCALLOPS

Ingredients:

¾ cup all-purpose flour   2 doz. scallops, rinsed, drained & patted dry

1 tbs. sea salt   ¼ cup olive oil

¾ cup dried thyme   ¼ cup chopped fresh parsley

3 tbs. lemon pepper   Lemon juice

Directions:

In a large bowl, mix together the first 4 ingredients. Toss in the scallops and coat on all sides.

Heat olive oil in a 12" skillet over medium-high heat. Place scallops in pan, making sure they do not touch each other. Sear on all sides. Add lemon juice to pan and sprinkle with parsley. Serve immediately.

MARCH 11 ITALIAN BAKED FISH IN PACKETS

Ingredients:

4-4 oz. fillets of white fish (cod, halibut, or haddock)

Extra virgin olive oil

Salt & freshly ground black pepper

4 garlic cloves, minced

1 tsp. dried oregano

8 plum tomatoes

Parchment paper

2 cups steamed rice or couscous

Directions:

Cut 4 pieces of parchment paper that are double the size of each fish. Place a piece of fish in the center of each piece of parchment paper. Lightly drizzle each piece of fish with olive oil, sprinkle with salt and pepper. In addition, evenly divide the minced garlic over each piece of fish. Then sprinkle ¼ teaspoon of oregano over each as well. Place the tomatoes in a bowl, gently squeeze each one and place 2 tomatoes on top of each fish.

Next, gather both ends of the parchment paper and bring them up to the top so they meet in the middle. Begin to fold over the fish but leave enough room to allow steam to flow. Tightly crimp the sides of the parchment paper so that the juices will not leak out. Place all four packets on a rimmed baking sheet, and place in a pre-heated 350 degree oven for approximately 20-25 minutes or until fish becomes flaky. Serve immediately with steamed rice or couscous. ***NOTE: Be careful when opening the packets because steam will release. It is best to have an adult open the packets when children are being served.

MARCH 12 PASTA E' LENTICA (PASTA AND LENTILS)

Ingredients:

3 tbs. extra virgin olive oil

4 garlic cloves, finely chopped

2 cups lentils, washed & drained

¼ tsp. crushed red pepper

1/8 tsp. black pepper

Salt, to taste

| 4 ½ quarts water | ½ lb. ditali, elbows, or farfalle pasta |
| 2 tbs. dried oregano | ¼ cup grated parmesan cheese, optional |

Directions:

In a 5 qt. sauce pan, heat oil on medium-low heat; add in garlic, stirring until golden. Do not overcook. Add lentils to the pot, stir, then immediately add in the water. Next, add remaining ingredients through salt. Increase heat bringing mixture to a boil, then cover and lower heat allowing mixture to simmer. Cook until lentils are tender about 20-30 minutes.

Once the lentils have cooked, prepare pasta as suggested on package directions until al dente. Be careful not to overcook the pasta. When pasta is done, drain and pour into a large bowl, then pour the lentil mixture over the pasta. Stir until completely mixed. Add cheese, if desired. Ladle into individual bowls while hot.

MARCH 13 **MATZO BALL SOUP (JEWISH)**

Ingredients:

For the matzo balls:

2 eggs, beaten	1 tbs. dried parsley
2 tbs. unsalted butter, melted	1 tbs. dried dill weed
2 tbs. vegetable stock	½ tsp. salt
½ cup matzo meal	

For the broth:

2 tbs. olive oil	48 oz. vegetable stock
1 onion, finely chopped	¼ cup chopped fresh parsley
1 celery stalk, finely chopped	Kosher salt
2 carrots, diced	Freshly ground black pepper
2 scallions, finely chopped	

Directions:

For the Matzo balls:

Using a medium sized bowl, combine together the eggs, butter, and vegetable stock. Add in the meal parsley, dill, and salt. Mix well. Cover bowl tightly with plastic wrap and set in refrigerator for 30 minutes.

Fill a 6 qt. pot with water, add a pinch of salt, and bring water to a boil. After 30 minutes or so, remove bowl from refrigerator and form dough into walnut-sized balls (they will be sticky so use wet hands). Drop the balls into the water, reduce heat, and cook for 30 minutes or so until plump.

For the broth:

In the meantime, using a Dutch oven over medium-high heat add in the olive oil. Once hot, toss in the onions, celery, and carrots, and sauté until tender and translucent. Add in the scallions and cook for an additional 5 minutes. Next, add in the stock, parsley, salt, and pepper. Bring to a boil then reduce heat and let simmer for 15-20 minutes. When matzo balls are done, ladle broth into individual bowls and add 2 matzo balls to each bowl.

MARCH 14 NEAR EASTERN CURRIED BUTTERNUT SQUASH AND RICE (INDIAN)

Ingredients:

3 tbs. olive oil	½ tsp. ground cumin
4 cups butternut squash, cubed	1 tbs. curry powder
1 tbs. grated fresh ginger	1-14.5 oz. container vegetable stock
½ cup dried cranberries	4 cups cooked brown rice
1 tsp. ground cinnamon	2 scallions, finely chopped
1 tsp. ground coriander	

Directions:

Heat the oil in a large skillet over medium heat. Add in the squash and cook until all sides begin to lightly brown. Add in the ginger, cranberries, cinnamon, coriander, cumin, and curry powder. Cook for an additional 2-3 minutes on low heat. Add the stock and bring mixture to a boil, then reduce heat, cover skillet and let simmer on low for about 15 minutes until squash becomes tender. Do not overcook. Serve over rice and sprinkle with scallions.

MARCH 15 **EGGPLANT NUGGETS**

Ingredients:

3 cups canola oil, pre-heated to 350 degrees

2-3 lg. eggs, beaten

2 lg. eggplants, peeled & cut into large cubes

2 cups Italian-style breadcrumbs

1½ tsp. sugar

½ tsp. black pepper

Your favorite marinara or Alfredo sauce

Directions:

Heat the oil in a medium saucepan over medium-high heat. Beat eggs in a large bowl and toss in the eggplants. Dip the eggplants in the eggs and coat well on both sides. Place bread crumbs, sugar, and pepper, in a large zip-lock bag. Shake to mix well, then using a kitchen spider, or slotted spoon, lift eggplants from the eggs allowing excess egg batter to drain back into bowl, and drop eggplants (a little at a time) into the bag with the breadcrumbs. Toss well to make sure they are completely covered with bread crumbs then place in hot oil. Brown eggplants on all sides then place on a platter lined with paper towels to absorb excess oil. Dip in your favorite marinara sauce or an Alfredo sauce.

MARCH 16 **CREAM OF PEANUT SOUP**

Ingredients:

¼ cup butter

½ cup finely chopped celery

½ cup finely chopped onion

1½ tbs. flour

1 cup smooth creamy peanut butter

6 cups vegetable stock

Salt & pepper, to taste

1 cup heavy cream

½ cup finely chopped unsalted peanuts

Directions:

Melt butter in a heavy 5 qt. saucepan over medium heat. Then add the celery and onion. Sauté until tender, but not browned. Sprinkle with flour and cook for one minute, stirring constantly. Turn off the heat, stir in the peanut butter, then add in the stock. Bring to a boil over high heat, then lower heat and simmer covered for 15 minutes. Season with salt and pepper. Add cream, and increase heat to medium for 5 minutes. Serve in individual bowls and garnish with chopped peanuts.

MARCH 17 *ST. PATRICK'S DAY* STEAMED CABBAGE

Ingredients:

1 head cabbage	¼ tsp. crushed red pepper flakes
½ cup olive oil	1 ½ cups water
6 garlic cloves, minced	Salt & pepper

Directions:

Cut cabbage head in half and remove the core. Then remove the leaves and rough chop. Heat the oil in a large pot or Dutch oven over medium heat. Add in the garlic, red pepper flakes, and cook until lightly golden. Place ¼ of the chopped cabbage in the pot along with ¼ cup water. Cover. When cabbage has wilted, add another ¼ to the pot and a little more water. Continue this process until all the cabbage has been used. Add remaining water and season with salt and pepper. Stir, then cover and allow to steam for 40-45 minutes or until leaves are tender, stirring occasionally. Serve hot along with sliced crusty bread.

MARCH 18 SHRIMP STIR-FRY WITH SESAME SEEDS

Ingredients:

½ tsp. ground ginger	3 tbs. sesame oil
¼ tsp. red pepper flakes	1 red bell pepper, sliced into thin strips
2 cloves garlic, minced	4 green onions, white & green parts, sliced
¼ cup teriyaki sauce	½ lb. snow peas
¼ cup sweet sherry	1 lb. med. raw shrimp, peeled & deveined
1/8 cup cornstarch	1 tbs. sesame seeds
1 tbs. honey	2 cups steamed rice

Directions:

Whisk the first 5 ingredients together in a medium bowl. Then add in the cornstarch and whisk together. Next, stir in the honey and set aside. Using a large wok or cast-iron skillet, heat the oil on medium-high heat. Add in the red pepper, onions, and snow peas. Sauté for 4 minutes while stirring continuously. Add in the shrimp and cook until they have turned pink and are no longer translucent. Finally, stir in the teriyaki mixture and incorporate all ingredients together for two minutes over high heat. Sprinkle with sesame seeds and serve over rice.

MARCH 19 ITALIAN PASTA SALAD WITH TUNA

Ingredients:

1 lg. red roasted pepper, finely chopped

2 cups cooked acine pepe or orzo pasta

1/3 cup extra virgin olive oil

8 sun-dried tomatoes, chopped small

1 lg. garlic clove, minced

1¼ tsp. dried oregano

1/3 cup black pitted oil cured olives, chopped small

2-6 oz. cans Italian tuna packed in olive oil

Salt & black pepper, to taste

Directions:

Roast the red pepper by either placing on an outdoor grill or by using an indoor grill. If you have a gas range, you can roast the pepper by using tongs and directly placing it on the grate over a high flame. Roast the pepper until completely blackened on all sides. Then remove from heat and transfer to the sink where you can remove all of the charred skin, seeds, and stem. Wash, dry, and slice into small pieces. Transfer to a medium-sized bowl.

Prepare the pasta as directed on package. Drain and add to bowl with red pepper. Immediately add the olive oil and stir so that the pasta will not stick together. Add in the remaining ingredients but separate the tuna with a fork before adding to the pasta mixture. Then combine.

MARCH 20 BROCCOLI QUICHE

Ingredients:

2 tbs. butter

1 medium onion, minced

2 garlic cloves, minced

2 cups fresh broccoli florets, chopped small

1-9" pie crust, unbaked

1 ½ cups shredded Gruyere

4 eggs, beaten

1½ cups, half & half

1 tsp. salt

1 tsp. freshly ground black pepper

1 tbs. butter, melted

Directions:

Melt butter in a medium saucepan over low-medium heat. Add in the onions, garlic, and broccoli. Cook until vegetables are soft, stirring occasionally. In the meantime, place pie crust in a greased 9" pie plate. Spoon vegetables into crust and sprinkle with cheese.

Whisk the eggs, half and half, salt, pepper, and butter together then pour mixture over vegetables and cheese. Bake in a pre-heated 350 degree oven until knife inserted in center comes out clean and crust has lightly browned (about 30-35 minutes).

MARCH 21 BAKED FISH WITH WALNUT, CURRANT, AND HERB STUFFING (MIDDLE EASTERN)

Ingredients:

1/2 cup + 2 tbs. olive oil	1 cup finely chopped walnuts
1-4 lb. whole striped bass/rock fish	½ cup flat leaf parsley, chopped
3 tsp. salt	½ cup fresh dill weed, finely chopped
1 cup finely chopped onions	1½ tsp. black pepper
4 cloves garlic, minced	3 tbs. fresh lime juice
¾ cup dried currants	2½ cups steamed rice

Directions:

Pour ¼ cup of oil in a large glass baking dish. Gut and scale the fish but leave on the head and tail. Pat dry the fish and sprinkle with 2 teaspoons of salt, in and out. Place fish in the baking dish and pour ¼ cup oil on top. Brush oil evenly over both sides. Set aside.

In the meantime, over medium heat, heat the remaining oil in a 10" skillet. Add in the onions and garlic, cooking until translucent. Add in the currants and continue to cook for 3 minutes. Then add in the walnuts; cook for 2 more minutes. Decrease heat to low and add in the parsley, dill, black pepper, and remaining teaspoon of salt. Stir well. Fill the fish with the stuffing. Close oral cavity by inserting crisscrossed wooden skewers. Pour lime juice over the fish and bake in a pre-heated 375 degree oven for 50-60 minutes until fish feels firm. Be sure to baste every 15-20 minutes. Serve with steamed rice.

MARCH 22 **CURRIED LENTILS AND RICE (INDIAN)**

Ingredients:

3 tbs. olive oil

1 lg. onion, finely chopped

4 lg. garlic cloves, minced

3 cups water

1 cup uncooked lentils

1 tsp. Kosher salt

1½ tsp. curried powder

2 cups steamed rice

Directions:

Heat the oil in a medium saucepan over medium heat. Add in the onion and garlic and cook until translucent. Add in the water, lentils, salt, and curry powder. Stir. Bring to a boil then reduce heat and cook until lentils are tender, about 35-40 minutes. Serve over steamed rice.

MARCH 23 **POTATO LEEK SOUP**

Ingredients:

3 leeks, white parts only, cleaned and finely chopped,

3 tbs. unsalted butter

2 shallots, finely chopped

1 qt. water

½ celery stalk, diced

4 potatoes diced

1 cup half & half

1 cup heavy cream

Salt & pepper

¼ cup fresh parsley, chopped

Directions:

Remove green portions from leeks. Cut the center of the leeks lengthwise and rinse thoroughly. Make sure all sand is washed away, and finely chop. In a Dutch oven, heat butter over medium-high heat and toss the chopped leeks and shallots into the pot. Sauté until translucent, stirring often. Add in the water and potatoes. Lower heat to medium and allow to simmer for 25-30 minutes. Turn off heat and using a stick blender, or potato masher, puree the soup. Next stir in the half and half, cream, salt and pepper. Turn on the heat to medium low and heat for 3-4 minutes. Ladle into individual bowls and garnish with parsley.

MARCH 24 **OMLET-E KHORMA/DATE OMELET (PERSIAN)**

Craving something sweet for dinner but want to eat light? Here is a wonderful sweet, light supper that I am sure you will enjoy.

Ingredients:

4 tbs. butter or margarine

1 cup pitted dates, roughly chopped

8 eggs, beaten

Directions:

Melt butter in a 10" non-stick skillet on medium-low heat. Add in the dates and sauté for about 5 minutes until they begin to soften. Spread dates evenly over the bottom of the skillet and pour the beaten eggs over the dates. Reduce heat to low, cover pan, and cook for 4-5 minutes until eggs have set. Serve with warmed flat bread.

MARCH 25 **MOUSSAKA (GREEK)**

Ingredients:

1 eggplant, thinly sliced	Salt & pepper, to taste
4 tbs. olive oil	2 cups crumbled feta cheese
1 lg. zucchini, thinly sliced	1½ tbs. butter
2 potatoes, thinly sliced	2 tbs. flour
1 onion, sliced	1¼ cups milk
3 garlic cloves, finely chopped	Black pepper, to taste
1 tbs. white vinegar	1/8 tsp. nutmeg
1-14.5 oz. can whole peeled tomatoes	1 egg, beaten
1 tsp. dried oregano	¼ cup freshly grated Parmesan
2 tbs. fresh parsley, chopped	

Directions:

Sprinkle eggplant with salt to release the acid and set aside. After 30 minutes or so, pat dry with paper towels. Pre-heat oven to 375 degrees.

Heat the oil in a large skillet over medium-high heat. Lightly brown eggplant and zucchini slices on both sides and transfer to a platter that has been lined with paper towels to absorb the excess oil. Next, brown the potato slices on both sides. (Add more oil if necessary). Transfer to a paper towel lined plate as well.

Sauté onions and garlic until lightly golden. Pour in the vinegar and cook until liquid has reduced. Stir in the tomatoes, oregano, and parsley. Cover; reduce heat to medium-low. Let simmer for 15 minutes.

Layer the eggplant, zucchini, potatoes, and feta cheese in a 9" X 13" casserole. Pour tomato mixture over vegetables, repeat layering process, finishing up with a layer of eggplant and zucchini on top. Cover with aluminum foil and bake in a pre-heated oven for 25 minutes.

In the meantime, in a small saucepan, melt butter, then whisk in flour and slowly add in the milk. Bring to a slow boil continuing to whisk constantly until sauce has thickened and is lump free. Add in the pepper and nutmeg. Remove from heat; allow to cool for 5 minutes, then stir in the beaten egg. Pour the sauce over the casserole, sprinkle with Parmesan cheese. Bake uncovered for 30 minutes until top is lightly golden. Serve hot.

MARCH 26 **BAKED EGGS, ITALIAN STYLE**

Ingredients:

4 cups marinara sauce	1/3 cup shredded mozzarella
8 eggs	Salt & pepper, to taste
1/3 cup grated Parmigiano-Reggiano cheese	½ cup fresh parsley, finely chopped

Directions:

Spoon marinara sauce into four individual casserole dishes. Crack 2 eggs (sunny-side up) into each dish. Divide the rest of the sauce equally and spoon around eggs in each of the 4 casseroles. Sprinkle with cheeses, salt, and pepper.

Bake in a pre-heated 350 degree oven for about 6-8 minutes. Remove from oven, garnish with parsley, and serve with crusty slices of Italian bread.

MARCH 27 **IRISH VEGETABLE SOUP**

Ingredients:

3 lg. carrots, peeled & diced	1 leek, washed well to remove sand, & sliced
3 lg. potatoes, peeled & diced	1 lg. onion, chopped

1 parsnip, peeled & diced   Salt & pepper, to taste

1 lg. turnip, peeled & diced   Water

Directions:

Place the first 6 ingredients in a large stock pot. Fill with water to cover the vegetables. Season with salt and pepper and bring to a boil over high heat. Cook until vegetables are soft. Add more water, if needed. When tender, puree in a blender or by using an immersion blender.

Return the puree to the stockpot and add more water to attain the desired consistency. Taste for seasoning. Serve hot.

MARCH 28 **SEAFOOD FRA DIAVOLO**

Ingredients:

4 tbs. olive oil, divided   1½ tbs. crushed red pepper flakes

6 garlic cloves, finely chopped   2 lobster tails

1-35 oz. can plum tomatoes   1 lb. linguine or spaghetti

1 ½ tsp. salt   8 oz. lg. raw shrimp, peeled & deveined

1 tbs. oregano   8 oz. clams, scrubbed

½ cup dry white wine   2 tbs. freshly chopped parsley

Directions:

In a saucepan, heat 2 tablespoons oil with garlic over medium heat. Add tomatoes, salt, oregano, wine, and red pepper flakes. Simmer on medium-low heat for 30 minutes. In another pot, bring 4 cups salted water to a boil. Add in the lobster and par-boil for 5½ minutes. Remove from pot and place on cutting board. Remove meat from shell and set aside.

Boil pasta until al dente and drain.

In a separate pan, heat the remaining 2 tablespoons oil. Add the shrimp and lobster and sauté for about 2-3 minutes. Remove from pan, transfer to saucepan containing sauce, add in the clams, and increase heat. Cover and cook until clams have opened, 4-6 minutes. Plate the pasta on a large serving platter. Ladle on the sauce and seafood. Sprinkle with parsley.

MARCH 29 SPICY MEXICAN CORN CHOWDER

Ingredients:

2 tbs. canola oil

1 med. onion, chopped

2 stalks celery, diced

1 red bell pepper, chopped

2 cups vegetable stock

4 cups frozen corn

1 lg. potato, peeled & diced

1 cup heavy cream

1 cup whole milk

2 jalapeno peppers, finely chopped

1 tbs. Kosher salt

1 tsp. black pepper

¼ tsp. crushed red pepper flakes

Directions:

Heat the oil in a medium skillet over medium-high heat. Add in the onion, celery, and red pepper. Sauté together until onion is translucent and celery and peppers are tender. Set aside. In a 5 qt. saucepan, heat vegetable stock over high heat until boiling. Then lower to medium heat, and add in the corn, potato, cream, milk, jalapenos, salt, and black pepper. Let simmer for 30 minutes over medium heat. Add in crushed red pepper flakes. Using an immersion blender or food processor, puree, then return to heat for an additional 15 minutes. Serve hot accompanied with cornbread.

MARCH 30 AROMATIC GYSPY SOUP

Ingredients:

3 tbs. olive oil

2 lg. onions, chopped

3 lg. garlic cloves, minced

1 lg. celery stalk, chopped

2 carrots, peeled and diced

1 lg. sweet potato, peeled & diced

1 cup butternut squash, diced

1¼ tsp. paprika

½ tsp. ground turmeric

½ tsp. dried basil

1 tsp. kosher salt

¼ tsp. ground cinnamon

¼ tsp. cayenne pepper

3 bay leaves

4 cups vegetable stock

¾ cup diced tomatoes

1 cup canned chick peas

1/3 cup green bell pepper, chopped

Directions:

Heat the oil in a large stock pot over medium-high heat. Add in the onion, garlic, celery, carrots, sweet potato, and squash. Stir well. Sauté until vegetables are tender. Then add in the next 7 seasonings. Mix well and stir in the stock. Cover and simmer on low heat for about 20-25 minutes. Add in the tomatoes, chick peas, and pepper. Simmer for an additional 15-20 minutes or until all vegetables are tender. Add more salt and pepper, if desired. Serve with crusty bread.

MARCH 31 RICOTTA GNOCCHI IN SAGE SAUCE

Ingredients:

1 lb. ricotta cheese	2 cups flour, plus extra for rolling
1 lg. egg	1 stick melted butter
1 tbs. olive oil	1½ tsp. rubbed sage
¼ cup freshly grated parmesan cheese	Black pepper
½ tsp. freshly grated nutmeg	½ cup grated parmesan cheese

Directions:

In a large bowl, combine egg, ricotta, and oil. Add the cheese and nutmeg to the mixture. Next, start adding flour, a little at a time, and thoroughly combine until a dough starts to form.

Dump dough on a clean work surface that has been generously floured. Knead dough into a smooth ball, adding flour so that dough is no longer sticky.

Break off pieces of dough and roll into long ropes. Using a knife, cut off 1" pieces. Roll off the back of a fork to get the imprints from the tines. Place on a floured baking sheet to prevent sticking.

In the meantime, bring a large sauce pan of salted water to a boil. Using a kitchen spider, gently lower the gnocchi into the boiling water. Gently stir using a wooden spoon. As the gnocchi rise to the top, scoop out with the kitchen spider, making sure to drain off excess water. Transfer to a large serving bowl or platter.

Melt butter in a small sauce pot. Add in sage and pepper, to taste. Pour over pasta. Mix well. Drizzle cheese over gnocchi and serve.

APRIL 1 **GREEK PIZZA**

<u>Ingredients:</u>

Spray olive oil	Salt & freshly ground black pepper
Flour, for dusting	12 oz. baby spinach
1 lb. store bought pizza dough	4 oz. crumbled feta cheese
3 tbs. olive oil	1/3 cup fresh mint leaves, chopped
1 lg. yellow onion, chopped	1/3 cup Kalamata olives, pitted & sliced
3 garlic cloves, minced	1½ tbs. dried oregano

<u>Directions:</u>

Pre-heat oven to 450 degrees. Spray a large pizza pan with oil and set aside. Roll out pizza dough to 12"-14" on a lightly floured surface. Transfer to pizza pan and lightly spray dough with oil. Set aside.

In a large skillet, heat olive oil over medium-high heat. Add in the onions and garlic. Season with salt and pepper, to taste. Cook, stirring frequently, until onions are soft and translucent. Slowly add in the spinach and cook until spinach has wilted. Mix well. Remove from heat and stir in the cheese and mint. Evenly spread over pizza dough. Arrange olives on top and sprinkle with oregano.

Bake until dough is golden and crispy for about 18-20 minutes. Slice into wedges and serve.

APRIL 2 **MUSHROOM BOURGUIGNON**

The best substitute for meat, I feel, is Portobello/cremini mushrooms. Their earthy, woodsy taste is a good replacement especially for meat but for beef in particular. For those of you who once were meat-eaters, and have now become vegetarians, you no longer have to give up your favorite dishes. Just substitute mushrooms for beef and vegetarian stock for beef or chicken stock.

<u>Ingredients:</u>

2 tbs. olive oil, divided	3 garlic cloves, minced
2 tbs. butter, room temperature, divided	1 cup dry red wine
32 oz. Portobello mushrooms sliced	2 tbs. tomato paste
1 med. onion, diced small	16 oz. vegetable stock

1 cup pearl onions

1 med. carrot, diced small

1 tsp. thyme leaves

Salt & pepper, to taste

1½ tbs. flour

12 oz. pkg. extra-wide egg noodles, cooked

Sour cream & chopped chives, for garnish

<u>Directions:</u>

Heat 1 tablespoon oil and 1 tablespoon butter in a large Dutch oven over medium-high heat. Add in the mushrooms and onion and cook until they start to turn brown. Stir occasionally to prevent them from burning or sticking to the pan. Once done, remove from pan and set aside in a bowl.

Add the remaining tablespoon of oil to the pan and reduce heat to medium. Add in the pearl onions, carrots, thyme, and season with salt and pepper. Cook until onions begin turning translucent and golden. Add in the garlic and cook mixture for 1 minute.

Pour in the wine while scraping the bottom of the pan to loosen any morsels. Increase heat to high to reduce liquid to half then stir in the paste and stock. Return mushrooms and onions along with their natural juices to the Dutch oven. Bring to a boil then reduce heat and let simmer until mushrooms become very tender.

In the meantime, combine the extra butter and flour to form a paste. Stir into the stew. Mix well to thicken juices, and simmer for an additional 10 minutes or until sauce has thickened and is not loose.

Serve the bourguignon over a bowl of noodles. Spoon 1 tablespoon of sour cream on top and garnish with chopped chives.

APRIL 3 **EGGPLANT PARMIGIANA WITH SPAGHETTI**

<u>Ingredients</u>:

Marinara Sauce:

3 tbs. extra virgin olive oil

4 garlic cloves, finely chopped

1-35 oz. can crushed tomatoes

1½ tbs. dried oregano

5 fresh basil leaves

Salt & pepper, to taste

¼ tsp. crushed red pepper flakes

1 tsp. sugar

Eggplants:

Olive oil

4 lg. eggplants, peeled & sliced round to ½"thick	1-1½ cups grated Parmigiano-Reggiano
2 lg. eggs, beaten	1 lb. shredded mozzarella
Salt and pepper, to taste	1 lb. spaghetti, cooked to al dente
Italian seasoned bread crumbs	5-6 basil leaves, for garnish

Directions:

Marinara Sauce:

Heat the oil in a 3 qt. saucepan over medium heat. Add in the garlic and cook until golden. Next add in the tomatoes and remaining ingredients. Stir then cover and simmer on low heat for 30 minutes.

Eggplant:

Peel eggplants and slice round (not lengthwise) to ½" thick. Next beat 2 eggs in a bowl and add in salt and pepper. Then generously pour bread crumbs onto a shallow plate or onto a sheet of wax paper for easy clean-up. Heat the oil in a 10" skillet on medium-high heat. In an assembly line manner, dip the eggplant slices one at a time into the eggs, draining off the excess, then coat with bread crumbs and fry until golden on each side. Transfer to a plate lined with paper towels to absorb excess oil. When all of the eggplants have been fried, spoon 2 cups of the marinara sauce into a 9" X 12" roasting pan and spread it around the entire bottom of the pan. Begin placing the eggplants into the pan. Once one layer has been put down, spoon sauce on top of each, then sprinkle with mozzarella and grated cheese. Repeat this layering process until all of the eggplants have been used. Top with sauce, mozzarella, and bake in a pre-heated 350 degree oven for approximately 30 minutes until cheese has melted and the top turns a light brown. Garnish with basil leaves and serve while hot.

If spaghetti is desired to serve alongside with the eggplant parmigiana, while eggplant is baking, prepare the spaghetti by following package directions. Drain. Transfer to a large platter, ladle the sauce on top and generously sprinkle with cheese. Serve alongside the eggplant.

APRIL 4 WEST AFRICAN YAM SOUP

Ingredients:

2 tsp. canola oil	¼ tsp. salt
2 cups chopped yellow onions	2-15.5 oz. cans garbanzo beans, drained

2/3 cup smooth peanut butter

32 oz. vegetable stock

6 cups yams, peeled & cubed into 1" pieces

1-28 oz. can diced tomatoes, undrained

1 tbs. ground cumin

Parsley springs, for garnish

½ tsp. freshly ground black pepper

Directions:

Heat the oil in a heavy Dutch oven over medium heat. Add onion and sauté until translucent and lightly browned. Add in the peanut butter, and the rest of the ingredients, with the exception of the parsley. Increase heat and bring to a boil. Then reduce heat, simmer uncovered for about 30 minutes or until potatoes are soft, but not mushy. Garnish with parsley and serve hot.

APRIL 5 **BEER-BATTERED COCONUT SHRIMP**

Ingredients:

1 lg. egg

2 2/3 cups flaked coconut

¾ cup all-purpose flour, divided

32 oz. lg. raw shrimp, peeled & deveined

1 cup beer

4 cups vegetable oil for frying

2 tsp. baking powder

Directions:

In a medium bowl, combine egg, ½ cup flour, beer and baking powder. Using 2 separate bowls, place ¼ cup flour in one and coconut in the other. Holding the shrimp by their tails, dredge in flour, then shake off excess flour. Next, dip in the egg/beer batter, allowing excess to drip off. Roll shrimp in coconut and place on a baking sheet lined with wax paper. Refrigerate for 30 minutes. Meanwhile, heat oil to 350 degrees in a deep fryer or sauce pan.

Fry shrimp in batches, turning once until golden brown on each side. Use a kitchen spider to remove shrimp and place on a plate lined with paper towels to drain excess oil. Serve warm.

Suggested dipping sauces: Orange marmalade, apricot preserves, sweet and sour sauce, spicy chili sauce, honey, or any of your favorites.

APRIL 6 SEAFOOD PAELLA VALENCIANA (SPANISH)

Ingredients:

3 cups water

1 cup dry white wine

½ tsp. crushed saffron

2-8 oz. bottles clam juice

1 cup chopped fresh parsley

1/3 cup freshly squeezed lemon juice

2 tbs. olive oil, divided

6 lg. garlic cloves, minced & divided

2 cups onion, finely chopped

1 cup red bell pepper, finely chopped

1 cup canned diced tomatoes + juice

1 tsp. paprika

½ tsp. crushed red pepper flakes

3 cups Arborio rice, uncooked

3 cups vegetable stock

1 cup frozen peas

16 little neck clams, scrubbed

16 mussels, scrubbed, beards removed

16 jumbo shrimp, peeled & deveined

1-7 oz. jar sliced pimento, drained

2 tbs. freshly squeezed lemon juice

4 lemons, each quartered

Directions:

Simmer the first 4 ingredients in a medium sauce pan over medium-low heat. Keep warm on very low heat.

Combine the parsley, lemon juice, 1 tablespoon oil, and 3 tablespoons garlic together in a bowl. Set aside.

Heat 1 tablespoon oil in a large paella pan over medium heat. Add in the onion and bell pepper, and sauté for about 5 minutes. Next, add in the tomatoes, paprika, crushed red pepper, and remaining garlic and cook for 5 additional minutes. Add in the rice and cook for 1 minute, stirring constantly. Pour in the stock, parsley mixture, and peas. Increase heat and bring mixture to a low boil. Cook for about 10 minutes, stirring frequently.

Add in the clams, mussels, and shrimp to the rice mixture. Cook for 5-7 minutes until shells are open and shrimp is no longer translucent. Discard any unopened clams and mussels. Stir well to combine all ingredients. Spoon mixture onto a very large platter and arrange pimentos in a decorative manner on top of the paella. Drizzle with lemon juice and arrange lemon wedges around the platter.

APRIL 7 ASH-E-RESHTEH (LEGUME AND NOODLE SOUP) PERSIAN

Ingredients:

1 bunch fresh parsley, chopped

2 bunches scallions, chopped

½ lb. fresh spinach, chopped

12 cups water

1 cup lentils

1 can chick peas, drained & rinsed

1 can dark kidney beans, drained & rinsed

1 can Northern white beans, drained & rinsed

2 tsp. turmeric

Salt & pepper, to taste

¼ lb. angel hair pasta, broken into 4" pieces

5 lg. garlic cloves, crushed

1 tbs. dried mint

¼ cup olive oil

Directions:

Combine parsley, scallions, spinach, water, and lentils in a large Dutch oven or sauce pot over medium-high heat. Bring to a boil until lentils and vegetables are tender. Add in the chick peas, kidney beans, white beans, turmeric, salt, and pepper. Cook for 20 minutes. Next, add in the pasta.

In the meantime, in a small saucepan, heat olive oil over low-medium heat and add in the garlic and mint. Cook on low until garlic turns golden then add to soup, stir, and serve while hot.

April 8 ESCAROLE AND BEAN SOUP

Ingredients:

½ cup extra virgin olive oil

1 cup finely chopped onion

8 garlic cloves, minced

½ tsp. crushed red pepper flakes

3-32 oz. pkg. of organic vegetable stock

1-19 oz. can cannellini beans, drained & rinsed

8 cups escarole leaves, roughly chopped

Salt, to taste

Italian seasoned croutons

Shaved parmesan cheese

Directions:

Heat olive oil in a 5 qt. sauce pan over medium heat then add onion, garlic, and red pepper flakes. When garlic is golden and onions translucent, add in the vegetable stock and increase heat to high to bring to a boil. When the liquid has come to a boil, lower heat back to medium and add in the beans, escarole, and salt. Simmer for about 30 minutes so that the flavors marry well. Serve in individual bowls, adding croutons on top. Sprinkle with shavings of Parmesan cheese.

APRIL 9 **EGGPLANT ROLLATINI**

<u>Ingredients:</u>

2 jars of your favorite tomato sauce

2 medium eggplants, approx. 1 lb. each

2 eggs, beaten

Italian-style bread crumbs for coating

1 cup Canola oil (more may be needed)

3 cups ricotta cheese

3 tbs. fresh Italian parsley, chopped

Salt & pepper

1 cup grated Parmigiano-Reggiano

8 oz. mozzarella cheese sticks

8 oz. shredded mozzarella

<u>Directions:</u>

Heat the sauce over low heat. Remove stems and skin from eggplant. Slice the eggplant lengthwise approximately ¼" thick. Whisk the eggs together and season with salt and pepper. Pour bread crumbs onto a platter or sheet of wax paper for easy cleanup. Next, pour the oil into a 10" or 12" skillet over medium-high heat. Dip the eggplant into the egg mixture, coating both sides evenly. Let excess egg drop back into bowl. Next, generously coat eggplant with bread crumbs on both sides. Place in skillet with heated oil (do not put the eggplants into the skillet until the oil is hot!) Fill the pan with the breaded eggplant slices and fry until golden on each side. Transfer to a platter lined with paper towels and allow excess oil to become absorbed by the paper towels. Set aside.

Place ricotta in a bowl. Add parsley and season with salt and pepper. Stir then set aside. Next, place about 2 cups tomato sauce into a 9" X 12" roasting pan or baking dish and spread sauce to cover entire bottom of the pan. Sprinkle with about 1 tablespoon grated cheese and set aside.

On a clean surface or tray, line up the eggplant slices, and spoon about 2 tablespoons ricotta mixture in the center. Place a stick of mozzarella on top of the ricotta and roll up the eggplant. Place the rolled up eggplant into the pan lined with sauce, seam side down. Repeat this process with each slice.

Spoon tomato sauce over each eggplant roll, sprinkle with the shredded mozzarella and grated cheese and bake in a pre-heated 350 degree oven for 30-40 minutes or until cheese has melted and started to turn golden. Serve hot.

APRIL 10 **MEDITERRANEAN GOAT CHEESE TART**

Ingredients:

1 pkg. (2 sheets/17.3 oz.) frozen puff pastry sheets, defrosted

11 oz. goat cheese

2 small red onions, sliced very thin

2 medium bell peppers, diced

8 oz. pkg. grape tomatoes, sliced

2 tsp. garlic powder

1 tbs. dried oregano

8 oz. pkg. Asiago cheese

Black pepper

Directions:

Unfold each sheet of puff pastry and place on parchment paper that has been lightly dusted with flour. Using a rolling pin that has been dusted with flour, roll out each sheet to form a rectangle measuring 11" X 13". Place each pastry sheet, including the parchment paper, onto 2 cookie sheets. Using a sharp knife, carefully score a ¼" border around the perimeter of each pastry sheet. DO NOT CUT THROUGH THE PASTRY BECAUSE IT WILL SEPARATE. YOU MERELY WANT TO CREATE A BORDER.

Divide the goat cheese in half and crumble 5.5 oz. onto each pastry sheet. Next, evenly divide the onions onto each sheet. Do the same with the peppers and, lastly, the tomatoes.

Sprinkle 1 teaspoon of garlic powder on each as well as ½ tablespoon oregano. Generously shave the Asiago cheese onto each sheet and top by sprinkling freshly ground black pepper. Bake in a pre-heated 350 degree oven for 20-25 minutes until pastry is golden. Halfway through the baking process, rotate pans so that the tarts will brown evenly. Remove from oven and cut each sheet into fours.

APRII 11 **QUICK AND EASY LINGUINE AND CLAM SAUCE**

Ingredients:

¼ cup extra virgin olive oil

4 garlic cloves, finely chopped

1 pint grape tomatoes, sliced

2-6.5 oz. cans chopped clams

1-8 oz. bottle clam juice

1 bunch fresh parsley, washed & chopped

½ tsp. crushed red pepper flakes

Salt, to taste

1 lb. linguine

Directions:

Prepare the pasta as directed on the package to al dente. While the pasta is cooking, heat olive oil in a 10" or 12" skillet and add in the garlic. Sauté garlic on medium heat, stirring constantly, until garlic is golden. Next, add in the grape tomatoes. Sauté for 2-3 minutes.

Add in the chopped clams, including the juice as well as the bottle of clam juice. Stir. Add in the parsley, pepper and salt. If you like it spicier, just add in more pepper.

Drain the pasta, and transfer to a large platter. Spoon the clam sauce evenly over the pasta. Garnish with fresh parsley sprigs and serve immediately.

APRIL 12 **15 BEAN SOUP**

Ingredients:

¼ cup extra virgin olive oil	1-16 oz. pkg. of 15 Bean Mix, washed & drained
4 lg. garlic cloves, finely chopped	1½ tbs. oregano
3 lg. carrots, peeled, sliced	64 oz. water or vegetable stock
2 lg. celery stalks, sliced	Salt & pepper, to taste
1 lg. onion, sliced	

Directions:

In a 5 qt. sauce pan, heat olive oil on medium heat, add in the garlic and sauté until golden. Add in carrots, celery, onions and 2 cups of water. Cover and simmer for 6-8 minutes. Then add in the bean mixture, oregano, and rest of the water or stock. Season with salt and pepper. Stir, cover and bring to a boil over high heat. Then reduce heat and let simmer for 2 hours.

APRIL 13 **ASPARAGUS FRITTATA**

Ingredients:

2 lbs. butter	¼ cup fresh parsley, finely chopped
1/3 cup shallots, finely chopped	1 tsp. sea salt
1 lb. baby asparagus, cut into 1" pieces	½ tsp. freshly ground black pepper
7 lg. eggs, beaten	1 cup shredded Gruyere cheese

<u>Directions:</u>

In a 10" non-stick skillet, melt butter over medium heat; add shallots and sauté until translucent. Add the asparagus, stir, and reduce heat to low. Cover and cook for about 4-5 minutes. When asparagus pieces are fork tender, mix parsley, salt, and pepper into the beaten eggs. Pour egg mixture over the asparagus. Cover and cook on low for 5-7 minutes until eggs are almost set. Uncover, sprinkle with cheese and place in pre-heated 350 degree oven for approximately 5-6 minutes. Cut into wedges and serve.

APRIL 14 **GRILLED TUNA STEAKS WITH SALSA**

<u>Ingredients:</u>

Salsa:

4 Roma tomatoes, diced	3 jalapenos, finely diced
1 lg. red bell pepper, finely diced	1 tbs. olive oil
1 green bell pepper, finely diced	1 tbs. chili powder
1 med. onion, finely diced	½ cup cilantro, chopped
4 garlic cloves, minced	Salt & pepper, to taste
1 lime, juiced	

Tuna Steaks:

4-6 oz. tuna steaks	Salt & pepper
Olive oil	Freshly squeezed lemon juice

<u>Directions:</u>

Salsa:

Place all ingredients in a bowl and mix together. Refrigerate for several hours so that the flavors will blend well.

Tuna Steaks:

Pat dry the tuna. Brush both sides with olive oil. Sprinkle with salt and pepper. Place on a pre-heated grill pan and grill each side for 6-8 minutes. Remove from grill, set on a platter, drizzle with lemon juice and top with salsa. Serve.

APRIL 15 **SPANOKOPITA/SPINACH PIE (GREEK)**

Ingredients:

¼ cup extra virgin olive oil

½ cup onions, finely chopped

¼ cup scallions (white & green sections), finely chopped

32 oz. fresh spinach (stems removed), finely chopped

¼ cup fresh dill weed, finely chopped

¼ cup flat-leaf parsley, finely chopped

½ tsp. sea salt

½ tsp. black pepper

1/3 cup milk

8 oz. crumbled feta cheese

4 eggs, beaten

½ lb. butter, melted

16 (12" X 16") filo

Directions:

In a heavy 10" or 12" skillet (preferably cast iron), heat olive oil over medium heat. Toss in the onions and scallions and cook until translucent. Add in the spinach, cover pan, and let steam for 5-6 minutes. Then add in the dill weed, parsley, salt, and pepper. Cook uncovered for about 8-10 minutes or until most of the liquid has evaporated. Remove from heat and transfer to a medium bowl. Add in the milk, stir well, and let cool for about 15-20 minutes. Next add in the cheese and eggs, mix well, and set aside.

Using a pastry brush, coat the inside of a 12" X 7" X 2" glass baking dish with the butter. Put down one sheet of filo, then brush the filo with the melted butter. Place another sheet of filo on top, brush with butter, and continue process until 8 sheets of filo have been used. Pre-heat oven to 300 degrees.

Using a spoon or spatula, evenly spread the spinach mixture over the filo, then place another sheet of filo on top, coat with butter and continue this process until remaining filo sheets have been used up. Trim any excess pastry around the edges of the pan or tuck in. Brush the top with melted butter and place in oven for about 1 hour or until filo is golden brown and crisp. Remove from oven; allow to cool for about 5-6 minutes, then cut into individual squares.

APRIL 16 **SHRIMP CREOLE**

Ingredients:

2 tbs. olive oil

1 cup diced green bell peppers

½ cup diced red bell peppers

1-14 oz. can diced tomatoes

1 tsp. crushed red pepper flakes

Salt, to taste

½ cup diced yellow pepper

1 lg. onion, diced

2 celery stalks, diced

1-14 oz. can Italian stewed tomatoes

2 tsp. garlic powder

1½ lbs. shrimp, peeled & deveined

3 cups steamed rice

Directions:

In a large 12" or 14" skillet, heat olive oil over medium heat. Add the peppers, onions, and celery. Cook until tender. Add tomatoes, pepper flakes, salt, and garlic powder. Cook for about 15 minutes. Add shrimp and continue to cook until shrimp turn pink and opaque on both sides. Serve over rice.

APRIL 17 **SPICY SHRIMP STEW**

Ingredients:

1 cup butter (2 sticks)

¼ cup all-purpose flour

1 lg. onion, finely chopped

4 celery stalks, finely chopped

1 lg. green bell pepper, seeded & finely chopped

5 garlic cloves, minced

3-14 oz. cans diced tomatoes

2½ cups frozen corn

5 cups low sodium shrimp or vegetable stock

2 tbs. salt

2 bay leaves

1½ tsp. dried basil

½ tsp. dried or fresh thyme leaves

1 tbs. cayenne pepper

½ tbs. crushed red pepper flakes

¼ tsp. paprika

4 lbs. med. raw shrimp, peeled & deveined

½ bunch Italian parsley, rough chopped

1 bunch scallions, finely chopped

Directions:

In a large sauce pot or Dutch oven, melt butter over medium heat. Whisk in the flour and continue to whisk until a roux is formed. Add in the onion, celery, bell pepper, and garlic. Let cook and constantly stir for about 5 minutes. Stir in the tomatoes, corn, stock, salt, bay leaves, basil, thyme, cayenne pepper, red pepper flakes, and paprika. Bring to a boil then reduce heat to low and simmer for 45 minutes, stirring occasionally. Stir in the shrimp, parsley, and scallions. Bring back to a boil then lower again and let simmer for another 20 minutes. Serve hot with corn bread.

APRIL 18 **BROCCOLI AND CHEESE FRITTATA**

Ingredients:

3 tsp. olive oil

½ tsp. sea salt

1 cup diced onion

Black pepper

2 cups broccoli florets, steamed but firm

¾ cup shredded extra-sharp Cheddar

8 lg. eggs, beaten

Directions:

In an oven-proof skillet, heat olive oil over medium heat and add onion sautéing until translucent. Add in the broccoli florets, stir, and cook for 2 minutes.

Whisk together the eggs, salt, and pepper and evenly pour the egg mixture over the vegetables. Cover and cook on low for 5-7 minutes until eggs are almost set. Then uncover, sprinkle with cheese and place in a pre-heated 350 degree oven for approximately 5-7 minutes. Cut into wedges and serve.

APRIL 19 **BROILED RED SNAPPER WITH ORANGE SAUCE**

Ingredients:

4 thick fillets of red snapper

2 tbs. lime juice

2 onions, grated

1 tsp. salt

5 garlic cloves, minced

1 tsp. black pepper

1/3 cup olive oil

1 lg. orange, thinly sliced

½ cup orange juice with pulp

2 cups steamed Basmati rice

Directions:

Place fish fillets in a glass baking dish. In a medium bowl, add the onions, garlic, oil, orange juice, lime juice, salt, and pepper. Mix well then pour over the fish. Cover with plastic wrap and marinate for 4-5 hours.

Pre-heat broiler to 400 degrees. Place baking dish under broiler for 5-7 minutes. Remove from broiler, place sliced oranges on top. Return to broiler for 1 additional minute then serve with rice.

APRIL 20 **TORTELLINI SOUP**

Ingredients:

¼ cup extra virgin olive oil

1 lg. onion, diced

2 garlic cloves, minced

1-8 oz. pkg. Baby Bella mushrooms, sliced

1-29 oz. can diced tomatoes

1-16 oz. pkg. fresh baby spinach

1-48 oz. container vegetable stock

1-19 oz. can cannellini beans

½ cup grated Parmigiano-Reggiano

Salt & pepper

1½ cups cheese tortellini

Directions:

In a 5 qt. sauce pan, heat oil over medium heat. Add in onion and garlic. Sauté for 2 minutes, then add in the mushrooms. Stir, cover, and reduce heat to medium-low. When mushrooms are tender, add in the tomatoes, spinach, vegetable stock and beans. Stir, then add in the cheese, salt, and pepper. Increase heat to high and bring to a boil. Add in the tortellini and cook until pasta is tender. Do not overcook the pasta. Serve in individual bowls. Sprinkle with additional cheese on top.

APRIL 21 **ARABIAN EGGPLANT SALAD**

Ingredients:

6 Asian eggplants

1 cup sunflower oil

2 roasted red bell peppers

1 cup pitted green olives, chopped lg.

2 garlic cloves, minced

Juice from 1 lemon

1 tsp. cumin

¼ tsp. crushed red pepper flakes

1 tbs. fresh dill weed, chopped

1 tbs. fresh mint, chopped

Salt

Directions:

Heat the oil in medium skillet over medium heat. Cut eggplants in quarters, then halve each quarter. Cook the eggplants until browned on both sides. Transfer to a plate lined with paper towels to absorb excess oil.

Using tongs, place peppers on an open flame and blacken on all sides. Allow to cool, then discard the blackened skin. Remove seeds and stem then cut into thin strips.

Place the peppers in a bowl. Rough chop the olives and add to bowl with peppers. Next, add in the garlic, lemon juice, cumin, crushed pepper, dill weed, mint, and salt. Add in the eggplants, Combine all ingredients well and serve at room temperature. Accompany with heated pita bread.

APRIL 22 **SPINACH AND CHEESE STUFFED SHELLS IN A CREAM SAUCE**

Ingredients:

10 oz. pkg. frozen chopped spinach,

  thawed, drained

2 cups ricotta cheese

1 cup shredded mozzarella cheese sliced

1/3 cup freshly grated Parmesan cheese

1 egg, beaten

Salt & pepper, to taste

12 oz. pkg. jumbo shell pasta

1 tbs. olive oil

2 tbs. butter

10 oz. pkg. cremini mushrooms, sliced

2 cups heavy cream

¾ cup grated Fontina cheese

Directions:

In a large bowl, combine the spinach, ricotta, mozzarella, Parmesan, egg, salt, and pepper.

Prepare the pasta as directed on pkg. Be sure not to overcook. Stuff the shells with spinach and cheese mixture and place in a 9" X 12" roasting pan. Bake in a pre-heated 400 degree oven for 15 minutes.

In a sauté pan, heat oil over medium heat then add the butter and melt. Add in the mushrooms and sauté until tender. Transfer to a plate lined with paper towels. Using same pan, wipe clean, and add in the cream. Heat over medium-high heat. When cream starts to bubble and thicken, whisk in the cheese. While stirring, toss in the mushrooms.

Remove pan from oven, pour mushroom-cheese sauce over shells and return to oven for another 5-6 minutes or until sauce starts to bubble. Serve immediately.

APRIL 23 **LENTIL SPINACH SOUP**

Ingredients:

3 tbs. olive oil	10 oz. pkg. frozen spinach, thawed
1 lg. onion, finely diced	1½ tsp. salt
5 garlic cloves, minced	¼ tsp. crushed red pepper flakes
7½ cups water	1 tbs. dried oregano
1½ cups lentils	

Directions:

In a 5 qt. sauce pot over medium heat, heat the oil, then add the onion and garlic. Cook until translucent. Add the water and lentils and cook for about 30 minutes, until lentils are tender. Next, add in the spinach, salt, pepper, and oregano. Cook for an additional 15 minutes. Serve with thick slices of crusty bread.

APRIL 24 **SALMON TERIYAKI**

Ingredients:

¼ cup low sodium soy sauce, divided	2 tbs. canola oil
¼ cup sherry	4-6 oz. salmon fillets
2 tbs. honey	1½ tsp. toasted sesame seeds
½ tsp. ground ginger	1 green onion, thinly sliced
4 garlic cloves, minced	2 cups steamed rice for serving
½ tsp. cornstarch	

Directions:

In a small sauce pan over medium heat combine the first 6 ingredients using only half of the soy sauce. Stir and let simmer for 2 minutes. Then remove from heat. Place salmon fillets in a glass baking dish and cover with the soy sauce mixture. Cover with plastic wrap and refrigerate for up to 4 hours to marinate.

Pre-heat the oil in a large non-stick fry pan over medium-high heat. When oil is hot, add in the salmon only, not the marinade and sear on each side for 4 minutes. In the meantime, heat the soy sauce marinade in a small sauce pan.

Once salmon is cooked, place on a platter, drizzle with soy sauce mixture, sprinkle with sesame seeds and green onion. Serve with steamed rice.

APRIL 25 **ROASTED PEARS WITH BLEU CHEESE**

Ingredients:

6 ripe unbruised Anjou pears	2/3 cup light brown sugar
Juice of 3 freshly squeezed lemons	½ cup olive oil
½ cup dried cranberries	12 oz. arugula
½ cup walnut halves, toasted and chopped	Kosher salt
1 cup apple cider	Freshly ground black pepper
6 tablespoons port wine	6 oz. crumbled bleu cheese

Directions:

Pre-heat oven to 375 degrees.

Peel the pears and slice in half lengthwise. Remove the core and using a melon baller, remove the seeds and create a small well. Toss the pears in some lemon juice so that they won't turn brown. Arrange them in a rectangular baking dish core side up and arrange so that they fit tightly in order to prevent them from turning on their sides.

In a bowl, toss the cranberries and walnuts together. Then divide evenly amongst all 12 halves. Using the same bowl, combine the apple cider, port, and brown sugar; stir until sugar dissolves. Pour the mixture over and around the pears and place in oven. Bake pears until tender for about 25-30 minutes, occasionally basting. Remove from oven and set aside.

In a large bowl, whisk together the olive oil, ¼ cup lemon juice, and ¼ cup of the basting liquid. Divide the arugula among 6 plates. Top each with 2 pear halves. Drizzle each with the liquid and sprinkle with salt and freshly ground black pepper. Finally, sprinkle the crumbled cheese over each. Serve while warm.

APRIL 26 **TACO PIZZA**

Ingredients:

1 lb. store-bought pizza dough	1 cup canned black beans, rinsed & drained
Flour, for dusting	2 cups shredded Four Cheese Mexican

Olive oil, for brushing

1 cup salsa

3 scallions, finely chopped

3 jalapenos, finely chopped

Toppings:

½ cup sour cream

Juice of 1 freshly squeezed lime

Thinly shredded lettuce

Cherry tomatoes, cut into thirds

Salt, to taste

½ cup chopped fresh cilantro

Directions:

Pre-heat oven to 425 degrees.

Roll out pizza dough on a lightly floured surface. Brush a 12" pizza pan with olive oil and transfer the dough to the greased pan. Brush the dough with the olive oil. Spread the salsa evenly over the dough leaving a half inch border. Next, spread black beans on top of the salsa. Sprinkle the cheese on top, then sprinkle the scallions and jalapenos. Bake in oven for about 10 minutes or until crust is golden.

In the meantime, while pizza is in the oven, combine the sour cream and half of the lime juice in a small bowl. Set aside. In another bowl, toss the lettuce, tomatoes, and remaining lime juice. Season with salt. Remove pizza from oven, top with salad mixture, then drizzle with sour cream mixture and cilantro. Cut into 8 slices.

APRIL 27 **HEARTY VEGETABLE SOUP**

Ingredients:

Olive oil

1 lg. onion, thinly sliced

3 garlic cloves, minced

4 zucchini, sliced thick

4 carrots, sliced thick

2 celery stalks, sliced

16 oz. fresh cut green beans

1-15 oz. can chick peas

6 baby golden Yukon potatoes

10 cippolini onions

1-35 oz. can crushed tomatoes

64 oz. unsalted vegetable stock

2 tbs. French tarragon

Salt & pepper, to taste

Directions:

In a large Dutch oven, heat oil over medium heat and add the sliced onion, garlic, zucchini, carrots, and celery. Toss and sauté for 3-4 minutes. Add in the remaining ingredients, stir well, and bring to a boil. Then reduce heat and simmer for approximately 2 hours until all the vegetables are tender.

APRIL 28 **ROASTED BEET AND GOAT CHEESE RAVIOLI**

Ingredients:

6½ cups diced beets (about 8 medium beets)	8 oz. goat cheese
Olive oil, for drizzling	14 oz. pkg. wonton wrappers (about 45)
1½ tsp. salt	Water
1½ tsp. crushed black pepper	5 tbs. butter, melted
1½ tsp. garlic powder	½ tsp. sage
2 tbs. heavy cream	½ cup grated Parmigiano-Reggiano cheese

Directions:

Peel the beets, dice them, and place on a large rimmed baked sheet. Drizzle with olive oil, sprinkle with salt, pepper, and garlic powder. Stir and place in a pre-heated 350 oven for about 45 minutes, but stir every 10 minutes. When beets are soft, remove from oven, and spoon into a blender on puree setting. Next, add heavy cream and goat cheese. Continue to puree. Remove mixture from blender, place in a bowl and refrigerate for 30 minutes.

On a clean dry surface, lay out wonton wrappers, 5 at a time. Pour some water in a bowl and have a pastry brush or silicone brush on hand. Place I teaspoon of the beet puree in center of each wonton wrapper. Dip brush in water and brush all four edges of each wonton. Fold each one over forming a triangle and be sure to press down the edges to seal in the puree. Set each individual ravioli on a sheet lined with wax paper. When done filling the ravioli, bring 5 quarts of salted water to a boil. Carefully place each one into the pot and let boil for 4-5 minutes.

In the meantime, melt the butter and add in the sage.

When ravioli are ready, drain and place on a large serving platter. Pour melted butter and sage over the pasta, and sprinkle with cheese. Serve immediately.

APRIL 29 **BAKED HADDOCK WITH OVEN ROASTED POTATOES**

<u>INGREDIENTS:</u>

Potatoes:

4 russet potatoes, peeled, & sliced ¼" thick   Garlic powder

Spray oil   Salt & pepper, to taste

Olive oil

Haddock:

¾ cup milk   ¾ cup Italian style panko

1 tsp. salt   ¼ tsp. dried thyme

¼ cup grated Parmesan cheese   ¼ cup melted butter

<u>Directions:</u>

Potatoes:

Pre-heat oven to 375 degrees.

Peel and slice potatoes to ¼" thickness and place on a baking sheet that has been sprayed with oil. Lightly drizzle olive oil on each slice then sprinkle with garlic powder, salt, and pepper. Place in oven for about 30-35 minutes until golden.

Haddock:

In a shallow bowl, combine the milk and salt. In another shallow bowl, mix together, the cheese, panko, and thyme. Dip the haddock fillets in the milk, then into the cheese mixture making sure to coat evenly on both sides. Place haddock fillets into a glass baking dish and drizzle with melted butter. Bake in a pre-heated 425 degree oven until the fish flakes easily about 15-20 minutes.

Serve with potatoes and a green vegetable or salad on the side.

APRIL 30 **CALZONE**

<u>Ingredients:</u>

1 lb. store-bought pizza dough   1/3 cup grated Parmesan cheese

2 lbs. ricotta   ½ cup fresh parsley, chopped

2 cups shredded mozzarella   1 egg, beaten

91

Directions:

Divide dough into 4 small balls and place on a clean and lightly floured work surface. Dust with flour and cover loosely with plastic wrap. Let rise until each one is double in bulk.

In the meantime, prepare the filling. In a large bowl, combine the ricotta, mozzarella, and Parmesan cheeses. Stir in the parsley and refrigerate.

Pre-heat oven to 400 degrees. Line 2 baking sheets with aluminum foil.

Roll out each dough ball, one at a time, and spoon ¼ of the filling onto each half of the dough, leaving a ½" border. Brush the edges of the dough with the egg wash and fold the dough over the side with the filling. Crimp the edges with a fork to seal in the cheese and place each calzone on the foil lined baking sheet. Brush the tops of each calzone with the egg wash and, using a fork, puncture a few holes on top of each to allow steam to escape. Bake for 20 minutes or until crust turns golden.

MAY 1 BAKED ZITI

Ingredients:

3 tbs. extra virgin olive oil	1 tsp. sugar
1 med. onion	3/4 cup grated Parmigiano-Reggiano, divided
4 med. garlic cloves, finely chopped	1 tsp. salt
1-35 oz. can crushed tomatoes	¼ tsp. crushed red pepper flakes
16 oz. water	1 lb. ziti
1 tbs. dried oregano	1 lb. ricotta cheese
6-8 basil leaves, julienned	1 cup shredded mozzarella

Directions:

In a medium saucepan, heat oil over medium heat, then add the onion and garlic. Sauté until golden. Add in the tomatoes and next 7 ingredients, but only ¼ cup grated cheese. Stir, cover, and simmer on medium-low heat for about 1 hour.

Next, prepare pasta as stated on package until al dente. Drain. Pour 2 cups of the tomato sauce into a 9" X 12" roasting pan and spread to cover the bottom of the pan. Add in the drained pasta. Stir in the ricotta cheese and 3 cups of sauce. Mix until pasta, cheese, and sauce have all been blended together. Add additional sauce on top and evenly sprinkle on the mozzarella cheese and the remaining grated cheese. Then bake in a pre-heated 350 degree oven for 30 minutes or until top has slightly browned, turning crisp, and the cheese is bubbling.

MAY 2 **DOLMEH-YE-BARG-E MO/STUFFED GRAPE LEAVES** (PERSIAN)

Ingredients:

About 50 grape leaves, fresh or canned may be used

1 cup uncooked basmati rice

½ cup yellow split peas

Salt

¼ cup olive oil

1 med. onion, finely diced

1 cup chopped scallions (both white & green parts)

2 tbs. dried dill weed

1 tbs. dried tarragon

1 tbs. dried mint

1 cup dried parsley

½ tsp. cinnamon powder

½ cup raisins or dried currants

1/3 cup pine nuts (optional)

1 cup water

2/3 cup sugar

1/3 cup lemon juice

Directions:

If using fresh leaves, select tender ones and blanch them in boiling water for just 2 minutes, then drain and rinse immediately in cold water. Pat dry. If using canned leaves, simply drain and rinse under cold water and pat dry.

In a sauce pan, cook rice in salted boiling water for about 15 minutes. Drain and set aside.

Then cook split peas in boiling water for about 20 minutes or until tender. Drain and set aside.

In a large skillet, heat oil over medium heat, then add onions and scallions. Sauté until golden and translucent. Add the rice, split peas, dill, tarragon, mint, parsley, cinnamon, raisins, and pine nuts. Mix thoroughly and let cook for about 3-4 minutes.

Drizzle oil on the bottom of a Dutch oven and line with 3 layers of grape leaves. On a clean surface lay out a few grape leaves at a time, remove stems, and spoon 1 or 2 tbs. of rice mixture in center of each leaf. Roll up, making sure to tuck in the sides to avoid spillage. Place onto leaves in Dutch oven, seam sides down. Repeat the process.

Mix together 1 cup of water, sugar, and lime juice and pour over the filled stuffed grape leaves. Cover and simmer on low heat for about 40-45 minutes, then serve.

MAY 3 STRIPED BASS WITH COUSCOUS AND ROASTED BRUSSEL SPROUTS

Ingredients:

1½ lbs. halved Brussel sprouts

¼ cup olive oil

¼ tsp. red pepper flakes

Kosher salt

Freshly ground black pepper

1 tsp. garlic powder

Olive oil

1/3 cup shallots, finely chopped

1/3 cup toasted pine nuts

¼ cup chopped dried apricots

1 cup couscous

4 basil leaves, julienned

Vegetable oil

4-6 oz. skinless striped bass fillets

Directions:

On a rimmed baking sheet, toss the Brussel sprouts with olive oil, red pepper flakes, salt, pepper, and garlic powder. Roast in a 375 degree oven for approximately 30-40 minutes until caramelized, but be sure to stir frequently.

In a small frying pan, heat olive oil on medium heat and add shallots. Sauté until golden. In another small frying pan on low to medium-heat, add in the pine nuts and toast until lightly golden on all sides. In the meantime, prepare the couscous as directed on package. When done, remove lid and add in the sautéed shallots, apricots, pine nuts, and basil leaves. Fluff with a fork and place lid back on pot; remove from heat and set aside.

In a non-stick skillet, heat the vegetable oil over medium heat. Sprinkle with salt and pepper on the fish and transfer fish to skillet. Cook until lightly browned on each side (4 minutes). Transfer to individual serving dishes along with Brussel sprouts and couscous.

MAY 4 FETTUCCINE ALFREDO

***Note: This is a very quick sauce to make. By the time the fettuccine has been prepared, the Alfredo sauce will be ready.*

Ingredients:

1 lb. fettuccine, cooked to al dente

½ cup unsalted butter, room temp.

2 tbs. flour

1 pint heavy cream

¾ cup freshly grated Parmigiano-Reggiano, divided

Freshly ground black pepper

Salt, to taste

Chopped fresh parsley for garnish

Directions:

Prepare the pasta as directed on package. Melt butter in a medium sauce pan over medium heat. Add in flour a little at a time and, using a whisk, incorporate the flour and the butter together. Gradually add in the cream and continue to whisk until mixture begins to thicken. Be careful not to burn. Next, stir in ½ cup cheese, salt, and black pepper.

Once the pasta has cooked, drain thoroughly and transfer the fettuccine to a very large platter. Pour on the sauce, a little at a time, and toss so that the pasta is completely coated with the sauce. Top with remaining cheese and parsley as a garnish. Serve immediately.

***Variation: You can add 1 lb. raw shrimp that has been peeled and deveined to the sauce while cooking. Cook until shrimp has begun to turn a light pink, approximately 2-3 minutes.**

MAY 5 **MOCK CRAB CAKES**

This recipe was contributed to me by my good friend and neighbor of 31 years, Mrs. Gale Kladitis.

Ingredients:

2 cups shredded, yellow squash, well drained	1 egg white
1½-2 tsp. Old Bay Seasoning	¼ tsp. garlic powder
4 slices toast, cut into cubes	¼ tsp. black pepper
1 tbs. baking powder	2 tbs. oil for frying

Directions:

Once squash has been shredded, allow to drain in a sieve. Squeeze well so that all of the liquid comes out and then place squash on paper towels to absorb any excess liquid. Pat dry. Mix all ingredients in a medium bowl.

In a large non-skillet, heat oil over medium-high heat. Shape mixture into patties and fry until golden brown on each side. Place on a paper towel lined platter to absorb excess oil. Patties may be served alone with sides or on a hamburger bun with mayonnaise, mustard, tartar sauce, or any sauce of your liking, plus lettuce and tomatoes.

MAY 6 SHRIMP TORTILLAS WITH MANGO SALSA

Ingredients:

1 mango-peeled, seeded, & diced

1 ripe avocado, peeled, pitted, & diced

2 tomatoes, diced

½ cup chopped fresh cilantro

¼ cup chopped red onion

3 cloves garlic, minced

½ tp. salt

2 tbs. lime juice

¼ cup butter

1lb. raw shrimp, peeled & deveined

4-10" tortillas, warmed

Directions:

In a medium bowl, stir together the first 8 ingredients. Cover with clear plastic wrap and let marinate in refrigerator for at least one hour.

In a medium skillet, melt butter over medium heat, add the shrimp, and cook until pink on both sides, 3-4 minutes. To serve, place some shrimp in a warmed tortilla, top with salsa, fold, and serve.

MAY 7 PIZZA MARGHERITA WITH BASIL PESTO

Ingredients:

1 prepared 12" pizza dough

2 cups fresh basil leaves

1/3 cup pine nuts

3 cloves garlic

1/3 cup olive oil

¼ cup grated Parmigiano-Reggiano cheese

½ tsp. salt

¼ tsp. black pepper

1/8 tsp. crushed red pepper

2 lg. tomatoes, thinly sliced

8 oz. fresh mozzarella, sliced

10 fresh basil leaves

Directions:

Pre-heat oven to 425 degrees. Roll out dough and place on 12" pizza tray that has been sprayed with non-stick oil. Set aside.

In a food processor, pack in the basil leaves, pine nuts, and garlic. Pulse a few times, then slowly add in the oil while processor is still running. Turn off the processor, scrape down the sides then add in the grated cheese, salt, pepper, and red pepper flakes. Pulse again until a creamy sauce is formed. Spread pesto on pizza dough. Starting from the outer edge, alternate the tomatoes and mozzarella slices in a circular pattern ending in the center. Place the pan in the oven and bake for about 15-20 minutes or until the crust is golden and cheese has melted and is bubbling. Remove from oven and let sit for 5 minutes then sprinkle the basil leaves on top. Slice and serve.

MAY 8 SWISS CHARD WRAPS

Ingredients:

4 large tender Swiss chard leaves

2 avocados

1 tsp. fresh lemon juice

½ tsp. hot sauce

Salt and pepper, to taste

1 cup diced tomatoes

1 cup diced sweet onion

1 lg. orange or yellow pepper, diced

4 whole wheat wraps, grilled

Directions:

Wash and dry the leaves and lay flat. In a large bowl, smash the avocados and add in the lemon juice, hot sauce, salt, and pepper. Blend until creamy.

Next, add the tomatoes, onion, and pepper and give a quick toss. Spoon the filling onto each Swiss chard leaf and roll into a wrap.

MAY 9 LINGUINE WITH BUTTER, CHEESE, AND BABY SPINACH

Ingredients:

Salt

1 lb. linguine, preferably whole wheat

½ stick (1/4 cup) butter, room temperature

1¼ cups grated Pecorino Romano cheese

1½ tsp. ground black pepper

1½ cups fresh baby spinach, rinsed & dried

Directions:

Using a 5 qt. pot, bring salted water to a boil over high heat. Add in the linguine and cook until al dente, stirring often, to prevent from sticking together. Drain the pasta but reserve 1 cup of the water used to cook the linguine.

Transfer the linguine to a large bowl and immediately add in the butter. Begin tossing the hot pasta so that the butter will quickly melt and coat the pasta. Next, add in the cheese, pepper, and the 1 cup reserved cooking liquid to moisten the linguine. Toss in the spinach and salt, to taste.

MAY 10 **SHRIMP FRIED RICE**

Ingredients:

2 cups cooked Basmati rice, preferably chilled

½ cup Marsala wine

¼ cup low-sodium soy sauce

1 tsp. salt

1 tsp. sugar

1 lb. cooked med. shrimp

2 tbs. vegetable oil

1 lg. onion, chopped small

½ cup frozen baby peas

¼ cup chopped green onion

Directions:

Crumble the rice to break up into individual grains for easy stir frying and set aside. In a small bowl, combine the Marsala, soy sauce, salt, and sugar and stir until salt and sugar dissolve. Next, chop the shrimp into small chunks and set aside.

Heat a wok or a large heavy cast iron skillet over high heat. Add the oil and swirl to coat the pan. Add the chopped onion, toss well and cook until translucent. Add the shrimp pieces and toss together for 1 minute. Next add the rice and toss. Cook for about 1 minute then add the wine mixture and peas. Continue to toss. Add in the green onions and cook for 1 minute more. Serve hot in individual serving bowls.

MAY 11 **ESHKENEH/EGG DROP SOUP (PERSIAN)**

This recipe was contributed to me by my husband's cousin, Mr. Hamid Sedigh.

Ingredients:

½ cup margarine

3 lg. onions, thinly sliced

4 cups water

2 medium potatoes, diced

2 tsp. salt

½ tsp. pepper

½ tsp. turmeric

¼ fresh cilantro, chopped

¼ cup fresh parsley, chopped

4 eggs

Directions:

In a medium-sized sauce pan, heat butter over medium heat. Add onions and sauté until translucent. Add water, potatoes, salt, pepper, turmeric, and cilantro. Bring to a boil, then reduce heat and simmer for 30 minutes on low heat.

Break the eggs, one by one, and slowly add to the soup while stirring. Allow to simmer for an additional 3 minutes then remove from heat. Serve with hot bread.

MAY 12 **FELAFEL PITAS (MIDDLE EASTERN)**

This recipe was contributed to me by my husband's cousin, Mr. Hamid Sedigh.

Ingredients:

1-15 oz. can chick peas, drained & rinsed	½ tsp. salt
1 small onion, diced small	¼ cup fresh parsley leaves, rough chopped
2 garlic cloves, minced	¼ tsp. cayenne pepper
2 tsp. ground cumin	¼ tsp. black pepper
½ tsp. ground coriander	1 tbs. olive oil, plus extra

*** **NOTE:** You will need pita pockets, lettuce, sliced tomatoes, cucumbers, yoghurt and dill sauce for serving

Directions:

Pre-heat oven to 400 degrees. Using a food processor, combine all of the above ingredients in the bowl of the processor and process for 15 seconds. Then stop machine and using a silicone scraper, scrape down sides of bowl. Pulse for another 15 seconds. Mixture will be coarse.

Form mixture into balls. Brush each with olive oil then pat down into patties and place on a greased baking sheet. Bake for about 20 minutes then flip over and bake for 20 minutes more or until falafel are golden and crispy.

Serve in warm pitas with lettuce, tomatoes, cucumbers, and a yoghurt and dill sauce.

MAY 13 **KUKU SABZI/GREEN VEGETABLE OMELET (PERSIAN)**

My husband and I prepare this dish quite frequently over the summer when the vegetables and herbs from our garden are in abundance. It is a very light meal, but one that is very healthy and delicious.

Ingredients;

¼ cup olive oil

½ cup scallions, finely chopped

1 cup garlic/onion chives, finely chopped

1 ½ cups parsley, finely chopped

¼ cup fresh dill weed, chopped

¼ cup fresh tarragon, chopped

½ tsp. turmeric

1 tsp. salt

½ tsp. black pepper

8 eggs, beaten

Directions:

Heat the oil in a 10" or 12" non-stick oven-proof skillet over medium heat. Once the oil is hot, toss in the scallions and chives and sauté for about 3-4 minutes.

In the meantime, in a medium bowl, add the parsley, dill, tarragon, turmeric, salt, and pepper. Add in the eggs and combine well. Pour mixture over the scallions and chives. Reduce heat, cover, and let cook on stovetop for about 5 minutes. Then uncover and place in a pre-heated 350 degree oven for about 8-10 minutes or until top is firm and set. Serve with a warm bread and plain yoghurt on the side.

MAY 14 **ROCKFISH ALLA MARINARA**

Ingredients:

3 tbs. extra-virgin olive oil

3 garlic cloves, minced

1-35 oz. can whole plum tomatoes

1 tbs. dried oregano

4-6 oz. pieces rockfish

Salt & pepper

1½ cups flour

3-4 tbs. olive oil

Directions:

In a medium skillet, heat olive oil over medium heat, add the garlic, and cook until lightly golden. Lower heat, and add in the tomatoes. Using a fork or the back of a spoon, gently crush the tomatoes. Add in the oregano, and season with salt and pepper. Allow to simmer for 20-25 minutes.

Meanwhile, in a medium non-stick skillet, heat 3-4 tablespoons of oil over medium-high heat. Pat dry both sides of each fish and season each side with salt and pepper. Put flour on a plate or piece of wax paper. Dredge fish in flour; shake off excess flour and place fish in pan. Fry until golden brown on each side. Once each fish has been browned, add the fish to the pan with the marinara sauce and let simmer for 5 minutes. Place on individual dinner plates. Spoon sauce over fish and serve immediately.

MAY 15 SUNNY SIDE UP EGGS OVER SAUTEED' VEGETABLES

My husband loves preparing this dish for himself, especially during the summer months when our garden is overflowing with sweet ripened vegetables.

Ingredients:

3 tbs. olive oil

10 grapes tomatoes, halved

1 lg. onion, chopped

4 eggs

4 cloves garlic, minced

Salt & pepper, to taste

1 lg. green bell pepper, diced

Tabasco sauce

2 chili peppers, seeds removed, finely chopped

1 tbs. fresh dill or tarragon

Directions:

Heat olive oil in a 10" or 12" non-stick skillet over medium heat. Toss in the onions, garlic, and peppers. Sauté until fairly tender but still firm (about 4-5 minutes). Add in the tomatoes and sauté over medium-low heat until most of the juice has evaporated (about 8-10 minutes). Stir, then evenly distribute the vegetables over the entire bottom of the skillet. Carefully crack the eggs over the vegetables being careful not to break the yolks. Season with salt and pepper and a few dashes of tabasco sauce (if desired). Sprinkle with either fresh dill or tarragon. Cover, reduce heat to low, and let eggs cook until the white part is opaque but the yolk is still loose. Enjoy with crusty bread. *****Suggestion: This recipe is especially nice if prepared and served in small individual cast iron skillets.**

MAY 16 AVOCADO TACOS (CALIFORNIA-MEXICAN)

Ingredients:

12 corn tortillas

2 cups shredded lettuce

3 avocados—peeled, pitted, & mashed

2 lg. tomatoes, diced

1 tbs. freshly squeezed lime juice

2 cups black beans, drained & rinsed

1/3 cup yellow onions, diced	2 cups cilantro leaves, finely chopped
1 tsp. garlic powder	Hot pepper sauce

Directions:

Pre-heat oven to 300 degrees. Arrange the tortillas on a baking sheet and when oven has reached desired temperature, place the sheet in the oven for about 5-7 minutes until tortillas are heated.

In the meantime, in a bowl combine the mashed avocados, lime juice, onions, and garlic powder. Remove tortillas from oven and place 2 tortillas per each dinner plate. Evenly divide the avocado mixture on each tortilla and spread. Top each with lettuce, tomatoes, black beans, cilantro, and hot pepper sauce.

MAY 17 **PASTA PRIMAVERA**

Pasta Primavera is a dish that consists of pasta and fresh vegetables in an Alfredo sauce. The focus, however, is on the fresh vegetables because "Primavera" means springtime and in the spring we start planting our gardens. When vegetables are ready to be harvested, they are gathered and prepared into this wonderful meal. In preparing Pasta Primavera, various types of pasta may be used, such as penne, rotelle, bowties, or rigatoni, but the best one to use is fettuccine because of it being a <u>wider</u> pasta, it absorbs the Alfredo sauce even more so.

This dish is versatile because many different types of vegetables may be used—whatever is in season at the time. Just remember that the vegetables must still be crisp when added to the sauce. Do not overcook them. My family personally enjoys using broccoli florets, peas, matchstick carrots, string beans, and red bell peppers. Experiment and enjoy adding in your own personal favorites!

Ingredients:

1 cup matchstick carrots	2 tbs. flour
2 cups broccoli florets	1 pint heavy cream
1 cup fresh or frozen peas	¾ cup grated Parmesan cheese, divided
1 cup fresh cut string beans	Freshly ground black pepper
1 red bell pepper, cut into thin strips	Chopped fresh parsley, for garnish
½ cup unsalted butter, softened	1 lb. fettuccini pasta, al dente

Directions:

In a medium sauce pan over high heat, bring approximately 4 cups salted water to a boil. Add in the carrots and broccoli and once tender but firm, remove from water using a kitchen spider and place into a colander. Next add in the peas, beans, and pepper doing the same thing. Add to colander with other vegetables, drain and set aside.

Prepare the pasta as directed on package.

While pasta is cooking, melt butter in a large 14" skillet. Whisk in the flour then gradually add in the cream and continue to whisk until mixture thickens forming a smooth sauce. Stir in ½ cup of cheese and pepper.

Drain the pasta and add to the skillet with the sauce. Combine. Next, add in the vegetables and gently toss. Generously sprinkle with remaining grated cheese and garnish with fresh parsley. Serve immediately.

MAY 18 **RED SNAPPER EN PAPILLOTE**

Ingredients:

¼ cup sesame oil	¼ cup low sodium soy sauce
1 tbs. minced garlic	¼ cups scallions, finely chopped
1 tbs. finely chopped ginger	4-4 oz. red snapper fillets
1 tbs. chili sauce	4 quarter sheets of parchment paper
2 tbs. brown sugar	

Directions:

In a bowl, whisk together the first 7 ingredients. Arrange the snapper into a deep dish and pour the marinade over the fish. Cover and refrigerate for 15 minutes. At the end of the 15 minutes, uncover and turn fish over. Cover and refrigerate for another 15 minutes.

Place the 4 sheets of paper on a work surface and place each snapper slice into the center of each square of paper. Bring the ends together in the center and fold. Then twist the ends together to completely close. Place packets onto a baking sheet and place in a pre-heated 400 degree oven. Steam until cooked for about 15-20 minutes.

In the meantime, heat the marinade. When fish is cooked, place one packet on each of 4 dinner plates. Carefully open each packet and pour remaining marinade over each slice. Serve with steamed vegetables on the side or a salad.

MAY 19 **BAKED ZUCCHINI, TOMATO, AND SQUASH CASSEROLE**

Ingredients:

2 medium zucchini, cut into ¼" slices

4 lg. garlic cloves, minced

2 medium yellow squash, cut into ¼" slices

2 lg. beefsteak tomatoes, thinly sliced

1 lg. egg, lightly beaten

Freshly ground black pepper

Italian-style Panko

8 oz. shredded white Cheddar cheese

Canola oil for frying

8 oz. grated Asiago cheese

2 lg. onions, diced

Directions:

Heat oil in a large coated skillet over medium high heat and in an assembly line fashion, dip the zucchini and squash in the egg (draining off excess) then coat with the Panko on each side and fry until golden on both sides. As the zucchini and squash turn golden, transfer to a large platter lined with paper towels to allow excess oil to absorb. Next, sauté the onions and garlic in the same skillet and cook until golden and onions are translucent. Set aside.

Grease a casserole dish and place 1 layer of zucchini on bottom. Season with salt and pepper. Place a layer of tomatoes on top, then layer with onion and garlic mixture. Next, add the yellow squash on top and, once again, season with salt and pepper. Layer with the remaining tomato slices, sprinkle on more Panko. Sprinkle the two cheeses on top and place in a 350 degree oven for about 45 minutes or until top is golden brown and cheese has melted and is bubbling.

MAY 20 **SHRIMP AND ORZO**

Ingredients:

2 cups orzo (rice-shaped pasta)

1½ tsp. dried oregano

3 tbs. olive oil, divided

¼ tsp. crushed red pepper

1-14.5 oz. can diced tomatoes, drained

Salt, to taste

3 cloves garlic, finely chopped

1 lb. small raw shrimp, peeled & deveined

1-28 oz. can crushed tomatoes

Sprigs of fresh parsley for garnish

Directions:

Cook orzo according to package directions, to al dente. Drain and transfer to an oven-proof baking dish and drizzle with 1 tablespoon olive oil over the orzo. Stir in the diced tomatoes (no juice) and place in a 200 degree oven to keep warm.

In the meantime, pour remaining olive oil into a skillet over medium heat and add in the garlic. Cook until a light golden color. Add in the crushed tomatoes, oregano, pepper, and salt. Stir and let simmer for about 10 minutes. Add in the shrimp, stir, and sauté until shrimp have turned pink on both sides.

Remove orzo from oven and immediately spoon the shrimp mixture over the orzo. Garnish with sprigs of parsley. Serve immediately.

MAY 21 **CHICKPEA SALAD SANDWICHES (MIDDLE EASTERN)**

Ingredients:

1½ cans chickpeas, drained & rinsed	1½ tsp. dill weed
1 lg. celery stalk, finely chopped	Salt & pepper
1 medium carrot, finely chopped	4 Romaine lettuce leaves
1 small onion, finely chopped	1 lg. tomato, sliced
3 tbs. mayonnaise	2 slices pita pockets, halved
1 tbs. lemon juice	

Directions:

Pour chickpeas into a medium bowl and mash with a fork. Add in the next 8 ingredients and blend well. Stuff pita pockets with the salad. Add in 1 lettuce leaf and 1 slice of tomato.

MAY 22 **MIRZA GHASEMI (PERSIAN)**

This is a peasant dish from northern Iran. It was contributed to me by my dear sister-in-law, Maria Movahedi-Karimi, who happens to be a wonderful cook herself!

Ingredients:

6 Asian eggplants, roasted with skin on, then small diced	4 lg. tomatoes, grated
3 tbs. olive oil	Salt & pepper, to taste

20 garlic cloves, minced   2 lg. eggs, beaten (optional)

Directions:

Place eggplants on the grate of a hot grill and roast on all sides until tender. Heat olive oil in a heavy skillet over medium-high heat. Add in the garlic and cook until lightly golden. Next, add in the eggplants, tomatoes, salt, and pepper and let simmer for about 10-12 minutes on medium-low heat. Once mixture has simmered, add in the beaten eggs stirring constantly. Let mixture cook for an additional 5 minutes.

Serve immediately with warm pita bread.

MAY 23 **ORIENTAL SHRIMP WRAPS**

Ingredients:

8 flour tortillas   8 oz. can tiny shrimp, drained

1-14.5 oz. can French style green beans   2 green onions, thinly sliced

1-14.4 oz. can peas & carrots   ¼ cup sweet & sour sauce

2 cups rice, prepared as directed on pkg.

Directions:

Wrap tortillas in foil and heat in a pre-heated 350 degree oven until warm.

In the meantime, heat the green beans and peas & carrots in a sauce pan in their own liquids. Once hot, drain, then return to sauce pan and, over low heat, stir in the rice, shrimp and onions. Keep warm.

Remove tortillas from oven and spread the sauce on one side of each tortilla. Stuff each one with shrimp mixture then roll up into a cone shape. Additional sauce may be poured on top. Serving size: 2 wraps per person.

MAY 24 **BROWN RICE CASSEROLE**

Ingredients:

3 cups organic vegetable stock, divided   3 garlic cloves, finely chopped

½ cup brown rice   1 carrot, peeled & diced small

¾ cup lentils   ½ tsp. English thyme

2 tbs. olive oil   ¾ cup grated Parmesan, divided

1 lg. onion, chopped   Salt & pepper, to taste

Directions:

In a small sauce pan, bring 1¾ cups vegetable stock to a boil over medium-high heat. Add rice; bring mixture to a boil, then lower heat and allow to simmer until rice is tender, stirring occasionally. Drain and set aside.

In another small sauce pan, bring remaining stock to a boil, add lentils, and cook until tender. In the meantime, heat olive oil in a small skillet over medium heat and toss in the onions, garlic and carrots. Sauté until tender, stirring often.

Transfer the rice, lentils, and onion mixture to an 8" X 10" casserole that has been sprayed with cooking spray and combine well. Add in the thyme, ½ cup of cheese, salt, and pepper, stir, and place in a pre-heated 350 degree oven for 20-25 minutes. Remove from oven, sprinkle with additional cheese and serve immediately.

MAY 25 **PASTA WITH SUN-DRIED TOMATOES**

Ingredients:

1/3 cup extra virgin olive oil   1 tbs. dried oregano

6 garlic cloves, minced   ½ tsp. crushed red pepper

5 oz. green Spanish olives with   Sea salt, to taste

  stuffed red peppers, chopped   1 lb. cooked fusilli

14 oz. sun-dried tomatoes, chopped plus

  some of the oil from the jar

Directions:

Pour olive oil and some of the oil from the jar of tomatoes into a large bowl and add in the garlic. Add in the next five ingredients and stir. Finally add in the pasta, and toss all ingredients combining well. If pasta seems dry, drizzle on additional oil.

Cover with plastic wrap and let stand about 30 minutes at room temperature before serving to allow ingredients to marinate. Stir well one more time before serving at room temperature.

MAY 26 GREEK LENTIL CASSEROLE

Ingredients:

1 cup lentils, rinsed	½ tsp. dried Greek oregano
1 lg. onion, chopped small	½ tsp. sea salt
4 garlic cloves, minced	1-14.5 oz. can stewed tomatoes, drained
1 1/8 cups organic vegetable stock	1 green bell pepper, diced
2 bay leaves	1 red bell pepper, diced
½ tsp. freshly ground black pepper	1 cup crumbled Feta cheese with herbs

Directions:

Pre-heat oven to 375 degrees. Using a casserole dish, combine the lentils, onion, garlic, vegetable stock, bay leaves, black pepper, oregano and salt. Cover and place in oven for 45 minutes.

In the meantime, mash the tomatoes, and seed and dice the bell peppers.

Remove lentils from oven at the end of 45 minutes. Add in the stewed tomatoes, and bell pepper along with 2/3 cup of Feta. Place back in oven for an additional 30 minutes or until Feta begins to melt and turn lightly golden. Remove from oven and crumble the rest of the Feta over the casserole. Serve hot with warmed Mediterranean pitas.

MAY 27 SPINACH AND BEAN CASSEROLE

Ingredients:

3 tbs. olive oil	2 tbs. thyme
1 lg. onion, diced	8 cups fresh baby spinach
4 garlic cloves, minced	Salt & pepper, to taste
3 cans cannellini beans, rinsed & drained	

Directions:

Heat the oil in a 10" skillet over medium heat. Add onion and garlic and sauté until lightly golden. Add in the beans and thyme and cook for 3-4 minutes. Stir in the spinach and immediately turn of the heat. Once spinach has wilted, season with salt and pepper and serve.

MAY 28 **TEX-MEX RANCHEROS**

Ingredients:

1-16 oz. pkg. mixed frozen vegetables

3 tbs. olive oil, divided

2 medium onions, diced

8 oz. pkg. Baby Bella mushrooms, small chopped

2 medium potatoes, diced

2 tomatoes, diced

2 hot jalapeno peppers, finely chopped

1 pkg. small raw shrimp, peeled & deveined

1 tsp. dried oregano

1 tsp. dried rosemary

1 tbs. fresh cilantro, finely chopped

1 pkg. Four Cheese Mexican

Tortilla chips or baked pita chips

Directions:

In a medium pot, bring the mixed frozen vegetable to a par-boil. Drain and set aside.

Next, pour 2 tablespoons of oil into a heavy skillet and heat over medium-high heat. Add in the onions and mushrooms. Cook until onions are translucent and mushrooms are tender.

In a small frying pan, heat the remaining 1 tablespoon of oil and; in the potatoes. Cook until golden on all sides. Transfer to onion-mushroom mixture, adding in the mixed vegetables, tomatoes, and next 5 ingredients. Simmer on medium heat for 6-8 minutes. Remove from heat. Serve on individual plates along with tortilla chips and sprinkle on cheese.

MAY 29 **EASY LOBSTER SALAD**

Ingredients:

2 steamed lobsters, halved

1 cup mayonnaise

1 tbs. freshly squeezed lemon juice

¼ tsp. salt

Freshly ground black pepper, to taste

2 tbs. fresh dill, finely chopped

3 celery stalks, cut into thirds

Rye loaf, sliced

Directions:

Place ice cubes on a large platter. Place the 4 lobster halves around the platter. In a serving bowl, combine the next 5 ingredients. Place bowl in the center of the platter. Put celery stalks in a clear decorative glass and place on platter. Slice bread and serve along with the lobster.

MAY 30 **ROTELLE WITH CHERRY TOMATOES POMODORO**

Ingredients:

1 lb. rotelle, prepared to al dente

3 tbs. extra virgin olive oil

3 garlic cloves, minced

10 oz. pkg. grape tomatoes, sliced

1 tbs. dried oregano

1 tbs. dried basil

Salt & pepper, to taste

1 tsp. sugar

¼ cup grated Parmesan cheese

6 oz. ciliegine (sm. round mozzarella balls), halved

10-12 fresh basil leaves, julienned

Directions:

Prepare pasta to al dente.

In the meantime, in a large, 14" skillet, heat olive oil over medium-high heat. Add in the garlic and sauté until lightly golden. Add in the tomatoes, oregano, dried basil, salt, pepper, and sugar. Cook until tomatoes soften (about 6-8 minutes).

Drain pasta and transfer to the skillet. Combine well and sprinkle with grated cheese. Toss well. Next, add the ciliegine and stir. Transfer to a large platter, sprinkle with the basil leaves. Serve immediately.

MAY 31 **GRILLED SHRIMP KABOBS AND RICE**

Ingredients:

½ cup chili sauce

1 tbs. honey

1 tbs. soy sauce

1 tsp. minced garlic

1 lb. raw shrimp, shelled and deveined

1 lg. green bell pepper, cut into 12 pieces

1 lg. yellow bell pepper, cut into 12 pieces

3 lg. onions, each quartered

2 med. yellow squash, cut into 8 pieces

2 cups cooked rice

Directions:

Heat grill and spray with oil. In a small bowl whisk the chili sauce, honey, soy sauce, and garlic. Set aside.

Alternately, thread shrimp, green pepper, yellow pepper, onions, and squash onto 4 long metal skewers. Brush the kabobs with half the sauce and place on hot grill. Cook for about 8-10 minutes until shrimp turn pink and vegetables are tender. Brush with reserved sauce once again before serving.

Spoon rice onto individual plates and place a skewer of kabob on each bed of rice.

JUNE 1 **GAZAPACHO**

Ingredients:

4 ripe tomatoes, peeled & diced

1 red onion, finely chopped

1 cucumber, peeled, seeded, & finely chopped

1 sweet red bell pepper, seeded & chopped

1 green bed pepper, seeded & chopped

2 stalks celery, chopped

2 tbs. chopped fresh parsley

2 tbs. chopped fresh chives

3 garlic cloves, minced

¼ cup olive oil

2 tbs. freshly squeezed lemon juice

2 tsp. sugar

Sea salt & black pepper

Tabasco sauce, to taste

3 cups tomato juice

Directions:

Combine all ingredients in a blender and store overnight in refrigerator to allow flavors to marry. Serve cold the next day.

JUNE 2 **PERCIATELLI WITH CRAB SAUCE**

Ingredients:

4 large live blue crabs

¼ cup extra virgin olive oil

4 large garlic cloves, crushed

1-35 oz. can crushed tomatoes

1 tbs. dried oregano

¼ cup fresh Italian parsley, chopped

½ tsp. crushed red pepper flakes

Salt, to taste

1 lb. perciatelli pasta

Directions:

Place the live crabs in a large Dutch oven and cover with cold water. Cover with lid and bring to a boil. Reduce heat and let simmer for 10 minutes. Remove crabs from pot and let cool so you can handle. Once cool, break off the legs and claws from each. Crack open the legs and claws, remove meat, and set aside in a bowl. Next, pull off the back shell and clean out the green matter, gills, and air sacs. Discard. Remove the meat and add to same bowl. Set aside.

Pour olive oil into a medium sauce pan over medium heat and add garlic. Sauté until golden. Add in the tomatoes, oregano, half of the parsley, red pepper, and salt. Stir, then cover pot and simmer on low-medium for 30 minutes. Next, add crab meat to the sauce and let simmer on low for another 10-15 minutes.

In the meantime, bring 5-6 quarts salted water to a boil. Add in the pasta and cook until al dente. Drain the pasta and place on a large platter. Pour sauce over pasta and toss very well to incorporate the crab meat and sauce into the pasta. Garnish with remaining parsley and serve at once.

JUNE 3 **SHRIMP ROLL UPS**

Ingredients:

1 lb. cream cheese, room temperature

Salt & pepper, to taste

2 tbs. lime juice

10 lg. flavored flour tortillas

1 cup cocktail sauce (salsa may be substituted)

1 bunch fresh cilantro, roughly chopped

½ lb. cooked small shrimp

Directions:

Using the paddle attachment of a mixer, blend together the cream cheese and the lime juice. Next add in the cocktail sauce or salsa, the shrimp, salt and pepper. Blend for 1 minute.

Place tortillas on a clean surface. Spread the mixture evenly on the tortillas, add some fresh cilantro and roll them up tightly. Wrap each roll up in a plastic wrap and refrigerate overnight. May be served with additional cocktail sauce or salsa for dipping.

JUNE 4 **GRILLED GOAT CHEESE AND HEIRLOOM TOMATO SANDWICHES**

Ingredients:

8 thick slices sourdough bread

8 tbs. softened butter

2 garlic cloves, minced

4 oz. goat cheese, room temperature

2 tbs. chopped fresh tarragon

12 slices heirloom tomatoes

Sea salt, to taste

Freshly ground black pepper

Directions:

Spread softened butter on one side of each slice of bread. Set aside. In a small bowl, combine the minced garlic, goat cheese, and tarragon. Blend well. Take 4 slices of bread and spread the cheese mixture onto the unbuttered side. Place 3 tomato slices on each slice of bread, sprinkle with salt and pepper, then cover each with the remaining bread slices, butter side up.

Place each sandwich on a pre-heated griddle pan and place a weight such as a grill press on top of each. When one side has browned, flip over and brown the other side. May be served alone or with soup or a salad. Serve while hot.

JUNE 5 **SIMPLY LINGUINE**

Ingredients:

1 lb. linguine, cooked to al dente & drained

1½ sticks butter, softened at room temperature

1 cup freshly grated Parmigiano-Reggiano cheese

1 tbs. ground rubbed sage

Freshly ground black pepper

¼ cup fresh Italian parsley, chopped

Directions:

Once pasta has cooked, drain, and place on a large platter or into a large pasta bowl. Add in the butter and mix well. Add in the cheese, sage, and pepper. Toss well to combine. Serve in 4 individual pasta bowls, garnish each with parsley and serve while hot.

JUNE 6 **TEX-MEX CORN AND BEANS WITH TOSTITOS**

Ingredients:

5 tsp. olive oil, divided

2 cups frozen corn, thawed

1-16 oz. can black beans, drained & rinsed

1-16 oz. can black-eyed peas, drained & rinsed

1 lg. onion, chopped	2 tbs. fresh lime juice
2 tsp. chili powder	1 family-sized bag of Tostitos with a hint of lime
1 tsp. ground cumin	1 cups shredded pepper jack cheese
1-16 oz. bottle salsa verde	1 bunch fresh cilantro, chopped
8 oz. chopped green chilies	2 ripe avocados, sliced

Directions:

In a large skillet, heat 3 teaspoons olive oil over medium heat and add in the corn. Cook until corn starts to turn slightly brown. Remove from skillet and set aside. Heat remaining oil in same skillet; add in the onion and sauté until translucent. Next, stir in the chili powder, cumin, salsa verde, and chilies. Cook for about 8-10 minutes, then add in the beans, peas, and lime juice. Cook for about 2-3 minutes.

Divide Tostitos on 6 plates. Spoon mixture over the chips, sprinkle with cheese and cilantro, then top with avocado slices. Serve while hot.

JUNE 7 GRILLED SALMON PITAS WITH CUCUMBER YOGHURT DILL SAUCE

Ingredients:

Olive oil	2 tbs. diced sweet onion
16 oz. salmon, cut into chunks	1 cup plain yoghurt
¾ cup lemon juice	1 tbs. fresh dill weed, chopped
1½ tsp. garlic powder	1 cup shredded lettuce
Salt and pepper	4 pita pockets, cut in half
1/3 cup diced cucumber	

Directions:

In a medium bowl, toss together the salmon chunks, lemon juice, garlic powder, salt and pepper. Cover tightly with plastic wrap and marinate in refrigerator for 3 hours. In the meantime, in a small bowl, mix together the cucumber, onion, yoghurt, dill weed, salt and pepper. Cover with plastic wrap and store in refrigerator.

Heat grill pan on medium-high heat, drizzle with olive oil and once oil is hot, place salmon on grill. Grill on all sides until edges begin to turn crispy and grill marks show. Remove from grill, divide into pita pockets and top with chilled cucumber-yoghurt dill sauce.

JUNE 8 GRILLED VEGETABLE KABOBS

Ingredients:

8 wooden skewers, soaked in water for at least 1 hour

2 med. eggplants cut into large chunks

4 lg. onions, cut into sixths

24 grape tomatoes

2 lg. zucchini, cut into ½" rounds

2 lg. green peppers, cut into 1" pieces

24 cremini mushrooms

Olive oil

Sea salt

Black pepper

2 cups steamed Basmati rice

Directions:

Pre-heat grill to medium-high heat. Then, alternately thread eggplants, onions, tomatoes, zucchini, peppers, and mushrooms on wooden skewers. Brush each skewer generously with olive oil. Season with salt and pepper.

Place skewers on grill and cook on each side for about 8-10 minutes or until vegetables are tender. Serve over steamed rice.

JUNE 9 QUINOA AND CORN SALAD

Ingredients:

1½ cups quinoa, rinsed & drained

2 cups canned corn, drained

1 lg. roasted red pepper

1 seedless cucumber, peeled & diced

¼ cup fresh lemon juice

1 tsp. ground cumin

1 tsp. chili powder

1 garlic clove, minced

¼ cup chopped flat leaf parsley

Mediterranean sea salt

1 head Romaine lettuce, cut in half

12 grape tomatoes, halved

1 ripe avocado, thinly sliced

1 lime, cut into wedges

1/3 cups toasted pumpkin seeds

Directions:

Cook quinoa as directed on package until water is absorbed. Once cooked, in a large bowl, mix with corn, red pepper, and cucumber and let cool or about 30 minutes. Set aside.

In a small bowl, whisk together the next 6 ingredients. Pour over the quinoa and corn. Stir well.

Arrange lettuce leaves around a large platter and spoon the quinoa mixture into the center of the platter. Arrange tomatoes, avocado slices, and lime wedges around the lettuce. Sprinkle with seeds and serve.

JUNE 10 **BAKED TOMATO TAPAS**

Ingredients:

2 lg. Roma (plum) tomatoes, chopped

12 sun-dried tomatoes in oil, chopped

1 cup shredded mozzarella and provolone blend

1/3 cup Gorgonzola cheese, crumbled

¼ cup finely chopped Vidalia onion

1 tbs. fresh basil, finely chopped

1 tsp. fresh rosemary, finely chopped

¼ tsp. garlic powder

¼ tsp. black pepper

1 long French baguette, sliced on a diagonal

Directions:

In a large bowl, combine the first 9 ingredients together. Using a large baking sheet, arrange the baguette slices onto the sheet. Spoon mixture over each slice and bake in a pre-heated 350 degree oven until cheese has melted. Serve with a garden salad.

JUNE 11 **CUCUMBER "SPAGHETTI" AND SCALLIONS**

***NOTE: You will need a mandolin for this recipe.*

Ingredients:

6 lg. seedless cucumbers

4 tsp. kosher salt

2/3 cup thinly sliced green onions, green parts only

½ cup plus 2 tbs. rice vinegar

2 tbs. honey

1 tsp. sesame oil

¼ cup toasted sesame seeds

2 tbs. chopped fresh dill weed

1 tbs. chopped fresh mint

<u>Directions:</u>

Peel cucumbers and cut into thin strips using a mandolin equipped with a julienne blade. Place strips in a large bowl, add salt, toss together, and then transfer to a colander. Drain for 30 minutes.

Transfer cucumber back to a large bowl; add in the green onions as well as the vinegar, honey, oil, and dill weed. Toss well. Serve on individual plates. Sprinkle with sesame seeds, dill weed, and mint. Serve.

JUNE 12 **SHRIMP SALAD**

<u>Ingredients:</u>

1 lb. cooked small shrimp

1 celery stalk, finely chopped

3 green onions (white and green parts), finely chopped

1½ tbs. fresh dill, chopped

1 cup mayonnaise

Pinch of kosher salt

Freshly ground black pepper

<u>Directions:</u>

Using a large salad bowl, combine all ingredients and mix well. Refrigerate for 1 hour before serving. May be served on bread or in pitas as sandwiches. May also be served on a plate lined with a lettuce cup and crackers on the side.

JUNE 13 **PARMESAN BABY SPINACH AND ASPARAGUS QUINOA**

<u>Ingredients:</u>

1 cup uncooked quinoa, rinsed well

1½ cups no sodium, vegetable stock

1½ tsp. freshly ground black pepper

1 tsp. sea salt

2 tbs. olive oil

1 medium yellow onion, chopped

1 cup baby asparagus, cut into small pieces

3 garlic cloves, minced

2 cups fresh baby spinach, chopped

1 tbs. freshly squeezed lemon juice

¾ cup freshly grated Parmesan cheese

¼ cup freshly shaved Parmesan cheese

Directions:

In a medium saucepan, over high heat, bring quinoa, stock, pepper, and salt to a boil. Then reduce heat to medium-low, cover, and cook until stock has been absorbed and quinoa is tender. Set aside.

Meanwhile, heat the oil in a large skillet over medium heat. Stir in the onion and asparagus. Cook for 2 minutes. Add in the garlic and cook for 1-2 minutes. Next, stir in the quinoa and spinach. When the spinach has wilted, add in the lemon juice and grated cheese. Mix well. Garnish with shaved cheese and serve immediately.

JUNE 14 **AVOCADO AND GRAPEFRUIT SALAD**

Ingredients:

Salad:

6 cups fresh baby spinach, washed & drained

2 pink grapefruits, halved, peeled, sectioned, & seeded

2 avocados, halved, seeded, peeled & diced

1/3 cup dried cranberries or currants

1 lg. Granny Smith apple, cored, & diced

Dressing:

1/3 cup champagne vinegar

6 tsp. canola oil

Freshly ground black pepper, to taste

Directions:

Divide spinach among 6 salad plates. Top with grapefruit, avocado, cranberries, and apple pieces.

In a small bowl, whisk together the vinegar, oil, and pepper, and drizzle over tops of each salad. Serve chilled.

JUNE 15 **MOROCCAN LENTIL CASSEROLE**

Ingredients:

4 cups organic vegetable stock

¼ tsp. red pepper flakes

2 cups dried lentils, rinsed

2-3 tbs. olive oil

1 lg. onion, chopped

4 garlic cloves, finely chopped

1-15 oz. can chick peas, drained & rinsed

1 tsp. sea salt

1 tsp. chili powder

½ tsp cinnamon

½ cup red wine

1 Delicious red apple, diced

¼ cup dried apricots, chopped

1 tbs. lemon juice

1 tsp. brown sugar

¼ tsp. ground ginger

1/3 cup slivered almonds, toasted

Directions:

In a medium sauce pan, bring vegetable stock to a boil over medium-high heat. Add in the lentils and cook until tender but not mushy. Set aside.

In a large skillet, heat olive oil over medium heat, then add in the onion and garlic and cook until slightly golden. Add in the chick peas, lentils with vegetable stock (if any), and the next 5 ingredients. If more liquid is needed, add in another ½ cup vegetable stock. Bring ingredients to a boil over high heat then transfer to a casserole dish that has been sprayed with cooking oil.

Mix together the next 5 ingredients, spoon over the lentil mixture, cover with aluminum foil, and place in a pre-heated 350 degree oven for 20-25 minutes. Remove from oven, and sprinkle with almonds. Serve hot.

JUNE 16 **SUMMER FARMER'S MARKET SALAD**

Ingredients:

Salad:

2 cups grape tomatoes, halved

1 small zucchini, thinly sliced in to half-moons

1 small yellow squash, thinly sliced into half-moons

1 small red bell pepper, cut into thin strips

1 small yellow bell pepper, cut into thin strips

1 cup fresh corn kernels

½ cup thinly sliced scallions

8 oz. penne pasta, cooked

1/3 cup torn fresh basil

½ cup mozzarella pearls

Vinaigrette:

½ cup freshly grated Parmesan cheese

2 tsp. coarse black pepper

½ cup extra virgin olive oil

4 tbs. balsamic vinegar from Modena

2 lg. garlic cloves

½ tsp. sea salt

¼ tsp. red pepper flakes

2 tsp. lemon zest

Directions:

In a large bowl, combine all the ingredients for the salad and gently toss.

Using a blender or food processor, pulse together all ingredients for vinaigrette and pour over salad. Toss well and serve immediately.

JUNE 17 FUSILLI WITH CHERRY TOMATOES AND FRESH BABY SPINACH

1 lb. fusilli

1 tbs. salt

8 oz. fresh baby spinach

1/3 cup organic vegetable stock

¼ cup extra virgin olive oil

2 cups halved cherry tomatoes

½ tsp. sea salt

1 tsp. crushed red pepper flakes

1/3 cup freshly grated Parmesan cheese

10-12 lg. basil leaves, julienned

Freshly shaved Asiago cheese

Directions:

Boil water in a 5 qt. pot over high heat. Add in the salt and pasta. Cook until al dente. Add in the spinach and cook together for 1 minute. Drain pasta and spinach and transfer to a large bowl.

Add in the stock, olive oil, and tomatoes then season with salt and pepper flakes. Toss well. Next, add in the Parmesan cheese and basil. Toss well again. Top with shaved cheese and serve.

JUNE 18 BAKED POLENTA AND VEGETABLE CASSEROLE

My maternal grandparents were quite poor and my grandmother had to be creative when preparing meatless meals, especially for her large family. She made several different meals using polenta or yellow corn meal. The following recipe is a variation of one of her polenta recipes.

Ingredients:

2 tbs. extra virgin olive oil

½ tsp. dried thyme

1 medium yellow onion, diced

1 cup polenta (cook according to pkg. directions)

3 lg. garlic cloves, minced

12 oz. can diced tomatoes, drained

1 medium green bell pepper, diced

¼ cup each Parmesan & Fontina cheese

Directions:

Heat olive oil in a medium skillet over medium heat. Add the onions, garlic, peppers, and thyme. Sauté until vegetables are tender (about 6-8 minutes). Turn off heat.

Prepare the polenta as directed on package. When polenta has thickened, transfer to a greased 9" X 9" baking dish and spread out evenly. Let cool for 30-40 minutes. Then evenly spread the tomatoes over the polenta. Next, pour the onion/pepper mixture on top of the tomatoes and spread evenly. Sprinkle with cheese and bake in a 375 degree oven for about 12-15 minutes until cheese has melted.

JUNE 19 COLD CUCUMBER SOUP

Ingredients:

3 cucumbers, peeled, seeds removed, rough chopped

1 tsp. freshly ground black pepper

¾ cup green onions, rough chopped

1½ cups organic vegetable stock

1 tbs. lemon zest

½ cup plain yoghurt

1 tsp. kosher salt

1 tbs. fresh dill weed chopped

Directions:

Place first 6 ingredients in a blender on a puree setting. Remove from blender and transfer to a bowl. Stir in the yoghurt and dill and chill for 1 hour. Serve topped with fresh dill weed.

JUNE 20 COBB SALAD STUFFED PITAS

Traditionally, Cobb Salad is made with chicken and bacon but substitutions were used in this vegetarian variation.

Ingredients:

3 cups cooked small shrimp

2 oz. crumbled bleu cheese

2 cups Romaine lettuce, chopped small	4 tbs. mayonnaise
1 lg. avocado, diced	1 tbs. fresh lemon juice
2 lg. Roma tomatoes, diced	2 tsp. ground black pepper
1 sm. red onion, diced	1 tsp. kosher salt
½ cup mock "bacon" bits	6-6" pitas, halved

Directions:

In a large bowl, combine the first 7 ingredients. In a smaller bowl, whisk together the next 4 ingredients. Pour over the salad and toss well. Fill each pita half with approximately a half cup of salad.

JUNE 21 MEDITERRANEAN GRILLED EGGPLANT AND TOMATO VINAIGRETTE

Ingredients:

2 medium eggplants, sliced lengthwise, ½" thick	1 tbs. dried oregano
Extra virgin olive oil for brushing	Sea salt
8 sun-dried tomatoes, chopped	Freshly ground black pepper
2 lg. shallots, finely chopped	½ cup olive oil
1 tbs. capers, minced	3 tbs. Spanish sherry vinegar
3 garlic cloves, minced	1 Italian loaf or French baguette

Directions:

Heat grill (indoor or outdoor). Brush each side of eggplant slices with olive oil and place on grill. Lightly brown each side and set on a large platter.

In the meantime, combine the tomatoes, shallots, capers, garlic, and oregano in a bowl. Season with salt and pepper.

Whisk together the oil and vinegar and pour over the tomato mixture. Stir together and taste to see if more seasoning is needed. Finally, spoon the tomato mixture over the eggplant slices. Serve immediately with sliced bread.

JUNE 22 **BAKED TILAPIA WITH CHAMPAGNE MUSTARD**

Ingredients:

4-4 oz. pieces of tilapia	Italian style bread crumbs
1 lg. egg	Champagne mustard
¼ cup milk	Spray oil

Directions:

Pre-heat oven to 375 degrees. Spray a casserole dish with oil. In a shallow baking dish, whisk together the egg and milk. On a sheet of wax paper, generously spread out the bread crumbs. Dip one piece of tilapia at a time into the egg mixture. Then generously coat with bread crumbs on each side. Place in casserole dish and using a spoon, spoon the mustard onto the tops of each fish. Bake for 10-15 minutes until golden and crisp.

JUNE 23 **APPLE AND CHEDDAR PANINI WITH FIG JAM**

Ingredients:

8 slices country style oatmeal bread	8 slices cheddar cheese
2 tbs. olive oil	2 Fuji apples, peeled, cored & thinly sliced
8 tbs. fig jam	

Directions:

Pre-heat a Panini press or griddle pan with a press.

Brush one side of each bread slice with the olive oil and lay the slices oiled side down on a cutting board. Spread each slice with 1 tablespoon fig jam. On four of the bread slices, place 2 slices of cheese then arrange the apple slices on top. Top each with the remaining bread slices, oiled side up.

Place the sandwiches on the Panini press or griddle pan and press down. Cook until bread is golden and cheese has melted. Serve with apple chips or any other fruit chips on the side.

JUNE 24 EGG SALAD AND CARAMELIZED ONION SANDWICHES

Ingredients:

¼ cup olive oil

½ cup finely chopped celery

2 lg. Vidalia onions, thinly sliced

¼ cup finely chopped yellow onion

2 tbs. balsamic vinegar from Modena

1 tsp. dried mustard

1¼ tsp. kosher salt, divided

¾ cup mayonnaise

½ tsp. freshly ground black pepper, divided

8 slices sour-dough bread, thickly sliced

8 lg. hard-boiled eggs, chopped

4 lg. iceberg lettuce leaves

Directions:

Heat oil in a medium skillet over medium heat and add onions. Stir occasionally and cook until soft and translucent. When onions turn golden brown, add in the vinegar, ¾ tsp. salt, and ¼ teaspoon pepper. Cook until onions turn deep brown and vinegar begins to dissipate. Transfer to a bowl and let cool.

In a medium bowl, combine the eggs, celery, onion, mustard and remaining salt. Add mayonnaise, season with remaining pepper and stir gently. Lightly toast bread and on each of 4 slices of bread, place lettuce leaves. Evenly divide the egg salad and place on lettuce beds, then top with caramelized onions. Top with remaining bread slices, cut in half and serve.

JUNE 25 SPAGHETTI AND CALAMARI SAUCE

Ingredients:

1½ lbs. calamari (squid), cleaned

Salt, to taste

3 tbs. extra virgin olive oil

½ tsp. crushed red pepper flakes

4 lg. garlic cloves, finely chopped

Pinch of sugar

1-35. oz. can crushed tomatoes

Chopped fresh Italian parsley, for garnish

1½ tbs. dried oregano

1 lb. spaghetti, cooked to al dente

Directions:

Heat oil in medium sauce pan over medium heat and add garlic. Cook until garlic is golden. Next add the tomatoes, oregano, salt, pepper, and sugar. Stir well, cover, and let simmer for 30 minutes. In the meantime, cut the squid into ¾" circles. If using tentacles, cut into small bits. Transfer to a colander and place on a dish to catch any liquid. Set aside in the refrigerator. Prepare the pasta.

When sauce is ready, add in the squid for 8-10 minutes. Do not overcook because the squid will turn rubbery. Transfer the pasta to a large platter and pour sauce over the pasta. Garnish with parsley. Serve immediately.

JUNE 26 SPANISH OMELET WITH MANCHEGO CHEESE AND OLIVES

Ingredients:

1/3 cup olive oil, divided	½ tsp. black pepper
1 medium yellow onion, thinly sliced	8 eggs, beaten
1½ tsp. salt	½ cup pitted green olives with pimento
5 medium red potatoes cut	¼ lb. manchego cheese, thinly sliced
into 1/8" thick slices, skin on	

Directions:

Using a 12" oven-proof non-stick skillet, heat 2 tbs. oil over medium heat. Add in the onion and ½ teaspoon salt. Cook until soft and translucent. Transfer to a large bowl when done.

In the same skillet, heat 2 tablespoons oil over medium heat. Add half of the potatoes in an even layer, ½ teaspoon salt, and ¼ tsp. pepper. Stirring occasionally, cook until potatoes are soft. Transfer to the bowl with the onions. Repeat process for remaining potatoes. Combine with the other potatoes and add in the eggs and olives. Stir gently to combine.

Heat remaining oil over medium heat in same skillet. Add half of the potato/onion/egg mixture and smooth to an even layer in pan. Top with cheese. Add the second half of the mixture. Cook on stove for approximately 10 minutes then transfer to a pre-heated 350 degree oven. Bake for approximately 30 minutes or until eggs are set. Remove from oven, invert onto a large round serving platter and cut into wedges.

JUNE 27 BEER BATTER FRIED SHRIMP

Ingredients:

½ cup all-purpose flour	1½ lbs. lg. shrimp
½ cup beer	Canola oil

1 tsp. salt

Directions:

In a medium bowl, combine the first 3 ingredients. Set aside and batter will start to thicken. In the meantime, shell and devein the shrimp. Rinse with cold water and pat dry with paper towels so that the batter will adhere to the shrimp.

Heat oil in a small sauce pan or deep fryer until oil is bubbling. Dip shrimp, one at a time, into batter and carefully drop into oil. Fry until lightly browned on each side. Place on a platter lined with paper towels to drain excess oil.

JUNE 28 SEARED GROUPER WITH A VEGETABLE MEDLEY

Ingredients:

4-6 oz. grouper fillets	1½ cups frozen corn kernels
1 tsp. salt	4 garlic cloves, minced
½ tsp. black pepper	1½ cups grape tomatoes, halved
2 tbs. olive oil	1½ cups frozen baby lima beans
2 med. zucchini, sliced	2 tbs. cold butter
1 lg. shallot, chopped	2 tbs. dried rosemary

Directions:

Sprinkle fish with salt and pepper. Heat oil in a large nonstick skillet over medium heat. Cook 4 minutes on each side or until browned and cooked to desired doneness. Remove from pan and keep warm.

Sauté zucchini and shallot until crisp and tender. Add in the corn and garlic and sauté for an additional 2 minutes. Reduce heat to low, and stir in the tomatoes, lima beans, butter and rosemary. Season, to taste. Cook until vegetables are tender. Spoon vegetables onto four individual dinner plates and top with fish.

JUNE 29 LEMON, ORZO, AND SHRIMP SOUP

Ingredients:

2 tbs. olive oil	2 tsp. lemon zest
1 med. sweet onion, chopped	½ tsp. rosemary

3 carrots, thinly sliced	¾ cup orzo pasta
2 garlic cloves, minced	1 lb. raw shrimp, peeled & deveined
64 oz. shrimp stock	½ cup fresh flat-leaf parsley
6 tbs. freshly squeezed lemon juice	

Directions:

Heat oil in a Dutch oven over medium heat. Toss in the onion and sauté until tender. Add in the carrots and garlic and sauté for 2 minutes. Stir in the stock, lemon juice, zest, and rosemary. Increase heat to high and bring to a boil. Add in the orzo. Reduce heat to medium, simmer, stirring occasionally. After 7 minutes, add in the shrimp, season with salt and pepper, to taste. Cook for 3 minutes and serve with seasoned crackers.

JUNE 30 **GRILLED MEDITERRANEAN VEGETABLE SANDWICHES**

Ingredients:

1 sm. eggplant sliced	Garlic powder
1 lg. onion, thickly sliced	4 hard rolls, sliced open
1 lg. red bell pepper, sliced	1 cup marinara sauce
4 lg. Portobello mushroom, halved	2 lg. tomatoes, sliced
Olive oil	Dried oregano
Salt & pepper, to taste	4 lg. slices fresh mozzarella

Directions:

Pre-heat oven to 375 degrees.

Place the eggplant, onion, pepper, and mushrooms on a large rimmed baking sheet. Drizzle with olive oil and sprinkle with salt, pepper, and garlic powder. Heat a grill pan and place vegetables on pan. Grill each side until grill marks form.

In the meantime, spread each side of the rolls with marinara sauce. Then layer with the grilled eggplant, onions, peppers, and mushrooms. Add on the tomatoes; sprinkle with oregano, and top with mozzarella. Leave rolls open and place on a baking sheet. Transfer sheet to oven for about 5-7 minutes or until cheese has melted. Close each roll and serve hot.

JULY 1 **FRUIT AND SPINACH SALAD**

<u>Ingredients:</u>

4 cups baby spinach, washed & dried	1/3 cup crumbled herbed feta cheese
1 cup sliced strawberries	2 tbs. extra virgin olive oil
1 cup yellow raisins	2 tbs. balsamic vinegar
1 cup diced apple	Freshly ground black pepper
½ cup chopped pecans	Croutons

<u>Directions:</u>

Wash spinach, remove stems, and dry by wrapping in a clean dish towel and patting dry.

Mix the first 6 ingredients in a large salad bowl.

In a small bowl, combine the oil, vinegar, and pepper. Pour over salad. Add croutons and serve.

JULY 2 **SUN-DRIED TOMATO, MOZZARELLA, AND BASIL PANINI**

<u>Ingredients:</u>

4 ciabatta rolls, halved	4 thick slices fresh mozzarella
4 tsp. olive oil	Sea salt
12 sun-dried tomatoes	Black pepper
8 lg. basil leaves	

<u>Directions:</u>

Drizzle the insides of both halves of bread with oil. Arrange 3 sun-dried tomatoes on each bottom half, 2 basil leaves, and one thick slice of mozzarella. Sprinkle with salt and pepper and place top half of roll on bottom half forming a complete sandwich. Put sandwiches on a hot Panini press for about 10 minutes, until the bread is crusty and cheese has melted.

Basic Recipe:

Ingredients:

1-15 oz. can garbanzo beans, drained, liquid reserved   ½ tsp. salt

1 lg. garlic clove, crushed   1 tbs. olive oil

2 tsp. ground cumin

Directions:

In a blender or food processor, combine beans, garlic, cumin, salt, and oil. Blend on low speed, gradually adding reserved bean liquid, until desired consistency is attained. Transfer to a serving bowl and refrigerate.

Roasted Red Pepper Hummus:

Ingredients:

1-15 oz. can garbanzo beans, drained   ½ cup roasted red peppers

2 garlic cloves, crushed   ¼ tsp. dried basil

1/3 cup lemon juice   Salt & pepper

Directions:

In a blender or food processor, combine beans, garlic, and lemon juice. Blend on low speed until mixture is smooth. Add in roasted peppers and basil; process until peppers are finely chopped. Season with salt and pepper. Transfer to a serving bowl and chill until ready to serve.

Black Bean Hummus:

Ingredients:

1-15 oz. can black beans, drained, liquid reserved   ½ tsp. black pepper

1 clove garlic crushed   ¼ tsp. cayenne pepper

2 tbs. lemon juice   ¼ tsp. paprika

¾ tsp. ground cumin   10 Kalamata olives

½ tsp. salt

<u>Directions:</u>

In an electric blender or food processor, add beans, garlic, 2 tablespoons of the reserved liquid, lemon juice, and the rest of the ingredients through the cayenne pepper. Process until smooth then transfer mixture to a serving bowl, cover, and chill. When ready to serve, garnish with the paprika and olives.

***NOTE:** When getting ready to serve, place all 3 bowls onto a large tray or serving platter and arrange warmed pita bread wedges and or vegetable chips around the tray as well.

JULY 4 *HAPPY INDEPEDENCE DAY* BAKED BEANS AND "HOT DOGS"

<u>Ingredients:</u>

2-15 oz. cans of navy beans, drained & rinsed	¼ cup brown sugar, firmly packed
2 tbs. oil	¼ cup dark molasses
2 cups sweet onions, chopped	2 tbs. cider vinegar
1 garlic clove, minced	1 tsp. dry mustard
32 oz. canned tomato sauce	¼ tsp. freshly ground black pepper

<u>Directions:</u>

Place beans in a pot or large casserole dish. Set aside. Pre-heat oven to 300 degrees. Heat olive oil in a medium skillet over medium heat. Add in the onions and garlic and cook until tender and golden. Remove from heat and stir into dish with beans. Next, stir in the tomato sauce and the rest of the ingredients. Cover and bake for 3 ½ hours, stirring often. If mixture starts to become dry, add water. At the end of the 3 ½ hours, uncover and let bake for 30 more minutes.

Serve with grilled soy "hot dogs" that can be purchased at your local grocer.

JULY 5 Joey's Pasta

<u>Ingredients:</u>

½ cup extra virgin olive oil, divided	¾ cup water
1 cup diced eggplant	1 tbs. garlic powder
1 cup diced zucchini	1 tsp. sugar

8 scallions, thinly sliced (white section & ½ of green stems)

10 oz. pkg. Baby Bella mushrooms, sliced

5 oz. grape tomatoes, sliced in half

8 oz. frozen peas

3 oz. tomato paste

½ tsp. dried oregano

6-8 basil leaves, julienned

Salt & pepper

2/3 cup grated Parmesan cheese

1 lb. fettuccine

1 cup mozzarella pearls

Directions:

Heat ¼ cup oil in a heavy 12" skillet over medium-high heat. Add in the diced eggplants and zucchini and lightly brown evenly on all sides. Remove from skillet and place on a plate lined with paper towels. Set aside.

Reduce heat to medium and add remaining oil to skillet. Add in the scallions and mushrooms. Sauté covered for 10 minutes. Add in the grape tomatoes and sauté for an additional 6-8 minutes. Next, add in the peas. Sauté covered for an additional 6-8 minutes. Remove lid, transfer the cooked eggplants and zucchini to the pan and stir. Create a well in the center of the pan and add in the tomato paste and water. Starting from the center of the well, stir in the paste and water gently, then begin to incorporate all the vegetables together. Add remaining ingredients, through the cheese, but only 1/3 cup of cheese. Simmer on low heat for an additional 15 minutes. Mixture will be dry and thick, not loose. If too dry, add a little more water.

In the meantime, using a 5 qt. pot, bring salted water to a boil, add in the pasta, and cook to al dente. Drain and transfer pasta to the skillet with the vegetables and sauce. Mix until pasta and sauce are completely blended. Transfer to a large platter; generously sprinkle with remaining cheese and mozzarella pearls. Toss well to combine.

JULY 6 **TUNA SALAD**

Ingredients:

2-6 oz. cans tuna packed in oil or water, drained

Approximately 6 tbs. mayonnaise

½ celery stalk, finely chopped

½ carrot, finely chopped

2 tbs. sweet pickle relish

2 tsp. fresh dill weed, chopped

2 tsp. fresh parsley, chopped

Pinch of salt & pepper

Directions:

In a medium bowl, empty the 2 cans of tuna and flake. Add in the mayonnaise and blend well. Next, add in the remaining ingredients and mix well. Chill for 1 hour before serving.

May be served on bread as a sandwich with lettuce and tomato or may be served on a plate by first creating a bed of lettuce in the center of the plate. Using a large ice cream scoop, place 1 scoop of tuna salad in the center of the lettuce bed. Arrange thinly sliced seasoned tomatoes and one halved pickle alongside the lettuce and serve with gourmet crackers.

JULY 7 **CRAB QUICHE**

Ingredients:

2 eggs, beaten	1½ tsp. Old Bay Seasoning
½ cup mayonnaise	1 cup diced Gruyere cheese
2 tbs. all-purpose flour	½ cup chopped green onions
½ cup milk	1 tsp. black pepper
1 cup crab meat	1-9" unbaked pie crust

Directions:

Pre-heat oven to 375 degrees.

In a medium bowl, whisk the eggs, mayonnaise, flour, and milk until blended well. Stir in the crabmeat, Old Bay, cheese, onions, and black pepper then pour into pie shell that has been set into a well-greased pie plate. Bake for about 40-45 minutes, or until a knife inserted in the center comes out clean. Cut into wedges. May be served with a salad on the side.

JULY 8 **GIAMBOTTA/SAUTEED' SUMMER VEGETABLES (ITALIAN)**

This is an excellent example of a healthy and nutritious recipe that may be served hot or chilled. It can be accompanied by a crusty loaf of Italian bread or it may also be served on a bed of pasta. Enjoy!

Ingredients:

½ cup extra virgin olive oil	1 lg. onion, sliced
4 garlic cloves, sliced	4 lg. Roma tomatoes, diced
2 med. zucchini, cut into 1" thick slices	1 tbs. fresh dill weed, chopped

2 lg. yellow bell peppers, cored,	Pinch of sugar
seeded, & cut into thick slices	Salt & pepper, to taste
2 lg. red bell peppers, cored,	1 lg. loaf of Italian bread
seeded, & cut into thick slices	

Directions:

In a large 12" or 14" skillet, add the oil and heat over medium heat. Toss in the garlic, zucchini, peppers, and onion. Stir. Cover and let simmer for 15 minutes. Add in the remaining ingredients. Stir then cover and continue to simmer for another 20-25 minutes until vegetables are softened. Serve with a crusty loaf of Italian bread.

JULY 9 FARFALLE (BOWTIES) AND BROCCOLI PESTO

Ingredients:

Pesto:

12 oz. frozen broccoli cuts	¼ tsp. sea salt
½ cup fresh basil leaves	¼ tsp. crushed red pepper
¼ cup walnuts	1/3 cup olive oil
3 garlic cloves	2 tbs. water
¼ cup grated Parmesan cheese	1 tsp. lemon juice

Farfalle:

| 1 lb. farfalle | 1 Roma tomato, chopped |
| 1 yellow bell pepper, cut into thin strips | Grated Parmesan for sprinkling |

Directions:

Pesto:

Cook broccoli until tender, but yet crisp. Drain. Set aside 1½ cups of broccoli. Place the remaining broccoli and all of the other pesto ingredients into a food processor and process until smooth.

Farfalle:

Prepare pasta as directed on package. During the last minute of cooking, add the 1½ cups of broccoli that had been set aside and the bell pepper slices to the boiling pasta. Drain and transfer to a large serving platter or bowl. Add in the tomato and incorporate the pesto into the pasta. Toss well. Generously sprinkle with additional cheese.

JULY 10 **YELLOW SQUASH CASSEROLE**

Ingredients:

6 medium yellow squash, sliced ¼" thick

2 lg. eggs, beaten

2-3 cups Italian-style panko

Olive oil, for frying

1 cup grated parmesan cheese

1 cup grated white cheddar cheese

1 cup grated mozzarella cheese

Directions:

In an assembly line fashion set up the sliced squash on one plate, the eggs in a shallow bowl, and the panko on a plate or sheet of wax paper for easy clean up. Heat oil in a 12" skillet over medium heat. Dip the squash in the eggs, draining off excess, and coat each side with the panko. Place in sizzling oil and fry each side until golden brown.

Place fried squash on a platter lined with paper towels to drain excess oil. Transfer 1 layer of the squash to a 9" X 9" baking dish. Sprinkle each of the cheeses on top then repeat process. Place in a pre-heated 350 degree oven for 35-40 minutes until cheese has melted and a golden crust has formed on top.

JULY 11 **GRILLED COD AND SALAD**

Ingredients:

1-8 oz. piece of filleted cod

1½ tbs. garlic infused olive oil

Sea salt

Freshly ground black pepper

1 bunch fresh baby spinach

1 cup baby arugula

1-15 oz. can garbanzo beans, drained & rinsed

1-15 oz. can dark red kidney beans, drained & rinsed

10 grape tomatoes, cut into thirds

1 sm. red onion, diced small

¼ cup olive oil

1 lemon, juiced & zested

2 tsp. honey

1 tbs. fresh dill weed, chopped

1 tsp. sea salt

1 tsp. black pepper

Directions:

Heat grill pan over medium-high heat. Brush cod with olive oil on both sides and season with salt and pepper. Grill until grill marks show on both sides. Remove from grill pan and cut into 1" cubes. Set aside.

In a large bowl, combine the spinach, arugula, garbanzo beans, kidney beans, tomatoes, and onion. In a small bowl, whisk together the oil, lemon juice, zest, honey, dill, salt, and pepper. Drizzle the dressing over the salad and toss. Add in the cod, give a quick toss and serve.

JULY 12 **CRAB & LOBSTER STUFFED SHELLS**

Ingredients:

1-12 oz. box jumbo shells	5 tbs. butter
1 cup ricotta cheese	½ cup flour
1 cup freshly grated Parmesan cheese, divided	4 cups half & half
½ cup fresh Italian parsley, chopped	½ tsp. garlic powder
1 lb. lump crab meat	½ tsp. white pepper
1 lb. lobster meat	¼ tsp. nutmeg
Salt and pepper, to taste	

Directions:

Prepare pasta according to package directions to al dente. Do not overcook! Drain and set aside.

In a large bowl, combine the ricotta, ½ cup Parmesan, parsley, crab, lobster, salt and pepper. Fill the shells with the crab/lobster mixture. Place in a buttered baking dish.

In the meantime, in a medium pan, melt the butter over medium-low heat. Whisk in the flour, then gradually pour in the half and half. Increase heat to medium; add in the garlic powder, pepper, and nutmeg. Continue to whisk until creamy. Immediately pour over the stuffed shells and sprinkle the remaining Parmesan cheese over top. Bake in a pre-heated 350 degree oven until cheese is bubbly and tops of shells begin to turn golden (about 25 minutes).

JULY 13 **GREEK SALAD**

<u>Ingredients:</u>

Salad:

1 bunch Romaine lettuce, washed, dried, & shredded

1 English cucumber, seedless, diced

1 red bell pepper, diced

1 yellow bell pepper diced

1 pint cherry tomatoes, halved

½ cup Kalamata olives, pitted

½ lb. feta cheese, diced

For the dressing:

2 cloves garlic, minced

1 tsp. dried Greek oregano

½ tsp. Dijon mustard

¼ cup lemon juice

1 tsp. sea salt

½ tsp. black pepper

½ cup extra virgin olive oil

Grilled pitas

<u>Directions:</u>

Salad:

Put the first five ingredients in a large bowl and toss. Do not include the olives and feta cheese.

Dressing:

In a small bowl, whisk together the first six ingredients for the dressing. Gradually add in the olive oil and continue to whisk until well-blended. Pour over salad, toss, then add the olives and feta. Toss lightly and set aside for about 30 minutes to allow flavors to blend. Serve at room temperature with grilled pitas.

For the grilled pitas, brush with olive oil and place on a heated outdoor or indoor grill. Once grill marks show, turn and do the same on the other side. Remove from grill, cut into quarters and serve with the salad.

JULY 14 CHILLED ZUCCHINI SOUP

Ingredients:

Olive oil

½ cup diced sweet onion

½ cup diced fennel bulb

4 garlic cloves, minced

5 cups diced zucchini

16 oz. vegetable stock

1 cup water

½ cup heavy cream

2 tsp. sea salt

1 tsp. black pepper

1 tsp. fresh lemon zest

1 tsp. freshly squeezed lemon juice

Directions:

In a large heavy Dutch oven, drizzle olive oil and swirl to cover bottom of pot. Heat the oil over medium heat. Add in the onion, fennel, and garlic and sauté until onions are translucent.

Next, add in the zucchini and sauté for about 5 minutes. Pour in the stock and water, stir, and increase the heat to high to bring mixture to a boil. Then reduce heat and let simmer for about 20 more minutes or until tender. Turn off heat and, using a handheld blender, puree until smooth. Add in the cream, salt, pepper, zest, and lemon juice and transfer to refrigerator to chill for at least 2½ to 3 hours. Serve cold.

JULY 15 TOMATO AND CHEESE PIE

Ingredients:

1-9" prepared pie crust

2¾ lbs. tomatoes (cut into ¼" slices)

2 tsp. kosher salt, divided

6 oz. Gruyere cheese, grated

½ cup grated Parmigiano-Reggiano cheese

½ cup mayonnaise

1 lg. egg, lightly beaten

2 tbs. chopped fresh chives

1 tbs. dried oregano

1 scallion, white & green parts, chopped

2 tsp. sugar

½ tsp. black pepper

1½ tbs. yellow cornmeal

Approx. 12 fresh basil leaves

Directions:

Place pie crust into a greased 9" tart pan (preferably fluted). Press crust into pan and cut off any excess along rim of pan. Refrigerate.

Place tomato slices on paper towels and sprinkle with 1 tsp. salt. Set aside for 30 minutes.

In a large bowl, combine the remaining salt and next 9 ingredients. Mix well. Remove crust from refrigerator. Sprinkle the corn meal over the crust. Spread ½ cup cheese mixture onto the crust then layer with half of the tomatoes in an overlapping pattern. Spread another ½ cup of cheese mixture then layer with tomato slices once again. Continue this process until all ingredients have been used, ending with the tomatoes on top.

Place in a preheated 375 degree oven for 30-40 minutes. Then place foil over the edges of the crust to prevent burning and bake for an additional 20 minutes or until crust is golden and tomatoes have baked. Remove from oven, place on a cooling rack for approximately 1 hour. Sprinkle with basil leaves and serve.

JULY 16 GRILLED POLYNESIAN SWORDFISH WITH PINEAPPLE MANGO SALSA

Ingredients:

Marinade:

1/3 cup low sodium soy sauce	¼ cup freshly squeezed lemon juice
¼ cup peanut oil	¼ cup minced ginger
2 tsp. lemon zest	2 tbs. Dijon mustard

Swordfish:

4-4 oz. swordfish steaks	Kosher salt

Salsa:

1 cup peeled mango, chopped small	1 jalapeno pepper, finely chopped
1 cup pineapple, sm. diced	½ cup chopped cilantro
½ cup sweet red pepper, diced	2 tbs. fresh lime juice
2 scallions, chopped	1 tbs. fresh lemon juice

Directions:

Marinade:

Whisk together all six ingredients in a bowl. Then pour half of the mixture into a casserole dish. Place swordfish steaks into casserole dish and pour the remaining marinade on top. Cover and place in refrigerator up to four hours. Pre-heat grill, brush oil onto grate, sprinkle salt on swordfish and place on hot grill. Cook for 5 minutes on each side.

Salsa:

Combine all ingredients together in a medium bowl. Stir well. Serve on the side with swordfish.

JULY 17 **SEAFOOD SALAD**

Ingredients:

½ lb. cooked crab meat

½ lb. cooked med. shrimp

½ lb. cooked lobster

1 lg. celery stalk, finely chopped

4 green onions (white & green parts), finely chopped

2 tbs. fresh dill weed, finely chopped

1½ cups mayonnaise

Pinch of kosher salt

White pepper, to taste

1 lemon cut into wedges

Parsley sprigs, for garnish

Directions:

In a large salad bowl, combine the first 9 ingredients. Mix well. Cover with plastic wrap and chill in refrigerator for 1 hour. When getting ready to serve, divide salad evenly among 4 dinner plates, garnish each with 1 lemon wedge and sprinkle parsley sprigs on each plate. May be served with bread or crackers of choice.

JULY 18 **ROASTED VEGETABLE TAPAS**

Ingredients:

6 cups of assorted sliced (½" thick) fresh vegetables:

    eggplant, zucchini, yellow squash

    red &yellow bell peppers

¼ tsp. dried thyme

¼ tsp. dried basil

Salt & pepper, to taste

cremini mushrooms & Vidalia onions

1 sm. jar Spanish olives

½ cup extra virgin olive oil

1 sm. jar Kalamata olives

¼ cup distilled vinegar

1 sm. jar artichoke hearts

½ cup freshly grated Parmesan cheese, divided

1 sm. wedge Provolone cheese

2 garlic cloves, minced

1 lg. loaf crusty Italian bread, sliced

¼ tsp. dried oregano, plus extra for sprinkling

Directions:

Slice vegetables and place in a large bowl. Whisk together the next 8 ingredients using only ¼ cup of the Parmesan cheese. Pour mixture over vegetables and toss well.

Using a slotted spoon, remove the vegetables from the bowl and place on a large baking sheet. Roast in a pre-heated 400 degree oven for about 40 minutes or until vegetables are tender and golden. (After 20 minutes, turn vegetables so they will get a golden color on each side).

Arrange like vegetables on a large serving tray or platter. Place olives in a decorative bowl and place in middle of platter. Place artichoke hearts in a small bowl as well and place in center of platter. Sprinkle vegetables with the remaining Parmesan cheese and accompany with olives, artichoke hearts, Provolone slices, and bread.

JULY 19 HUEVOS RANCHEROS SALAD

Ingredients:

1-15.5 oz. can black beans, rinsed & drained

1 tsp. salt

1½ cups diced tomatoes

8 oz. mixed salad greens

¼ cup red onion, chopped

6 corn tortillas

¾ cup extra virgin olive oil

6 lg. eggs

½ cup fresh lime juice

Black pepper

3 tbs. fresh cilantro, chopped, plus more for garnish

½ cup crumbled queso fresco

1 tsp. hot sauce

Directions:

In a medium bowl, gently stir together the first 8 ingredients. Set aside.

Evenly divide the salad greens among 6 dinner plates. Set aside.

Lightly brush olive oil on all 6 tortillas. Sprinkle with salt and toast over an open flame on each side. Cut into quarters and wrap in foil to keep warm.

Evenly divide half of the salsa on each of the plated salad greens.

Pour remaining oil into a large non-stick skillet and over medium heat gently crack eggs into pan. Season with salt and pepper and cook until whites are opaque. Transfer 1 egg onto each plate. Sprinkle with queso fresco and remaining salsa. Garnish with cilantro. Serve with warm tortillas.

JULY 20 **MARINATED VEGETABLE SALAD**

Ingredients:

2 cups broccoli florets, steamed until tender but crisp

1/3 cup olive oil

2 cups cauliflower florets, steamed until tender but crisp

1/3 cup fresh lemon juice

1 cup Italian green beans, steamed until tender but crisp

1 tsp. sea salt

1 cup cherry or grape tomatoes, halved

½ tsp. crushed red pepper

1 cup pitted oil cured olives, halved

1½ tsp. oregano

1½ cups canned garbanzo beans, drained and rinsed

¼ cup Parmesan cheese

½ cup sun-dried tomatoes, diced

Directions:

Place first 7 ingredients in a large bowl. Toss well.

Whisk together the oil, lemon juice, salt, pepper, and oregano. Pour dressing over salad and toss well. Refrigerate 2-3 hours. Before serving, sprinkle with cheese, toss well. Serve in individual serving bowls. Top with seasoned croutons, if desired.

JULY 21 **UPSIDE DOWN DINNER/WHOLE WHEAT BLUEBERRY PANCAKES**

Ingredients:

1¼ cups whole wheat flour

1 tbs. sugar

2 tsp. baking powder

½ cup fresh blueberries

1 lg. egg

Maple syrup, heated

1 cup whole milk (may need extra)

Pats of butter

Directions:

Mix together the flour and baking powder. Add in the egg, milk and sugar. Mix well. If batter seems thick, add additional milk. Stir in the blueberries. Set aside.

Pre-heat a large non-stick griddle pan. Spray with cooking oil. Pour batter in pan for each pancake. Cook until bubbly, then carefully flip and cook until golden on each side.

Serve 2 pancakes topped with 2 pats of butter and drizzled with syrup.

***NOTE: May be accompanied by fresh fruit such as strawberries, honeydew or cantaloupe.**

JULY 22 **SWISS CHARD AND HERB OMELET**

Ingredients:

2 tbs. olive oil, divided	2 tbs. dried French tarragon
1 med. red onion, thinly sliced	2 tbs. fresh parsley, chopped
2 cups Swiss chard leaves, chopped	2 tbs. chopped fresh chives
6 lg. eggs, beaten	½ cup grated Gruyere cheese
1½ tsp. garlic powder	

Directions:

Using a 10" oven-safe non-stick skillet, heat 1 tablespoon oil over medium-low heat. Add in onion and sauté until soft. Next, add in the Swiss chard and cook until tender. Generously season with pepper.

Meanwhile, in a medium bowl, whisk the eggs, then add in the garlic powder, tarragon, parsley, chives, and half the cheese. Combine well.

Add remaining oil to the skillet and turn up heat to medium. When oil is hot, add in the egg mixture and stir to combine with onion and chard. Reduce heat to low, cover, and cook until eggs are set for about 10 minutes. Then sprinkle remaining cheese on top of omelet and place skillet in a pre-heated 400 degree oven for about 5-7 minutes. Remove from oven, divide into wedges and serve with your favorite salad (fruit or vegetable) on the side along with sliced French baguette.

JULY 23 **GRILLED PIZZA BLANCA**

Ingredients:

1 prepared 1 lb. pizza dough

Small bowl olive oil

1 cup ricotta

1 lg. onion, thinly sliced

1 cup sliced cremini mushrooms

Sea salt

Black pepper

2 cups arugula

Directions:

Pre-heat grill and brush grates with olive oil. Roll out the dough and place on a pizza peel that has been dusted with corn meal. Slide dough onto grill, cover the grill, and cook for 2 minutes.

Using your peel, flip dough over, and lift dough back onto peel. Quickly brush with oil, and spread ricotta over dough. Then place onion and mushrooms over the ricotta, season with salt and pepper and place dough back onto grill for 3-4 minutes (check to make sure dough does not char). When cooked, sprinkle arugula over top, drizzle with a little more oil, slice and serve.

JULY 24 **HEIRLOOM TOMATO SALAD WITH BLEU CHEESE AND WILD RICE**

Ingredients:

2 cups steamed wild rice

¼ cup extra virgin olive oil

3 tbs. fresh lemon juice

1 tsp. sea salt

¼ tsp. crushed red pepper flakes

4 heirloom beefsteak tomatoes, cut into wedges

1 cup cherry tomatoes, halved

1 cup fresh basil

2 cups arugula

1/3 crumbled bleu cheese

Directions:

Steam the wild rice according to package directions, drain and place on a large platter. Set aside. In a small bowl, whisk together the oil, lemon juice, salt and pepper. Set aside.

In a medium bowl, toss together the tomato wedges, cherry tomatoes, basil, and arugula. Add in the oil and lemon juice dressing, mix well, then place tomato mixture over rice. Sprinkle on the crumbled cheese. Serve chilled or at room temperature.

JULY 25 MUSHROOM, SPINACH, AND CHEESE STRATA

This dish may be prepared in the morning and left to chill in refrigerator while at work and then can be baked in evening upon returning home.

Ingredients:

1 tbs. butter

1 tbs. olive oil

1½ cups onion, finely chopped

½ tsp. freshly ground black pepper, divided

8 oz. cremini mushrooms, cleaned & sliced

16 oz. fresh baby spinach, chopped small

8 cups cubed French baguette

1 cup grated Jarlsberg cheese

½ cup shredded mozzarella cheese

½ cup grated Parmigiano-Reggiano cheese

2¾ cups milk

10 lg. eggs

2 tbs. Dijon mustard

Directions:

In a large skillet, melt butter and heat oil over medium heat. Add in the onion, ¼ teaspoon black pepper, and mushrooms. Cook for 4-5 minutes, stirring constantly. Stir in the spinach and cook until wilted. Remove from heat.

Spray a medium-sized deep ceramic baking dish with spray oil and spread with 1/3 of the bread cubes on bottom. Layer with ½ of the spinach mixture and sprinkle with 1/3 of each cheese. Repeat the layering process ending with the cheeses.

Whisk together the milk, eggs, mustard, and remaining ¼ teaspoon of black pepper. Pour evenly over the bread, spinach, and cheese. Cover with plastic wrap and refrigerate for at least 8 hours. Pre-heat oven to 350 degrees. Remove strata from refrigerator and let stand at room temperature for 30 minutes. Bake on middle rack, uncovered for 45 minutes or until puffy and cooked through. Let stand for a few minutes before slicing and serving.

JULY 26 ITALIAN TUNA SALAD

Ingredients:

2-6 oz. cans of Italian tuna in olive oil, reserve the oil

1-15 oz. can of cannellini beans, drained & rinsed

1/3 cup pitted Spanish olives, chopped

4 cups baby spinach

Fresh lemon juice

Salt & pepper, to taste

1 medium red onion, diced

1 pt. cherry or grape tomatoes, halved

1 tsp. dried oregano

1½ cups Italian flavored croutons

Directions:

In a large salad bowl, add tuna but put the reserved oil from the tuna in a small bowl. Using a fork, flake the tuna. Add in the beans, olives, onions, tomatoes, and spinach. Toss well and set aside.

In the small bowl with the olive oil, add lemon juice using the following ratio: one part lemon juice to two parts oil and season with salt, pepper, and oregano. Whisk together then pour over salad and toss gently. Sprinkle croutons on top. Give one quick toss and serve immediately on individual dinner plates.

July 27 CRAB CAKES

Ingredients:

1 lb. crab meat

1 cup plain bread crumbs

3 green onions (green & white parts), finely chopped

¼ cup mayonnaise

1 egg

1 tsp. mustard

1 tsp. garlic powder

2 tsp. Old Bay Seasoning

½ tsp. baking powder

2 tsp. parsley flakes

½ cup Italian style bread crumbs

Canola oil for frying

Directions:

In a large bowl, mix all the ingredients through the parsley flakes and form into patties. Place remaining ½ cup bread crumbs on a plate or piece of wax paper and, one by one, carefully put each patty onto the breadcrumbs and pat down to coat each side. Transfer breaded crab cakes to a platter and refrigerate for about 2 hours or until firm. Heat the oil in a skillet over medium-high heat. Fry the crab cakes in the hot oil until golden brown (about 3-4 minutes) on each side.

***NOTE:** They can also be baked in a pre-heated 400 degree oven for about 8-10 minutes if you prefer not to fry.

JULY 28 **CAPRESE PANINI**

<u>Ingredients:</u>

4 ciabatta rolls, halved

Extra virgin olive oil

2 large tomatoes, sliced

8 oz. pkg. fresh mozzarella, sliced

16 basil leaves

Salt & pepper, to taste

<u>Directions:</u>

Brush the bread with olive oil on both sides. On one slice of bread, layer the tomato, mozzarella, and basil and season with salt and pepper. Do the same for all. Close with the other slice of bread and place the sandwiches two at a time into a pre-heated Panini press. Cook until golden and cheese has melted.

JULY 29 **CURRIED SHRIMP WITH SNOW PEAS**

<u>Ingredients:</u>

1½ tbs. sesame oil

1½ lbs. large shrimp, peeled & deveined

8 oz. snow peas

1 tbs. curry powder

½ tsp. garlic powder

½ tsp. salt

1-13.6 oz. lite coconut milk

2 tbs. white wine

2 tsp. lemon juice

1 tbs. cornstarch

3 scallions (green parts only), sliced

2 cups steamed rice

<u>Directions:</u>

In a large heavy skillet or wok, heat oil over medium-high heat. Add the shrimp, snow peas, curry powder, garlic powder, and salt. Stir constantly and cook until shrimp turn pink on both sides (about 5 minutes).

In a small bowl, stir together the coconut milk, wine, and lime juice into cornstarch until a smooth consistency is reached. Add to the pan with the shrimp and bring to a boil while continuing to stir. Then reduce heat and let simmer for a minute or two. Garnish with the scallions. Serve over prepared rice.

JULY 30 **AB DOUGH KHIAR/YOGHURT SALAD (PERSIAN)**

This is a very light summer yoghurt salad that will be sure to cool your palate on a warm summer evening!

Ingredients:

3-32 oz. containers of plain yoghurt	1 bunch scallions, white & ½ of
1 bunch radishes, chopped	the green parts, chopped
1 cucumber, grated, and drained	1½ cups walnuts, rough chopped
1 bunch mint, finely chopped	1½ cups white raisins
1 bunch basil, finely chopped	Flat breads, grilled

Directions:

Empty all 3 containers of yoghurt into a large bowl and stir. Add in each of the remaining ingredients through raisins, and using a large spoon, mix all ingredients together. Refrigerate for at least 2 hours. Remove from refrigerator, add a few ice cubes, stir, then serve in individual soup bowls along with grilled flat breads on the side.

JULY 31 **ROASTED RED ASIAN PEPPERS STUFFED WITH GOAT CHEESE**

Ingredients:

Roasted red peppers:

4 lg. red peppers

17 oz. goat cheese, softened at room temperature

Spray oil

Couscous:

1 cup uncooked couscous	1 tsp. olive oil
1 cup water	½ cup toasted pine nuts
¼ tsp. sea salt	8 basil leaves, julienned

Directions:

Red peppers:

Place peppers on a very hot pre-heated grill rack. As each side becomes completely charred, turn onto the other side. Once all four peppers have become blackened, let cool then removed the charred skin. Rinse under cool water, remove tops and seeds. Set on paper towels to dry.

Next, place the goat cheese in a bowl and stir with a spoon. Carefully stuff each pepper with the goat cheese and set into a medium casserole dish that has been sprayed with oil. Once all peppers have been stuffed, place casserole dish into a pre-heated 350 degree oven for 10-15 minutes to allow cheese to melt slightly. Remove from oven and serve on individual plates with couscous on the side.

Couscous:

In a medium sauce pan bring the water, salt, and oil to a boil. Add in the couscous, stir well, then immediately cover and remove from heat. Let stand for 5-6 minutes.

In the meantime, place the pine nuts into a small frying pan and toast until golden over medium heat using no oil. Be careful not to burn. Julienne the basil leaves. Remove lid from couscous, fluff with a fork and add in the pine nuts and basil. Give a quick stir and serve on the side with the stuffed peppers. May be accompanied by a small tossed salad.

AUGUST 1 **WILD RICE SALAD**

Ingredients:

2 cups wild rice, cooked according to pkg. directions

1 cup parsley, fine chopped

½ cup mint, fine chopped

½ cup tarragon, chopped

1 cup radishes, chopped

½ cup dried cranberries

½ cup dried apricots, chopped small

1 cup baby arugula

½ cup golden raisins

½ cup minced shallots

½ cup olive oil

¼ cup balsamic vinegar

¾ cup pecan halves

Directions:

Combine all ingredients from rice to shallots in a large bowl. Whisk together the oil and vinegar. Pour over salad. Top with pecans and serve.

AUGUST 2 **PANZANELLA SALAD**

Ingredients:

½ loaf Italian bread, cut into ½" cubes

Olive oil

2 small red onions, thinly sliced

½ seedless cucumber, cut into sm. cubes

1 pint grape tomatoes, sliced

½ cup pitted oil cured olives, chopped

½ cup basil leaves, julienned

1 lg. garlic clove, minced

½ cup ciliegine (1" mozzarella balls), halved

Salt & pepper

4 tbs. olive oil

1 tbs. balsamic vinegar

Directions:

Cut bread into ½" cubes and place on a baking sheet. Drizzle lightly with olive oil. Place in pre-heated 400 degree oven. Bake until golden brown on all sides. Be sure to toss so all sides will crisp evenly. Remove from oven and set aside.

In a large salad bowl, add the remaining ingredients except for the oil and vinegar. Toss well.

In a small bowl, whisk together the olive oil and vinegar. Pour over salad and toss. Finally, add the bread cubes, toss lightly and serve.

AUGUST 3 **SUMMER SEAFOOD STEW**

Ingredients:

¼ cup extra virgin olive oil

1 lg. onion, diced

4 garlic cloves, minced

1½ tbs. tomato paste

32 oz. vegetable stock

2-14 oz. cans diced tomatoes

½ cup white wine

3 bay leaves

1 cup diced carrots

1 cup fresh string beans

1 cup corn kernels

2 lbs. cod cut into 2" cubes

¼ cup chopped fresh parsley, plus extra for garnish

Kosher salt & coarse black pepper

1½ lbs. lg. raw shrimp, peeled & deveined

Pinch of sugar

1 tbs. fresh thyme   Sliced French baguette, grilled

1½ cups diced potatoes

Directions:

Heat oil in a large heavy pot over medium heat, then add in the onion and garlic. Cook until golden. Add in the tomato paste, stir, and let cook for about 1-2 minutes.

Next, add in the stock, tomatoes, wine, bay leaves, and thyme. Increase heat bringing mixture to a boil. Reduce heat back to medium; add in the potatoes, carrots, beans, and corn. Simmer for 45 minutes. Then add in the cod, parsley, salt, pepper, and sugar. Allow to simmer for 6-8 minutes. Toss in the shrimp and cook for an additional 3 minutes. Ladle into individual bowls. Garnish with parsley and serve with grilled bread slices.

AUGUST 4 **CHILLED STRAWBERRY SOUP**

Looking for something to do with your children in the late spring or summer? How about strawberry picking? What a wonderful way to spend time with the early part of a weekend and then returning home with the bounty to prepare a delicious chilled strawberry soup in the heat of the late afternoon sun! Family time is quality time and what better way to get the kids (and mom and dad, too) to leave the cell phones at home and spend quality time in a red and green strawberry patch looking for those large red berries that are ripened, sweet, and juicy.

Ingredients:

3 pints hulled strawberries, divided   1 tbs. olive oil

¼ cucumber, peeled   1 tbs. lemon juice

2 tbs. fresh mint   Salt & pepper

2 tbs. fresh dill   Thinly sliced scallions, for garnish

Directions:

In a blender, puree' 2 pints of the strawberries, the cucumber, mint, and dill. Next, add in the olive oil, lemon juice, salt and pepper, to taste. Chill for 1 hour.

Remove from refrigerator, and transfer to a large serving bowl. Chop the remaining pint of strawberries into small pieces and add them into the pureed mixture. Give a quick stir then garnish with scallions and serve in individual bowls. *****NOTE:** Ice cubes may be added.

AUGUST 5 **BAKED SPAGHETTI SQUASH WITH FONTINA**

For those of you backyard gardeners who have an abundance of squash during the summer months and don't know what to do with it, here is a recipe that will satisfy your taste buds and help you with your overflow. You may want to share your abundance along with this recipe with friends and neighbors.

Ingredients:

1 lb. spaghetti squash	1½ tsp. rubbed sage
½ cup grated Fontina cheese	½ tsp. minced garlic
3 tbs. sweet butter, softened at room temperature	1 tbs. black pepper
¼ cup Italian parsley, chopped	½ tsp. sea salt

Directions:

Pre-heat oven to 375 degrees.

Line a rimmed baking sheet with aluminum foil that has been lightly sprayed with cooking spray and set aside. Cut the squash in half lengthwise and place on baking sheet (cut sides down). Place pan in oven and cook until the squash is soft. Remove seeds and discard. Using a fork, drag fork through the flesh, separating flesh into long strands resembling spaghetti. Place in a large bowl, add in the next five ingredients and toss well. Season with pepper and salt. Give a quick toss and serve.

AUGUST 6 **SANDWICH NIGHT**

Ingredients:

8 slices whole wheat bread	1 lg. tomato, thinly sliced
1-8 oz. pkg. roasted red pepper hummus	8 thin slices of domestic Provolone cheese
1 seedless cucumber sliced with skin on	8 lettuce leaves

Directions:

Place 4 slices of bread on a clean surface. Spread hummus on each of the 4 slices. Evenly divide the cucumber slices among each of the 4 slices of bread. Do the same with the tomatoes. Next, place 2 slices of cheese on each as well as 2 lettuce leaves. Top each sandwich with the remaining 4 slices of bread. Serve with your favorite chips and pickles on the side.

AUGUST 7 GARIDES ME SALTSA/SHRIMP IN TOMATO AND FETA SAUCE (GREEK)

Ingredients:

6 tbs. olive oil

1 med. onion, finely chopped

2 cups plum tomatoes + juice, chopped

½ cup dry white wine

2 tbs. finely chopped flat leaf parsley, divided

1 tsp. dried Greek oregano

1 tsp. sea salt

1 tsp. black pepper

25-30 med. shrimp, peeled & deveined

2 oz. feta cheese, diced into cubes

Directions:

In a heavy (preferably cast iron) 10" or 12" skillet, heat oil over medium heat. Add in the onions and cook until translucent.

Next, stir in the tomatoes and their juice, wine, parsley, oregano, salt, and pepper. Increase heat to medium-high and bring mixture to a boil. The mixture should start to thicken to a puree'. Immediately add in the shrimp and cook until light pink on both sides over medium heat. Stir in the cheese. Serve immediately with crusty bread to absorb the sauce.

AUGUST 8 ROASTED VEGETABLE FRITTATA

Ingredients:

1-10 oz. container cremini mushrooms, sliced

1 red bell pepper, seeded, 1" diced

1 green bell pepper, seeded, 1" diced

1 medium yellow squash, 1" diced

1 onion, diced

2 garlic cloves, minced

1/3 cup olive oil

Sea salt, to taste

Black pepper, to taste

1 doz. lg. eggs, beaten

½ cup grated Fontina cheese

1½ tbs. olive oil

Directions:

Place the first 6 items on a sheet pan, drizzle with olive oil, and season with salt and pepper. Toss well and place in a pre-heated 400 degree oven for 15 minutes. Remove from oven, give another quick toss then return to oven for another 15 minutes.

In a large bowl, beat the eggs, add the cheese, and season with salt and pepper.

Heat 1½ tablespoons of olive oil into a 10" or 12" oven-proof non-stick skillet over medium heat. Remove roasted vegetables from oven and spoon into skillet. Pour the egg mixture into the skillet, stir quickly, and cook for about 4-5 minutes on medium-low heat. Then place in a 350 degree oven for about 15 minutes until set in the middle. Cut into wedges and serve.

AUGUST 9 **COOL WATERMELON SALAD**

Ingredients:

8 cups mixed salad greens

6 thickly sliced (2") cold seedless watermelon slices

1 lg. red onion, very thinly sliced

¾ cup salted sunflower seeds

1½ cups feta cheese

1 cup store bought Raspberry Vinaigrette

Directions:

In a large bowl, combine the first 3 ingredients. Toss well.

Place the watermelon slices on individual dinner plates. Evenly divide the mixed greens by topping each watermelon slice with a generous portion of the greens. Sprinkle with sunflower seeds and drizzle with vinaigrette.

AUGUST 10 **TOMATO AND CHEESE TART**

This is a delectable summer dish to make in July or August when tomatoes are ripe and very sweet!

Ingredients:

1 pie crust to fit into a 10" pan (preferably with a removable bottom)

3 tbs. extra-virgin olive oil

1 lg. garlic clove, minced

¾ cup grated Gruyere cheese

2 very lg. tomatoes (Big Boy or Beefsteak), sliced thin & placed on paper towels to absorb moisture

1 lb. fresh mozzarella cheese, thinly sliced

1 tsp. fresh rosemary, finely chopped

¼ cup basil leaves, julienned

<u>Directions:</u>

Pre-heat oven to 375 degrees. Lightly grease the bottom of the tart pan then place the pie crust into the pan, pressing dough into the sides of the pan. Trim the overhang but leave a little extra because crust will shrink when baking.

Whisk together the olive oil and garlic. Sprinkle gruyere cheese over the entire bottom of the crust. Starting on the outer edge and working your way to the center, begin to arrange the slices of tomatoes and mozzarella by alternating 1 tomato slice then one mozzarella slice. Drizzle with 2/3 of the garlic and oil mixture then sprinkle with the rosemary. Bake for about 40 minutes until crust has browned and cheese is bubbling. Remove from oven, sprinkle with remaining garlic and oil then top by sprinkling the basil leaves over the entire tart.

AUGUST 11 **HALIBUT AND SUMMER VEGETABLES EN PAPILLOTE**

<u>Ingredients:</u>

2 cups corn kernels	¼ cup chopped fresh dill weed, divided
2 cups halved cherry tomatoes	1 tbs. chopped fresh thyme, divided
12 oz. cut green beans	4-4 oz. pieces halibut fillets
¼ tbs. finely chopped shallots	Salt & pepper
2 tbs. olive oil	4 squares of parchment paper

<u>Directions:</u>

In a bowl, toss together the corn, tomatoes, beans, shallots, olive oil, and half of the dill weed and thyme. Season with salt and pepper.

Place the 4 sheets of parchment paper on a clean work surface. Divide the vegetable mixture into 4's and spoon into the center of each sheet. Place 1 halibut fillet on each, drizzle with olive oil and season with salt and pepper.

Bring the long ends of the parchment paper together in the center and fold several times. Twist the ends to form a tight seal and place each packet onto a baking tray. Transfer to a pre-heated 400 degree oven for 15-20 minutes. Serve immediately.

AUGUST 12 TUNA CASSEROLE WITH A "TWIST"

Ingredients:

1-16 oz. pkg. of rotelle pasta

6 tbs. butter, divided

1 lg. sweet onion, finely chopped

1-8 oz. pkg. cremini mushrooms, thinly sliced

¼ cup flour

3 cups heavy cream

1 cup low-sodium vegetable stock

2 cups shredded extra-sharp white cheddar

1/3 cup grated Parmesan cheese, divided

1 tsp. kosher salt

½ tsp. black pepper

1-12 oz. can solid white tuna, drained

2 tbs. fresh chives, finely chopped

1 tbs. fresh parsley, finely chopped

1-12 oz. pkg. frozen peas

½ cup Italian-style breadcrumbs

2 tbs. butter, melted

Fresh chives, for garnish

Directions:

Prepare rotelle pasta according to package directions to al dente; drain and set aside. Cook peas in boiling salted water until crisp, yet tender. Drain and set aside.

In a very large skillet melt 2 tablespoons butter over medium-high heat. Add in the onions and mushrooms and sauté until tender and onions are translucent, about 7 minutes. Transfer onion/mushroom mixture to a bowl. Wipe skillet clean. Melt 4 tablespoons butter in same skillet over medium heat. Whisk in the flour. Whisking constantly, gradually add in the cream and vegetable stock while bringing mixture to a boil. Reduce heat to medium-low and gradually whisk in the cheddar cheese and half of the Parmesan cheese until smooth. Season with salt and pepper.

Stir in the tuna, chives, parsley, and peas. Combine well and transfer to a buttered 9" X 13" baking dish.

In a small bowl, combine the bread crumbs, melted butter, and remaining Parmesan cheese. Sprinkle over the pasta mixture. Bake in a pre-heated 350 degree oven for about 45 minutes until bubbly. Remove from oven and let stand for 5 minutes before serving. Garnish with chives and serve hot.

AUGUST 13 **TRI-COLOR COUSCOUS WITH APRICOTS AND PINE NUTS**

Ingredients:

1/3 cup dried apricots, chopped small

¼ cup pine nuts, toasted

1 tsp. olive oil

1 lg. shallot, finely chopped

2 cups water

½ tsp. salt

2 tsp. unsalted butter

2 cups uncooked, tri-color couscous

8 basil leaves, julienned

Directions:

Chop dried apricots into small bits and set aside. Place pine nuts in a small skillet over low heat and toast until lightly golden, stirring occasionally. Do not burn. Remove from heat and set aside. Using the same small skillet, heat the olive oil over medium heat. Add in the shallot and cook until tender and lightly golden. Remove from heat.

In the meantime, in a medium saucepan, bring water, salt, and butter to a boil. Add couscous, stir quickly, then remove from heat, cover, and let stand for 5 minutes. Fluff with a fork and add in the apricots, pine nuts, and shallots. Combine using a fork. Transfer to a platter; sprinkle basil on top and serve.

AUGUST 14 **OATMEAL AND SPINACH**

Some people may think oatmeal is only a breakfast food, but they are wrong. It can be eaten for dinner, especially if you are looking for a warm, fast, and healthy meal.

Ingredients:

4 ½ cups milk

1 cup chopped baby spinach

1 tsp. salt

1½ cups rolled oats

Directions:

Bring milk to a boil in a medium sauce pan over medium-high heat. Add in the spinach and salt and let boil for 2-3 minutes. Stir in the oats, reduce heat, and let simmer for 5 minutes, or until thick. Serve hot.

AUGUST 15 **STUFFED FLOUNDER ROLL-UPS**

Ingredients:

6 oz. crab meat, drained

½ cup Italian flavored bread crumbs, divided

½ tsp. crushed red pepper flakes

3 tbs. mayonnaise

4-4 oz. flounder fillets

Cooking spray

Paprika, to taste

1 lemon, cut into 4 wedges

Directions:

In a medium bowl, combine the crab meat, ¼ cup bread crumbs, red pepper flakes, and mayonnaise. Set aside.

Spray a large baking sheet with cooking spray and set aside. Place ¼ cup bread crumbs on a piece of wax paper, set aside.

Next, lightly spray each fillet with the cooking spray and coat both sides with the bread crumbs. Evenly divide the crab mixture onto each fillet and spread over the fillets. Roll up and secure with toothpicks.

Place on baking sheet, sprinkle with paprika and bake in a pre-heated 425 degree oven for 15 minutes or until fish is no longer translucent. Squeeze fresh lemon juice over each and serve immediately. Accompany with a salad or fresh vegetable of choice.

AUGUST 16 **FALAFEL #2 (MIDDLE EASTERN)**

Ingredients:

1-15.5 oz. can of garbanzo beans, rinsed & drained

1 lg. onion, halved

2 garlic cloves

3 tbs. fresh parsley

1 tsp. coriander

1 tsp. cumin

2 tbs. flour

1 tsp. salt

1 tsp. black pepper

Canola oil for frying

Tahini, for serving

Directions:

With the exception of the oil, combine all ingredients in a food processor until a thick paste has formed. Form the mixture into patties.

Heat the oil in a non-stick skillet over medium-high heat until very hot. Fry falafel until golden brown on both sides. Serve by placing in pita bread with lettuce, tomatoes, tahini, salt, and pepper.

AUGUST 17 **MUENSTER AND APPLE OPEN-FACED SANDWICHES**

Ingredients:

1½ tbs. olive oil mayonnaise

1 tsp. Dijon mustard

4 thick slices of artisanal oatmeal whole wheat bread

8 slices Muenster cheese

1 very lg. Granny Smith apple, peeled, cored, & very thinly sliced

2 cups baby spinach, washed & drained

¼ cups chopped shallots

1 tbs. oil

1 tbs. Dijon mustard

1 tsp. champagne vinegar

½ tsp. black pepper

Directions:

Combine the first 2 ingredients together in a very small bowl. Lightly toast each of the 4 slices of bread. Spread mayonnaise/mustard on each slice of bread. Place 2 slices of Muenster cheese on each slice along with the apple slices.

Next, in a medium bowl, toss in the spinach and shallots. Mix well. In a small bowl, whisk together the last 4 ingredients. Pour over spinach mixture. Toss well then evenly divide over each sandwich.

AUGUST 18 **BEER STEAMED CLAMS**

Ingredients:

2 lbs. littleneck clams, scrubbed & rinsed

2½ tbs. olive oil

5 garlic cloves, minced

20 oz. beer

1 lemon, thinly sliced

Salt & pepper, to taste

1 tbs. fresh lemon juice

Directions:

Place clams in sink and cover with cold water. Discard any that are chipped, cracked, or opened. Scrub well. Drain water and rinse again in cold water. Refrigerate.

In a large Dutch oven, heat oil over medium heat. Add in the garlic and stir. Cook until lightly golden. Once garlic is ready, immediately add in the lemon juice, clams, and beer. Stir well. Place lemon slices over the clams, cover and let simmer for about 8-10 minutes or until clams open. Remove and discard any unopened shells. Give one more quick stir before serving. Serve hot.

***SERVING SUGGESTION:** Serve with corn on the cob, hush puppies, or fries on the side.

AUGUST 19 **TOMATO AND FRUIT SALAD**

Since tomatoes are classified as a fruit, why not combine with sweet, ripe fruits that are available in the summer and create a cool summer salad that is not only colorful but delicious enough to serve as a main course?

Ingredients:

4 cups large diced watermelon (seedless)

2 cups honeydew melon (lg. diced)

2 cups cantaloupe melon (lg. diced)

2 nectarines or peaches, cut into thin slices

2 cups cherry tomatoes, halved

½ cup mandarin oranges

8-10 basil leaves, julienned

1 cup toasted pecans

¾ cup raspberry vinaigrette

Directions:

Add first 6 ingredients to a large bowl and mix well. Cover and place in refrigerator for 1 hour to chill. At the end of the hour, remove from refrigerator, sprinkle with basil and pecans, then toss gently. Slowly drizzle the vinaigrette over the salad. Give a quick stir and serve.

AUGUST 20 **GREEK SALAD WRAPS**

Ingredients:

1 cup shredded Romaine lettuce

2 cups baby spinach

4 whole wheat tortillas, warmed

8 tbs. plain yoghurt

1 cup sliced grape tomatoes	2 tbs. olive oil
1 cup seedless cucumber, diced	2 garlic cloves, minced
1 med. onion, diced	3 tbs. lemon juice
1 cup pitted Kalamata olives, chopped	1 tsp. lemon zest
1/3 cup feta cheese, crumbled	¼ tsp. black pepper
8 sm. Pepperoncini, chopped	

Directions:

In a large bowl, combine the first 8 ingredients.

Warm the tortillas according to package directions. Then spread 2 tablespoons of yoghurt over each one.

In a small bowl, whisk together the last 5 ingredients. Pour over salad and stir well. Spread each tortilla on a plate. Top each with the salad and roll up each wrap.

AUGUST 21 GRILLED SWORDFISH WITH SUN-DRIED TOMATOES AND OLIVE TAPENADE

Ingredients:

Swordfish:

4-6 oz. swordfish steaks

Olive oil, for brushing

Salt and pepper, to taste

Tapenade:

1 cup sun-dried tomatoes, in oil (reserved)	¼ cup capers, rinsed & drained
½ cup Kalamata olives, pitted	2 tsp. reserved oil
5 garlic cloves	¼ tsp. crushed red pepper flakes
2 tbs. dried oregano	1/3 cup freshly grated Parmesan cheese
2 tbs. fresh lemon juice	Salt & pepper, to taste

Swordfish:

Pre-heat grill.

Place swordfish steaks on a platter. Brush each side with olive oil. Season with salt and pepper. Once grill is hot, place fish on grill cooking 5 minutes on each side.

Tapenade:

Place all ingredients for tapenade in a blender or food processor and puree' until a rough paste-like consistency.

When swordfish is done, spoon tapenade on each and coat evenly. Serve immediately.

AUGUST 22 **KIDNEY BEANS IN TOMATO SAUCE WITH SAFFRON ON RICE (MIDDLE EASTERN)**

Ingredients:

2 tbs. extra-virgin olive oil	1 tsp. turmeric
6 garlic cloves, minced	1/8 tsp. saffron
1-12 oz. can tomato paste	Salt, to taste
30 oz. water	2 cups uncooked Basmati rice

2-15 oz. cans dark red kidney beans, rinsed & drained

Directions:

Heat the oil in a large heavy skillet over medium heat. Add in the garlic and cook until lightly golden. Spoon in the tomato paste and spread around skillet continuously stirring for 1 minute. Add in 30 oz. water. Stir, then reduce heat to medium-low. Cover and let simmer for 20 minutes. Add in the beans, turmeric, saffron, and salt. Let simmer for 45 minutes or until sauce thickens.

In the meantime, steam rice according to package directions. Place on a large platter. Spoon beans and sauce over rice. Serve hot.

August 23 COUSCOUS WITH GREEN PEAS AND PARMESAN

Ingredients:

1½ cups frozen peas, defrosted

2 cups water

½ tsp. salt

2 tsp. extra virgin olive oil

2 cups couscous

2 tbs. fresh dill, chopped

1 tsp. fresh grated lemon zest

Black pepper, to taste

¼ cup grated Parmesan cheese

Directions:

Cook peas according to package directions. Drain and set aside.

In a medium sauce pan, over medium heat, bring the water, salt, and olive oil to a boil. Add in the couscous stirring quickly, then cover. Remove from heat and set aside for 5 minutes.

At the end of the 5 minutes, uncover the couscous, fluff with a fork and add in the peas, dill, and lemon zest. Fluff again, mixing thoroughly. Transfer to a platter, sprinkle with Parmesan and serve.

AUGUST 24 GRILLED TUNA STEAKS WITH ANCHOVIES, OLIVES, AND CAPERS TAPENADE

Ingredients:

Tuna Steaks:

4-6 oz. tuna steaks

Olive oil, for brushing

Salt & pepper, to taste

Tapenade:

5 anchovy fillets

1 cup pitted black olives, rinsed & drained

½ cup capers, rinsed & drained

1 cup fresh parsley (leaves only)

2 garlic cloves

½ cup olive oil

2 tbs. fresh lime juice

Salt & pepper, to taste

Directions:

Tuna Steaks:

Pre-heat grill.

Pat dry tuna steaks with a paper towel. Brush olive oil onto each side of fish. Sprinkle with salt and pepper. Set aside until grill is hot then place on grill for 2 minutes per side or until preferred doneness.

Tapenade:

Place all ingredients for tapenade in a blender or food processor and puree'. When fish are off the grill, spoon tapenade onto each and serve immediately.

AUGUST 25 **MOZZARELLA OMELET WITH PARSLEY AND TOMATO SAUCE**

Ingredients:

2 tbs. olive oil, divided	1 tsp. crushed red pepper flakes
8 lg. eggs	1/3 cup fresh parsley, chopped
½ cup tomato sauce	¾ cup shredded mozzarella
1 tsp. salt	4 tbs. grated Parmesan cheese

Directions:

Divide oil evenly among 2 lg. non-stick skillets. Swirl to coat. Heat over medium-low heat.

In a large bowl, whisk together the eggs through the parsley. Increase heat to medium and evenly divide one-half the eggs mixture among the two pans. Cook the egg mixture for about 1 minute or until edges begin to set. Divide cheese equally and sprinkle over half of each omelet. Then fold other half of egg mixture over the side with the cheese. Do the same for the other pan. Cook until eggs have set. Cut each omelet into halves and divide among 4 plates. Sprinkle 1 tablespoon Parmesan over each before serving.

AUGUST 26 **BEET, CHEDDAR, AND APPLE TARTS**

Ingredients:

12 puff pastry shells	2 med. beets, peeled & diced
1½ cups grated extra sharp white cheddar	1½ tbs. fresh rosemary, chopped

2 lg. Fuji apples, peeled, cored, & diced   Salt & pepper, to taste

Directions:

Pre–heat oven to 375 degrees. Place puff pastry shells on a cooking sheet lined with parchment paper. Divide half the cheese among the 12 pastry shells.

Next, divide the diced apples and beets among the pastry shells. Top each with the remaining cheese; sprinkle with rosemary and season with salt and pepper. Bake until pastry turns golden and slightly puffed, about 15-17 minutes.

AUGUST 27 SHRIMP AND COLLARDS PILAU (CAJUN)

Ingredients:

3 tbs. olive oil	2 lbs. med. raw shrimp, peeled & deveined
1 cup chopped onion	3 cups organic vegetable broth
1 cup diced celery	4 cups fresh collard greens
1 cup diced carrot	2 cups uncooked Basmati rice
2 garlic cloves, minced	Salt & crushed red pepper, to taste

Directions:

Heat the oil in a large Dutch oven over medium-high heat. Add in the onion, celery, carrot, and garlic. Stir frequently and cook for about 7 minutes or until onions are translucent. Add in the shrimp and continue to cook for 2-3 minutes or until shrimp turn pink on both sides. Stir in the broth, collards, and Basmati. Season with salt and red pepper flakes. Bring to a boil over high heat. Remove from heat and cover with an oven-proof lid.

Place Dutch oven in a pre-heated 350 degree oven and bake for about 20-25 minutes or until liquid is absorbed. Fluff with a fork and serve immediately.

AUGUST 28 PENNE WITH SWISS CHARD AND EGGPLANT

Ingredients:

2-3 tbs. olive oil	1 lb. penne pasta
1 lb. eggplant, peeled & cubed	1 cup diced mozzarella cheese
3 garlic cloves, minced	½ cup grated Fontinella cheese

2-28 oz. pkgs. cremini mushrooms, sliced

1 lb. Swiss chard, washed, drained & cut

Salt & pepper, to taste

Directions:

Heat olive oil in a large skillet over medium heat. Add in the eggplant and garlic and sauté for 3 minutes. Next, add in the mushrooms and sauté for an additional 7 minutes. Toss in the Swiss chard and cook for 2 minutes until wilted.

In the meantime, cook pasta according to package directions, to al dente. Drain. Transfer to a large bowl; add in vegetables, mozzarella, and Fontinella. Season with salt and pepper; toss while hot and serve.

AUGUST 29 **LEMON AND HERB CRUSTED BASS**

Ingredients:

4-4 oz. bass fillets

1 lemon, zested & squeezed

½ tsp. chili powder

1 tbs. fresh thyme leaves

2 tbs. chopped flat-leaf parsley

1½ tbs. olive oil

Sea salt & black pepper

Directions:

Season fish with lemon zest, chili powder, thyme, and parsley. Cover with plastic wrap and refrigerate for 15-20 minutes.

Heat a 12" non-stick skillet over medium-high heat. When pan is hot, drizzle in olive oil and heat for 1 minute. Place fish in pan, season with salt and pepper; reduce heat to medium-low and cook until no longer translucent. Place on individual plates and drizzle with lemon juice.

AUGUST 30 **GRILLED CHEESE SANDWICHES WITH SUN-DRIED TOMATOES TAPENADE**

Ingredients:

1 cup oil-packed sun-dried tomatoes & 2 tbs. oil from jar

½ cup pitted green olives stuffed with pimentos

¼ cup grated Parmigiano-Reggiano cheese

2 garlic cloves

4 onion rolls, sliced in half

Olive oil for brushing

12 slices Gruyere cheese

8 thick slices beefsteak tomatoes

Directions:

Place sun-dried tomatoes, olives, grated cheese, and garlic in a blender or food processor and process until smooth. Set aside.

On a clean work surface, line up the 4 bottom slices of the rolls. Brush with olive oil on outer side of rolls. Flip over and spread the tapenade evenly over the four slices. On each, place 3 slices of Gruyere on top of the tapenade then put 2 slices of tomatoes on top of the cheese. Top each with the 4 remaining top halves of the rolls and brush oil on the tops of each.

Heat a grill pan or large skillet over medium-high heat (a Panini press could also be used). Place sandwiches on pan and place a grill press or any other heavy object on each to flatten. Cook approximately 2 minutes on each side allowing bread to toast and cheese to melt. Cut each roll in half and serve hot.

AUGUST 31 **SPICY HOT FRUIT KABOBS**

Ingredients:

4 cups pomegranate juice	1 papaya, cut into lg. 1½" chunks
1½ tbs. cayenne pepper	1 pineapple, cut into lg. 1½ chunks
2 mangoes, lg. diced	1 pt. strawberries
2 Fuji apples, lg. diced	1 head romaine lettuce, halved

Directions:

Combine juice and pepper in a bowl. Place all fruit in the bowl and marinate for 30 minutes.

In the meantime, pre-heat in-door or out-door grill on low. When grill is warm, place fruit on skewers and grill until fruit begins to caramelize, about 20 minutes. Place fruit on beds of lettuce and serve.

SEPTEMBER 1 **SHRIMP TERIYAKI**

Ingredients:

1 lb. med. shrimp, peeled & deveined	½ cup diced red bell pepper
¾ cup Teriyaki Sauce	½ cup diced green bell pepper
3 tbs. sesame oil	½ cup baby carrots, julienned
½ cup diced yellow onion	Steamed white rice, for serving

Directions:

Place shrimp and teriyaki sauce in a glass bowl. Stir and place in refrigerator for 1 hour to marinate. After 1 hour, remove from refrigerator, drain the shrimp but reserve the teriyaki sauce.

Heat a wok or large cast iron skillet over high heat and add 1½ tablespoons of the sesame oil to the pan. Swirl the oil around to coat the sides of the pan. When the oil is hot, add the shrimp and cook each side for 1 minute, stirring constantly. Remove shrimp from pan and set aside.

Add remaining oil to pan, heat, then add the onion, peppers, and carrots. Stir constantly and cook for 4 minutes. Next, return the shrimp to the pan along with the reserved sauce and cook for an additional 5 minutes or until sauce thickens, but stir frequently.

Serve individual portions over a bed of rice.

SEPTEMBER 2 **FISH TACOS WITH CORN SALSA**

Ingredients:

1 cup corn	2 tbs. salt
½ cup diced red onion	6-4 oz. tilapia fillets
½ cup diced red bell pepper	2 tbs. salt
1 cup fresh cilantro leaves, finely chopped	2 tbs. olive oil
1 lime, zested and juiced	12 corn tortillas, warmer
2 tbs. cayenne pepper	1 cup sour cream
1 tbs. black pepper	3 tbs. chopped chives

Directions:

In a medium bowl, mix together corn, red onion, red bell pepper, and cilantro. Stir in lime juice and zest.

Pre-heat an indoor grill pan on high heat and spray with oil.

In a small bowl, combine cayenne pepper, ground black pepper, and salt. Brush each fillet with olive oil and dust with spices on all sides.

Arrange fillets on grill and cook for 4 minutes on each side. Serve each person 2 corn tortillas stuffed with a fillet, and accompany with the corn salsa, sour cream, and sprinkle with chives.

SEPTEMBER 3 **ROASTED VEGETABLES**

Ingredients:

1-35 oz. can crushed tomatoes

2 zucchini with skin, cut thick

2 yellow squash with skin, cut thick

2 sm. eggplants, diced large

2 red onions, thickly sliced

2 potatoes, diced large

1 pkg. cremini mushrooms, cleaned & halved

¼ cup olive oil

1½ tsp. sea salt

1 tsp. freshly ground black pepper

1 tbs. oregano

1 tbs. garlic powder

Directions:

In a 9" X 13" roasting pan, pour in the tomatoes and spread evenly around the pan. In a large bowl, mix all vegetables together and drizzle the olive oil on top. Sprinkle with salt, pepper, oregano, and garlic powder. Toss well. Place vegetables in the roasting pan, cover with aluminum foil, and bake in a pre-heated 400 degree oven for 40 minutes. After 40 minutes, lower oven to 375 degrees, uncover, stir the vegetables incorporating the tomatoes.

When the vegetables are tender and juicy, they are ready to serve. Serve with Italian bread that has been sliced and grilled on both sides of garlic bread.

SEPTEMBER 4 **BEET SOUP**

Ingredients:

¼ cup olive oil

1 lg. onion, chopped

4 garlic cloves, minced

1 lg. carrot diced

2 stalks celery, diced

1 lg. potato, peeled and diced

3 lg. beets, peeled & diced

1 sm. red cabbage, shredded

2 cups water

¼ cup fresh dill

Salt & pepper, to taste

6 cups water

Directions:

Heat oil in a Dutch oven over medium heat. Stir in the onion and garlic and sauté until onions are translucent. Next, add in the carrots, celery, potatoes, beets, and cabbage along with 2 cups water. Cover; increase heat to medium-high, stir, and let cook for 8-10 minutes. Uncover, add in the dill, salt, pepper, and remaining water. Bring to a boil then lower heat and simmer covered for 30 minutes. Serve warm.

SEPTEMBER 5 **LEMON SHRIMP EN PAPILLOTE**

Ingredients:

1 tbs. garlic paste	½ tsp. freshly ground black pepper
1½ tbs. olive oil	1 lb. lg. shrimp, peeled & deveined
1½ tsp. paprika	1 lemon, cut into very thin slices
1 tsp. Kosher salt	2 half sheets of parchment paper cut in half

Directions:

In a medium bowl, add in garlic paste, then whisk oil, paprika, salt, and pepper. Next add in the shrimp, and lemon slices. Toss to cover evenly. On a clean work surface, spread out the 4 sheets of parchment paper. Divide the shrimp and lemon slices evenly and place in center of each sheet. Bring the long ends of the paper together in the center and fold together several times. Then twist side ends to tightly close and seal together. Set the 4 packets on a tray and place in a pre-heated 375 degree oven for about 10-15 minutes or until shrimp are pink and no longer translucent. Serve with steamed rice.

SEPTEMBER 6 **BAKED TOMATOES AND CHEESE**

Ingredients:

4 very lg. tomatoes, seeds & pulp removed	1 tsp. black pepper
10 oz. ricotta cheese	1/3 cup Italian flavored bread crumbs
1 tbs. fresh basil, finely chopped	Olive oil for drizzling
1 tsp. sea salt	2 cups steamed rice

Directions:

Wash tomatoes; remove tops, seeds and pulp. Place on a roasting pan lined with aluminum foil. In a medium bowl, mix together the cheese, basil, salt, and pepper. Stuff each tomato with the cheese mixture. Generously sprinkle bread crumbs on top of each and lightly drizzle with olive oil. Bake in a pre-heated oven at 375 degrees for about 15- 20 minutes until bread crumbs are crispy and golden. Accompany with rice.

SEPTEMBER 7 STEAMED WILD RICE WITH TOASTED HAZELNUT BUTTER

Ingredients:

1½ cups toasted hazelnuts, coarsely chopped

2 cups steamed wild rice, prepared according to pkg. directions

2 tbs. extra virgin olive oil

1 med. onion, finely chopped

5 garlic cloves, minced

1 tsp. salt

1 tsp. black pepper

1 stick butter

½ cup fresh parsley, chopped

Directions:

Toast hazelnuts in a medium skillet over medium heat. Stir often so they won't burn. Remove from heat and place in a food processor until coarsely chopped. Set aside.

Prepare rice according to package directions. While rice is steaming, in a small skillet heat oil over medium heat, add in onion, garlic, salt, and pepper, and sauté until golden. Set aside.

In another small skillet over medium heat, cook butter, stirring until it turns golden brown. Add in the parsley and nuts; mix together well. Place steamed rice in a casserole dish. Stir in the onion/garlic mixture and toss. Pour the hazelnut butter over the rice, stir to combine, and serve immediately.

SEPTEMBER 8 TEX-MEX CORN CASSEROLE

Ingredients:

6 ears yellow sweet corn, shucked

½ cup whole milk

½ cup heavy cream

1 tsp. cayenne pepper

2 eggs, beaten

Salt & freshly ground black pepper

½ cup shredded pepper jack cheese

½ red bell pepper, seeded & diced small

½ green bell pepper, seeded & diced small

½ jalapeno pepper, seeded & diced small

Directions:

Pre-heat oven to 350 degrees. Spray a casserole dish with cooking spray.

Shuck the corn kernels and place in a bowl. Set aside.

In a bowl, whisk together the milk, cream, cayenne pepper, eggs, salt and pepper. Next, add in the corn, cheese, and peppers to the milk mixture and stir well. Pour into the casserole dish and bake for at least 30-40- minutes or until set. Serve hot with a tossed salad on the side.

SEPTEMBER 9 MIXED GREENS WITH ASIAN PEARS, APPLES, PECANS AND HERBED FETA

Ingredients:

3 tbs. extra virgin olive oil

2 bags salad greens

2 tbs. raspberry vinegar

1 lg. Asian pear, cored & sliced into wedges

2 tbs. orange juice

1 lg. Granny Smith apple, cored & sliced into wedges

1/3 cup pecans, chopped

1/3 cup dried cranberries

2 tbs. honey

10 mint leaves, julienned

Sea salt, to taste

½ cup crumbled herbed feta cheese

Freshly ground black pepper

Directions:

To prepare the dressing, in a large bowl combine the oil, vinegar, orange juice, pecans honey, salt and pepper. Mix well.

Add the greens to the dressing and toss until coated with dressing.

Divide the salad on 4 plates. Arrange pear and apple slices on each plate. Sprinkle with cranberries, mint, and feta.

SEPTEMBER 10 MUSHROOM AND PAPPARDELLE SOUP

Ingredients:

3 tbs. olive oil

1 can condensed cream of mushroom soup

1 lg. onion

1½ cups cut green beans

2 garlic cloves, minced

6 oz. pappardalle pasta

2 cups cremini mushrooms, sliced thin

½ cup freshly grated parmesan cheese

½ tsp. dried thyme

¼ cup fresh parsley, finely chopped

¼ tsp. oregano

Salt and pepper, to taste

171

2-32 oz. containers organic vegetable stock

Directions:

Heat oil in a large sauce pot over medium-high heat. Add in the onion, garlic, and mushrooms. Sauté for 5-7 minutes. Stir in the thyme and oregano. Next, add in the stock, condensed soup, and green beans. Stir and bring to a boil.

Cook pasta until al dente. Remove from heat and drain. Add the pasta to the mushroom sauce then add in the cheese, salt, and pepper. Garnish with parsley and serve.

SEPTEMBER 11 KUKU BADEMJAN/EGGPLANT OMELET (PERSIAN)

Ingredients:

2 med. eggplants, peeled, sliced round into ¼" slices

1 tsp. turmeric

Salt for sprinkling

½ tsp. garlic powder

¼ cup olive oil

2 tbs. fresh lemon juice

1 med. onion, finely grated

8 eggs, beaten

1 tsp. salt

¼ cup olive oil

½ tsp. black pepper

Directions:

Sprinkle eggplant slices lightly with salt. Heat oil in a non-stick skillet and, once oil is hot, place eggplant slices in skillet browning on both sides. Allow to cool on a plate lined with paper towels to absorb excess oil.

Once cooled, place in a bowl and mash very well. Add in the onions, seasonings, and lemon juice. Combine. Next, add in the beaten eggs. Heat oil in a 10" or 12" non-stick oven-proof skillet over medium heat. When oil is hot, add mixture to skillet, lower heat and cook on stove top for about 5 minutes. Then place in a 350 degree oven for about 8-10 minutes or until top is firm and set. Serve with warm bread and plain yoghurt on the side.

SEPTEMBER 12 LENTIL AND ONION SOUP WITH BROWN BASMATI RICE

Ingredients:

3 tbs. olive oil

1 cup Basmati brown rice

1 cup white onions, chopped

2 tbs. dried oregano

6 garlic cloves, minced

¼ cup fresh parsley, chopped

1 cup dry white wine

1 tbs. balsamic vinegar

64 oz. low sodium organic vegetable stock

Salt & freshly ground black pepper, to taste

¾ cup brown lentils, rinsed & drained

Directions:

Heat oil in a 5 quart sauce pan over medium-high heat. Add in the onions and garlic and cook together until onions are translucent. Next, add in the wine, stock, lentils, and rice. Simmer for approximately 50 minutes over medium heat. Stir in the oregano, parsley, vinegar, and season to taste.

Cover and let cook for 1 hour. If more liquid is needed, add a cup of water. Serve with hard crusty bread.

SEPTEMBER 13 **COD IN TOMATO BROTH CASSEROLE**

Ingredients:

4 tbs. extra virgin olive oil

Ground black pepper, to taste

2 med. red potatoes, unpeeled, each sliced into 4 slices

1 lb. cod fillets, cut into 2" chunks

2 yellow onions, each sliced into 4 round slices

1 cup fresh Italian parsley, chopped

4 celery stalks, thinly sliced

1 tsp. dried oregano

8 Roma tomatoes, sliced in half

½ cup chopped fresh cilantro

Sea salt, to taste

1 cup dry white wine

Directions:

Pre-heat oven to 400 degrees. Drizzle 1 tablespoon olive oil along the bottom of 4 individual deep casserole dishes. Equally divide and layer the potato slices, onion slices, celery and tomato slices on top of the olive oil in each of the casseroles. Season with salt and pepper and bake for 5 minutes in the oven.

Next, arrange the cod chunks on top of the vegetables and sprinkle the herbs over the fish. Pour ¼ cup wine in each casserole. If more liquid is needed, use vegetable stock to barely cover. Cover each dish with aluminum foil and bake for an additional 15-20 minutes or until vegetables are tender. Remove foil and bake for another 5 minutes or so until fish browns to a light golden color. Serve hot.

SEPTEMBER 14 BOILED RICOTTA AND SPINACH BALLS

Ingredients:

1 cup ricotta cheese

1 cup freshly grated Pecorino-Romano cheese

1 cup chopped spinach

1 tbs. dried parsley

2 garlic cloves, minced

Salt and pepper, to taste

4 eggs

2 cups Italian-style bread crumbs

5 qts. boiling water

4 tbs. butter

Directions:

In a large bowl, combine the first 8 ingredients. Form into balls and carefully slide each ball into a pot filled with salted boiling water. Cook for about 5 minutes, or until ricotta balls begin to float to the top.

Serve in bowls with some of the boiling water. Add 1 tablespoon butter to each individual bowl. Serve hot.

SEPTEMBER 15 BROCCOLI SOUP

Ingredients:

1½ cups broccoli, cut small

2 celery stalk, chopped

1 onion, chopped

1 cup unsalted vegetable broth

2 cups milk

2 tbs. cornstarch

¼ tsp. thyme

1 oz. shredded Swiss cheese

Directions:

In a large sauce pan or Dutch oven, cook broccoli, celery, onion and broth over medium-high heat. Bring to a boil, then cover and let simmer on medium heat for about 8 minutes or until vegetables are fork tender. In the meantime, using a 2 qt. sauce pan, combine the milk, cornstarch, and thyme and stir constantly until mixture thickens. Remove from heat, add in the cheese and stir until melted. Add cheese mixture to vegetable mixture and stir until soup has thickened. Serve hot.

SEPTEMBER 16 EGG FRIED RICE

Ingredients:

2 ½ cups water

½ tsp. salt

2 tbs. low sodium soy sauce

2 cups rice

2 tsp. sesame oil

1 sm. onion, finely chopped

1 cup petite frozen peas, thawed

1 egg, lightly beaten

Freshly ground black pepper, to taste

2 tbs. green onions, cut on a diagonal

Directions:

In a medium sauce pan over medium-high heat, bring water, salt, and soy sauce to a boil. Add rice and stir. Remove from heat, cover and set aside for 5-7 minutes.

Heat oil in a wok or heavy frying pan over medium-high heat. Sauté onions and peas for about 3 minutes, stirring constantly. Pour in the egg, cook for 2 minutes, scrambling the egg while cooking.

Stir in the rice, toss well and sprinkle with pepper and green onions. Serve immediately.

SEPTEMBER 17 CHANNA MASALA (INDIAN)

Ingredients:

2 tbs. coconut oil

1 lg. onion, chopped

3 garlic cloves, minced

1 tbs. fresh ginger, finely chopped

1 jalapeno pepper, seeded and chopped

3 tbs. tomato paste

1 tbs. coriander

1 tsp. cumin

½ tsp. cayenne pepper

1 tsp. turmeric

1-15 oz. can diced tomatoes

2-15 oz. cans chick peas, drained and rinsed

1 tsp. garam masala

Directions:

Heat the oil in a heavy skillet over medium-high heat. Add in the onions and garlic and lower heat to medium-low. Cook until onions have caramelized. Next, add in the ginger and jalapeno. Cook for 2-3 minutes. Add in the tomato paste, stir, and allow to cook for 4-5 minutes until paste begins to turn a deep reddish brown.

Next, add in the coriander, cumin, cayenne, and turmeric. Stir well to blend all ingredients. Then add in the tomatoes, chickpeas (garbanzo beans) and garam masala. Cook for about 5-7 minutes.

Serve with basmati rice and warm naan (flat bread).

SEPTEMBER 18 **MUSHROOM LASAGNA**

Ingredients:

1 cup boiling water

1 oz. dried porcini mushrooms

1 tbs. butter

3 tbs. olive oil, divided

1¼ cups chopped shallots

1-8 oz. pkg. cremini mushrooms, cleaned & thinly sliced

4 oz. shitake mushrooms, cleaned & thinly sliced

1 tsp. salt, divided

½ tsp. ground pepper, divided

1½ tbs. chopped fresh thyme

1 tsp. chopped fresh rosemary

6 garlic cloves, minced & divided

½ cup dry white wine

4 oz. mascarpone

2 tbs. chopped fresh chives, divided

3 cups light cream

¼ cup flour

Cooking spray

9 lasagna noodles, cooked al dente

¾ cup grated Parmigiano-Reggiano

Directions:

In a small pot over medium-high heat, bring 1 cup water to a boil. Add in the porcini, cover, and remove from heat. Let stand for 30 minutes. Then strain mixture over a bowl, reserving the liquid and porcini.

Next, in a large skillet, over medium-high heat, melt butter and add in 2 tbs. oil to pan. Add in the shallots and sauté for 2-3 minutes. Add in the cremini and shitake mushrooms, ½ teaspoon salt, and ¼ teaspoon pepper. Sauté until mushrooms are tender. Add in the thyme, rosemary, half of the minced garlic and sauté for 2 additional minutes. Stir in the wine and bring mixture to a boil. Cook until most of the liquid evaporates. Remove from heat, stir in the mascarpone cheese and 1 tablespoon of the chives. Add in the porcinis and stir.

Over medium-high heat, add 1 tablespoon oil to a saucepan, then add in the rest of the garlic and sauté until lightly golden. Next, add in the reserved porcini liquid, 2¾ cups light cream, remaining salt and pepper. Bring to a boil

In a small bowl, whisk the remaining ¼ cup cream and flour together. Add the flour mixture to the cream mixture, and whisk together until slightly thickened.

Spoon ½ cup sauce into a 7" X 11" glass baking dish that has been coated with cooking spray and place 3 lasagna noodles in dish. Next, layer with mushroom mixture, sauce, and cheese. Continue this process ending with remaining sauce and cheese. Bake in a pre-heated 350 degree oven for 45 minutes. Top with remaining chives and serve hot.

SEPTEMBER 19 **SHRIMP FETTUCCINE**

Ingredients:

1½ cups heavy cream	Freshly ground black pepper
½ cup white wine	1 lb. raw shrimp, peeled & deveined
5 garlic cloves, finely chopped	2 tbs. finely chopped fresh parsley

Directions:

In a large skillet over medium-high heat combine cream, wine, garlic and black pepper. Reduce heat to medium-low and let simmer 7-10 minutes. In the meantime, prepare the fettuccine according to package directions until al dente.

At the end of 10 minutes, add the shrimp to the sauce and cook for 3-5 minutes until pink and opaque.

Drain pasta. Transfer to a large platter and add sauce. Thoroughly toss together so that the sauce and pasta are completely incorporated. Add parsley and give one more quick toss. Serve immediately.

SEPTEMBER 20 **PECAN AND DILL CRUSTED SALMON**

Ingredients:

1½ cups pecan halves	1-3½ lb. boneless, skinless salmon (wild caught)
6 tbs. butter, softened at room temperature	1¼ tsp. kosher salt
2 lg. garlic cloves	½ tsp. freshly ground black pepper
1 tbs. dried dill weed	Parchment paper, half sheet

Directions:

Using a food processor, pulse together the first 4 ingredients until the mixture resembles coarse crumbs.

Pat dry the salmon and sprinkle with salt and pepper. Place salmon on a baking sheet lined with parchment paper and spread the pecan mixture over the salmon. Bake in a pre-heated 400 degree oven for approximately 20 minutes or until salmon flakes with a fork.

SEPTEMBER 21 **EGGPLANT PIZZAS**

Ingredients:

2 lg. eggplants, cut lengthwise in ½" thick slices	½ tsp. sugar
Salt	1 tsp. salt
¼ cup extra virgin olive oil	½ tsp. black pepper
1 med. onion, diced	½ cup grated Parmigiano-Reggiano, grated
4 med. garlic cloves, minced	2 cups grated mozzarella
1-35 oz. can crushed tomatoes	1-10 oz. pkg. cremini mushrooms, sliced
6-8 fresh basil leaves, julienned	1 lg. green bell pepper, diced
1 tbs. dried oregano	½ cup chopped onion

Directions:

Slice eggplants, sprinkle with salt and place on a baking sheet that has been sprayed with non-stick spray oil. Bake for about 15-20 minutes in a pre-heated 375 degree oven until soft, but still firm. Set aside.

In the meantime, heat oil in a medium-sized pan over medium heat. Add onion and garlic and sauté until golden. Add in the tomatoes, basil, oregano, sugar, salt, pepper and ¼ cup grated cheese. Stir, cover, and let simmer for 30 minutes.

When sauce is done, evenly spread tomato sauce over the eggplant. Sprinkle each slice with mozzarella, grated cheese, and top with mushrooms, green pepper, and onion. Return tray to oven for an additional 8-10 minutes or until cheese has melted. Serve hot.

SEPTEMBER 22 JAMBALAYA (CREOLE)

Ingredients:

2 tbs. canola oil

1 lg. onion, diced

1 cup celery, diced

1 lg. green bell pepper, diced

4 garlic cloves, minced

2 bay leaves

1½ tsp. Creole seasoning

1 tsp. dried oregano

1 tsp. dried thyme

1-28 oz. can diced tomatoes

1 cup organic vegetable stock

1 cup uncooked long-grained rice

2 lbs. med. raw shrimp, peeled & deveined

1 tbs. dried parsley

Directions:

Heat oil in a large Dutch oven over medium heat. Add in the onion and next 7 ingredients. Sauté for 5-7 minutes until vegetables are tender. Stir in the tomatoes, stock, and rice; bring to a boil over medium-high heat. Then, lower heat, simmer and cover until rice is tender, stirring occasionally. Stir in the shrimp and parsley and cook for an additional 5 minutes until shrimp has turned pink on both sides.

Serve over rice.

SEPTEMBER 23 KHORESH-E KADU/ZUCCHINI STEW (PERSIAN)

Ingredients:

8 med. zucchini, peeled, sliced round ½" thick

3-4 tbs. olive oil

1 lg. onion, sliced thin

1-16 oz. can whole peeled tomatoes, reserve juice

1 tsp. salt

½ tsp. black pepper

1 tsp. turmeric

1 tbs. dill weed

2 cups steamed white rice

Directions:

Heat oil in a medium skillet over medium heat. Brown zucchini slices well on both sides. Transfer to a medium-sized sauce pan. Next, add onions to skillet and sauté until golden and translucent. Add more oil, if necessary. Transfer to pot with zucchini.

Cut tomatoes in half and arrange cut side down over zucchini and onions. In a medium bowl, combine juice from tomato can, salt, pepper, and turmeric. Pour over zucchini mixture and sprinkle dill weed on top. Cover and let simmer on low-medium for 45 minutes. Serve over rice.

SEPTEMBER 24 **SWEET AND SPICY INDIAN SEAFOOD STEW**

Ingredients:

1 tbs. canola oil

1 lg. onion, chopped

1 lg. green bell pepper, chopped

½ tsp. granulated garlic

1 tbs. curry powder

¼ tsp. crushed red pepper flakes

1-14 oz. can diced tomatoes, undrained

14 oz. seafood stock

1 Granny Smith apple, cored & diced

½ cup golden raisins

1 lb. lg. raw shrimp, peeled & deveined

1 lb. scallops

2 cups cooked brown Basmati rice

Toasted sliced almonds, for garnish

Directions:

In a medium sauce pan, heat oil over medium-high heat. Add in the onion, pepper, garlic, curry powder, and red pepper flakes. Cook and stir for 3-4 minutes. Add in the tomatoes and stock. Stir. Bring to a boil. Reduce heat to low and let simmer for 5 minutes. Add in the apple, raisins, shrimp, and scallops. Stir well. Simmer for 7 minutes.

Ladle into individual bowls. Top each bowl with 1/3 cup rice and garnish with almonds. Serve warm naan, cut into wedges.

SEPTEMBER 25 **WILD RICE WITH ROASTED BUTTERNUT SQUASH**

Ingredients:

1 cup uncooked wild rice

2 lbs. pre-cut butternut squash

¼ tsp. kosher salt

¼ tsp. ground cinnamon

1/8 tsp. ground nutmeg

3 tbs. balsamic vinegar

2 tbs. honey

1/8 tsp. crushed red pepper flakes

1 shallot, minced

2 cups radicchio, chopped

1/8 tsp. ground black pepper

6 tbs. olive oil, divided

¼ cup roasted, unsalted, slivered almonds

1 cup fresh parsley, chopped

3 oz. crumbled Feta cheese

Directions:

Prepare rice according to package directions. Drain and set aside.

Pre-heat oven to 375 degrees. On a large baking sheet, combine the squash, salt, cinnamon, nutmeg, and black pepper. Drizzle on 2 tablespoons of oil. Stir well. Bake until tender (about 40 minutes).

Stir together the almonds, vinegar, honey, red pepper, and shallots in a small bowl. Add in the remaining olive oil and add in the salt. Stir well. In a large bowl, combine the radicchio and parsley. Pour almond mixture on top and toss well to combine. Place rice on a large serving platter. Top with the squash, and salad mixture. Sprinkle with Feta cheese and serve.

SEPTEMBER 26 EGGPLANT, MUSHROOM, AND RICE CASSEROLE

Ingredients:

¼ cup olive oil

1 cup chopped onion

5 garlic cloves, minced

2 cups eggplant, peeled & diced

2 cups cremini mushrooms, sliced

2 tbs. fresh basil, chopped

1-14.5 oz. jar sun-dried tomatoes

8 oz. tomato sauce

4 cups no-sodium vegetable stock

2 cups Basmati rice, par-boiled

1½ tsp. sea salt

1 tsp. freshly ground black pepper

½ cup grated Parmesan cheese plus

additional for sprinkling

Directions:

Heat the oil in a large heavy skillet over medium-high heat. Add in the onion, garlic, eggplant, and mushrooms. Cook until eggplant and mushrooms are soft. Stir in the basil, tomatoes, sauce, stock, and rice. Bring to a boil. Season with salt and pepper, add cheese, and stir well. Remove from heat and transfer to a 9" X 13" baking dish. Cover with aluminum foil and bake in a pre-heated 350 degree oven for 1 hour. Remove foil and generously sprinkle with additional cheese. Bake uncovered for an additional 7-10 minutes until top becomes crispy.

SEPTEMBER 27 **GREEK LENTIL SOUP**

Ingredients:

4 tbs. olive oil	1 tbs. rosemary
5 garlic cloves minced	15 oz. can diced tomatoes
1 lg. onion, chopped	3 cups dried lentils
2 celery stalks, diced	12 cups water
2 lg. carrots, peeled & diced	Salt & pepper, to taste

Directions:

Heat oil in a large pot over medium-high heat. Add in the garlic and onion and sauté until onion is translucent and garlic is golden. Next, add in the celery, carrots, and rosemary. Reduce heat to medium, stir, and cover for 20 minutes. Add in the tomatoes and lentils; simmer for 10 minutes. Add in water, salt, and pepper and let simmer for 1 hour until lentils are tender. Serve hot. Accompany with feta cheese that has been drizzled with olive oil and sprinkled with Greek oregano, Greek olives, and pita bread or an olive focaccia. *****NOTE:** Lemon juice may also be served for those who like to add it to their soup.

SEPTEMBER 28 **MUSHROOM OMELET**

Ingredients:

1 tbs. olive oil + 2 tbs. unsalted butter	12 eggs
1½ cups mushrooms, cleaned & sliced	½ cup heavy cream
½ cup shallots, diced	½ cup grated Parmesan cheese

Directions:

Heat the oil and butter in a 10" non-stick oven-proof skillet. Add mushrooms and shallots and sauté until mushrooms are tender and shallots translucent. In the meantime, whisk together the eggs, cream, and cheese. When mushrooms and shallots are cooked, pour egg mixture into skillet with mushrooms, mix together, and cook on medium-low for about 5 minutes. Then, place in a pre-heated oven for 6-8 minutes or until eggs have set on top. Cut into wedges and serve.

SEPTEMBER 29 **POTATO AND EGG HEROES/SUBS/HOAGIES**

Ingredients:

¼ cup olive oil

4 lg. russet potatoes, peeled & cut into thick wedges

1 lg. onion, sliced

½ tsp. salt

1 tsp. black pepper

1 tsp. garlic powder

5 lg. eggs beaten

4 Italian long sandwich rolls

¼ cup fresh Italian parsley, chopped

Directions:

In a large heavy skillet, heat oil over medium heat. Add in the potato wedges, onion slices, salt, pepper, and garlic powder. Fry the potatoes until lightly browned on all sides, stirring frequently but gently so as not to mash the potatoes. When the potatoes are browned and fork tender, beat the eggs, add parsley, salt, and pepper and evenly pour the eggs over the potatoes. Lower heat and stir frequently. In the meantime, cut rolls lengthwise. When eggs are firm and not runny, spoon generous portions into the Italian sandwich rolls. Serve warm.

SEPTEMBER 30 **CREAM OF MUSHROOM AND BARLEY SOUP**

Ingredients:

3 tbs. butter

1 med. onion, diced small

1-10 oz. pkg. cremini mushrooms, sliced thin

½ tsp. garlic powder

48 oz. mushroom stock

½ cup pearl barley

1/3 cup dry sherry

1 tsp. salt

1 tsp. black pepper

1½ cups heavy cream

Directions:

In a large sauce pan or Dutch oven, melt butter over medium heat and stir in onions and mushrooms. Cover and sauté over medium-low heat, stirring occasionally (approximately 6-8 minutes). Remove cover, sprinkle in garlic powder and add in the mushroom stock, barley, sherry salt, and pepper. Stir well. Cover and bring to a boil over medium-high heat, then reduce heat to medium-low and let simmer for about 40 minutes, or until barley has softened. Add cream, stir, and let simmer on low for 10 more minutes, uncovered.

OCTOBER 1 **PUMPKIN LASAGNA**

Ingredients:

3 tbs. extra virgin olive oil	2 med. yellow squash, peeled, cut into ¼" rounds
1 lg. onion, thinly sliced	2 med. zucchini, peeled, cut into ¼" rounds
3 garlic cloves, minced	1 lb. lasagna, cooked to al dente
1-28 oz. can pumpkin puree	1 lb. ricotta cheese
1½ cups heavy cream	¼ cup chopped fresh parsley
1 tsp. grated nutmeg	1 tbs. rubbed sage
Salt and pepper, to taste	2 cups grated Fontina cheese

1 cup grated Parmigiano-Reggiano, divided

Directions:

Heat 2 tablespoons oil in a medium saucepan over medium-high heat. Add in the onion and garlic and cook until onions are translucent and garlic is lightly golden. Add in the pumpkin and stir. Allow to cook for 2 minutes. Next, add in the cream, nutmeg, salt, pepper, and Parmigiano-Reggiano cheese. Stir, lower heat, and let simmer for 20-25 minutes.

In the meantime, drizzle ½ tablespoon oil onto a baking sheet and place squash and zucchini on sheet in a single layer. Drizzle with remaining oil, season with salt and pepper and place in a pre-heated 425 degree oven until fork tender and golden for about 20 minutes.

Prepare the pasta as directed.

In a bowl, combine the ricotta, parsley, and sage. Set aside.

Using a deep lasagna pan or roasting pan, spread about ½ cup of sauce onto the bottom of the pan and arrange 1 layer of pasta on top. Ladle sauce over noodles then layer with vegetable mixture and, next, the ricotta mixture. Sprinkle with the Fontina cheese and Parmigiano-Reggiano cheese. Continue with layering process 3 more times in this order. On top layer, only add sauce, Fontina cheese, and Parmigiano-Reggiano cheese.

Bake in a pre-heated 375 degree oven for 45 minutes until sauce is bubbling and pasta starts to crisp. Remove from oven. Let rest for 15 minutes; sprinkle with parsley and serve.

OCTOBER 2 STUFFED EGGPLANT

Ingredients:

8 sm. eggplants	2 tbs. lemon juice
1½ cups cooked rice	1 tbs. dried oregano
3 tbs. olive oil, plus extra for drizzling	1 tsp. dried mint
1 lg. onion, finely chopped	1 tsp. dried parsley
2 garlic cloves, minced	Salt and pepper
2 tbs. tomato paste	1-12 oz. can diced tomatoes

Directions

Cut off tops of eggplants; scoop out center with a melon baller, season inside of eggplant with salt. Set aside.

Cook rice as directed on package. Set aside.

In a skillet, heat olive oil over medium heat, add onion and garlic. Sauté until onion is translucent. Add in tomato paste and lemon juice. Stir well. Next, add in the rice, oregano, mint, parsley, salt, and pepper. Combine well.

Using a small spoon, stuff eggplants with the rice mixture. Place stuffed eggplants in a 9" X 13" roasting pan. Pour the can of tomatoes over the eggplants. Cover with aluminum foil and bake in a pre-heated 375 degree oven for 30 minutes. Remove foil from pan and continue to bake until eggplants are fork tender.

OCTOBER 3 SPICY HOT TEX-MEX RICE AND BEANS

Ingredients:

1-15 oz. can black-eyed peas, drained & rinsed	2 cups steamed Basmati rice
1-15 oz. can black beans, drained & rinsed	1¼ cups grape tomatoes, halved
1-15 oz. can dark red kidney beans, drained	6 oz. shredded pepper jack cheese
1 roasted red bell pepper, finely chopped	1 cup fresh cilantro, washed & drained
1 oz. can corn	1/3 cup thinly sliced scallions
Spicy hot vinaigrette (recipe below)	Sliced jalapeno peppers

Directions:

Add the first 5 ingredients into a medium-sized sauce pan and ¼ cup of the vinaigrette. Stir together over medium heat. Once heated, turn off heat but allow to sit for 30 minutes to allow flavors to blend.

Once the rice has been cooked, add the tomatoes to the rice.

Get 4 individual dinner plates and on each one spoon a serving of rice and tomato mixture, a serving of the bean/corn mixture, a serving of the cheese, then garnish with cilantro, scallions, and jalapeno peppers. Drizzle with additional vinaigrette over entire plate. May be served with corn bread or tortilla chips.

Spicy Hot Vinaigrette:

Ingredients:

½ cup olive oil	1 tsp. chili powder
¼ cup fresh lime juice	½ tsp. ground cumin
2 tbs. fresh cilantro leaves, chopped	Kosher salt
2 lg. garlic cloves, minced	Black pepper
1 tbs. hot sauce	¼ tsp, crushed red pepper

Directions:

Whisk all of the above ingredients together in a medium bowl. Allow to marinate for at least 45 minutes at room temperature.

OCTOBER 4 **ITALIAN SWISS CHARD SOUP**

Ingredients:

3 tbs. olive oil, divided	1½ tsp. dried oregano
1 lg. onion	64 oz. low sodium vegetable stock
1 lg. carrot, diced	1 cup orzo
3 garlic cloves, minced	1-15.5 oz. can cannellini beans, drained & rinsed
10 oz. cremini mushrooms, cleaned	½ lb. Swiss chard, chopped
1 tsp. ground black pepper	½ cup grated Parmigiano-Reggiano cheese

Directions:

Heat 1½ tablespoons olive oil in a large sauce pot over medium heat. Add in the onion, carrot, and garlic. Sauté until onions are translucent. Remove and set aside in a bowl.

Add remaining oil to sauce pot, heat, and toss in mushrooms, black pepper, and oregano. Cook until tender.

Next, add in the stock and sautéed vegetables, increase heat to high, and bring to a boil. Stir in the orzo and cook until pasta is done. Reduce heat to medium; add in the beans, and Swiss chard. Cover and cook for an additional 5 minutes. Ladle into individual serving bowls and top with the grated cheese.

***NOTE:** May add seasoned croutons, if desired.

OCTOBER 5 **STIR-FRY WITH SPICY PEANUT SAUCE (ORIENTAL)**

Ingredients:

1 tbs. sesame oil	½ cup baby carrots sticks
4 garlic cloves, minced	½ cup dry sherry
¾ cup sliced scallions (white part)	1 tbs. soy sauce
¼ cup sliced scallions (green part)	2 tbs. creamy peanut butter
1 tbs. grated fresh ginger	2 tbs. rice wine vinegar
1 cup chopped broccoli florets	2 tsp. crushed red pepper
1 cup fresh snow peas	2 cups steamed rice

Directions:

Heat oil in a wok or large heavy skillet over medium-high heat. Add garlic, scallions, and ginger. Cook for 30 seconds, stirring continuously. Toss in the broccoli, snow peas, and carrots. Cook for 2 minutes, while stirring, until vegetables are tender but crisp.

Whisk together the sherry and soy sauce and add to vegetables. Next, stir in the peanut butter, vinegar, and pepper flakes. Garnish with green scallions and serve over steamed rice.

OCTOBER 6 **PORTOBELLO "STEAKS" WITH CAULIFLOWER PUREE'**

Ingredients:

6 cups chopped cauliflower

Black pepper

2½ cups water

4 lg. Portobello mushrooms (caps only), cleaned

1½ cups half & half

Olive oil for brushing

4 tbs. melted butter

Thyme leaves for garnish

Sea Salt

Directions:

Combine cauliflower and water in a sauce pan over medium-high heat and bring to a boil. Cook until very tender. Drain and transfer cauliflower to a blender; puree' until smooth. Add in 1 cup of the half and half. Return puree' to sauce pan over low heat. Pour in the melted butter. Season with salt and pepper. (If more liquid is needed, add in the remaining half and half.) Keep warm on stove.

Generously brush both sides of mushroom caps with olive oil. Season with salt and pepper. Place on a pre-heated indoor or outdoor grill and grill each side until tender and grill marks appear.

Divide the cauliflower puree' among 4 plates. Top each with a mushroom cap; garnish with thyme and serve.

OCTOBER 7 **SALMON AND SQUASH EN PAPILLOTE**

Ingredients:

1 lemon, zested + 2 tbs. fresh juice

2 tbs. olive oil, plus extra

1 med. yellow squash, cut lengthwise into ½" slices

1 tsp. kosher salt

1 med. zucchini, cut lengthwise into ½"slices

½ tsp. coarse ground black pepper

½ cup thinly sliced green onions

4 pieces parchment paper

1 tbs. chopped fresh dill

4-4 oz. pieces salmon

Directions:

In a medium bowl, combine the first 8 ingredients.

Place parchment squares on a clean work surface. Divide the zucchini mixture evenly and place in center of each sheet. Top each with a salmon filet, drizzle with olive oil, and season with salt and pepper.

Bring the long ends of the parchment sheets together and fold several times at the top. Then twist the ends to completely close. Place packets on a baking sheet and bake in a pre-heated 375 degree oven for 15-20 minutes. Serve immediately.

OCTOBER 8 **PEPPER AND EGG HEROES**

Ingredients:

¼ cup olive oil

1½ tsp. garlic powder

8 lg. bell peppers (any color), sliced lengthwise

6 lg. eggs, beaten

Salt and pepper, to taste

6 Italian sandwich rolls, sliced lengthwise

Directions:

Over medium heat, heat oil in a large skillet. Add the peppers to the pan and sprinkle with salt, pepper, and garlic powder. Cover the skillet; reduce heat to low-medium and sauté peppers for about 6-8 minutes. Remove cover, stir peppers and continue to cook uncovered until peppers are soft and tender.

Next, beat the eggs, season with salt and pepper, and slowly pour the eggs evenly over the peppers. Stir. Once the eggs have firmed and are not runny, remove from heat and spoon generous portions into the Italian sandwich rolls.

OCTOBER 9 **EASY NO-COOK DINNER NIGHT**

Grocery List:

1 French baguette or Italian loaf, heated and sliced

Black pepper

8 oz. imported Italian Provolone cheese

7 oz. jar oil cured olives

8 oz. Asiago cheese

7 oz. jar pepperoncini

8 oz. Fontinella cheese

2 apples, cored & cut into 8" wedges

8 oz. fresh Mozzarella ball in water

4 Campari tomatoes, sliced

Olive oil, for drizzling

1 lb. seedless grapes, rinsed

1 sm. pkg. dried figs

Red wine of choice (optional)

Directions:

Arrange the various cheeses on a large platter. Place the tomatoes slices onto a smaller platter, drizzle with olive oil, and season with salt and pepper.

Spoon olives and pepperoncini into 2 separate small bowls and arrange on platter with cheese. Place fruit on a serving plate and Voila! Dinner is ready.

***NOTE:** You may also like to include mixed nuts along with this meal.

OCTOBER 10 **PASTA E'PESILLI/PASTA AND PEAS**

Ingredients:

¼ cup extra virgin olive oil

1 med. onion, chopped

4 med. garlic cloves, finely chopped

35 oz. can crushed tomatoes

16 oz. water

6-8 fresh basil leaves, julienned

1 tbs. dried oregano

½ tsp. sugar

1 pkg. frozen peas

1 tsp. salt

¼ tsp. crushed red pepper

¾ cup grated Parmigiano-Reggiano, divided

1 lb. ditalini pasta, cooked to al dente

Directions:

In a medium sauce pan, heat olive oil over medium heat then add onions and garlic. Sauté until golden. Add the crushed tomatoes and the remaining ingredients through the red pepper flakes but only ¼ cup of the cheese. Stir; cover with lid, and simmer for 1 hour.

When sauce is almost done, cook pasta according to package directions to al dente. Do not overcook! Drain and pour pasta into a large bowl. Add in all of the sauce and mix well. Sprinkle with the reserved ½ cup of cheese and serve into individual bowls.

OCTOBER 11 **QUINOA WITH PEAS AND GREEN ONIONS**

Ingredients:

1 cup uncooked quinoa

2 cups cold water

1 cup frozen peas

2 tbs. olive oil

2 tbs. fresh lemon juice

2 tsp. Dijon mustard

¼ tsp. salt

1/8 tsp. black pepper

2 green onions, white & green parts, sliced thin

1 cup fresh dill weed, finely chopped

Directions:

Rinse quinoa; drain. Place in pot with cold water and bring to a boil over high heat. Then reduce heat to medium-low and let simmer. Place lid on pot but do not completely close. Simmer until water is completely absorbed and quinoa is plump. Remove from heat and let sit covered for 5 minutes. Then remove lid, fluff with a fork and set aside.

Boil peas until tender; drain and set aside.

In a small bowl, whisk together the oil, lemon juice, mustard, salt and pepper.

In a large bowl, combine the quinoa, peas, green onions, and dill. Pour the dressing over the quinoa mixture and serve warm or cold.

OCTOBER 12 **LEMON TILAPIA PICATA**

Ingredients:

4-6 oz. tilapia fillets

½ tsp. kosher salt

¼ tsp. black pepper

1/3 cup flour

2 tbs. butter

1/3 cup sauvignon blanc

½ cup no sodium vegetable stock

1/3 cup freshly squeezed lemon juice

2 tbs. capers, rinsed & drained

¼ cup flat leaf parsley, chopped

Directions:

Pat dry the tilapia. Sprinkle each side with salt and pepper. Place flour on a sheet of wax paper. Dredge fish in flour on both sides.

Heat butter in a large non-stick skillet over medium-high heat. Place the fish in the pan and fry until crispy on both sides. When cooked, transfer to a large platter lined with paper towels.

Add wine to skillet and over medium-high heat, bring to a boil. Cook until almost evaporated. Pour in the stock and bring to a boil. Stir in the lemon juice and capers. Transfer fish to a large serving platter. Pour juice and capers over the fish. Sprinkle with parsley and serve.

OCTOBER 13 KUKU-YE GOL-E KALAM/CAULIFLOWER OMELET (PERSIAN)

Ingredients:

1 sm. head cauliflower (florets only), washed & drained

1 yellow onion, peeled & thinly sliced

2 garlic cloves, minced

¼ cup olive oil

4 eggs, beaten

1½ tsp. salt

½ tsp. black pepper

½ tsp. turmeric

¼ tsp. red pepper flakes

½ tsp. ground cumin

½ tsp. baking powder

Directions:

In a non-stick skillet, heat about 2 or 3 tablespoons olive oil over medium-low heat, then add the cauliflower, onion, and garlic. Sauté until lightly browned. Cover, lower heat, and allow steam to form in pan to soften the cauliflower (about 5 minutes). Remove from heat, mash, and set aside.

In a medium bowl, beat the eggs and add in the remaining ingredients. Combine. Next, add in the mashed cauliflower, onion, and garlic mixture. Pour the remaining oil into an 8" X 8" oven-proof baking dish and spread evenly around dish. Pour the egg mixture into the dish and place in a pre-heated 350 degree oven uncovered for 30 minutes or until top is set and a light golden brown. Serve with plain yoghurt on the side.

OCTOBER 14 COLLARD GREENS AND BROWN RICE PILAF

Ingredients:

1 tbs. olive oil

1 med. onion, thinly sliced

4 garlic cloves, minced

1 lg. bunch of collards, washed, drained, chopped

2 cups salted water

4 green onions, chopped fine

2 tbs. olive oil

4 tbs. toasted pine nuts

½ cup Bulgarian cheese, crumbled

Sea salt

2 cups cooked brown Basmati rice

Freshly ground black pepper

1 lemon, zested & juiced

Directions:

Using a 5 qt. sauce pot, heat olive oil over medium-high heat, then add in the onion and cook until translucent. Toss in garlic and cook for an additional minute. Add in the greens and water. Cover and simmer until leaves are tender (about 45 minutes).

In the meantime, prepare rice according to package directions. Drain and set aside.

In a large bowl, combine the lemon zest and juice, green onions, olive oil, pine nuts, and crumbled cheese. Toss gently. Add in the brown rice, drained collards, season with salt and pepper, to taste. Combine and serve at room temperature.

OCTOBER 15 **MEDITERRANEAN VEGETABLE BAKE**

Ingredients:

3 tbs. olive oil	¼ cup fresh basil, chopped
1 lg. onion, diced	¼ cup fresh parsley, chopped
5 garlic cloves, minced	2 cups Basmati brown rice, cooked
1 cup chopped fennel bulb	½ cup toasted pine nuts
2 cups cremini mushrooms, finely chopped	1 tsp. sea salt
½ cup sun-dried tomatoes, chopped	½ tsp. black pepper
½ cup Bulgarian sheep's milk cheese, crumbled	½ cup grated Fontina cheese
2 eggs	Spray oil

Directions:

Heat oil in a large skillet over medium heat then add onions, garlic, and fennel to pan. Sauté until onions and fennel are tender. Next, add in the mushrooms and tomatoes. Cook until all of the liquid has evaporated from skillet. Remove pan from heat and allow vegetables to cool completely.

In a large mixing bowl, mix together the cheese and eggs. Add the remaining ingredients as well as the cooled vegetables. Mix well.

Lightly coat a large loaf pan with spray oil. Place mixture in pan and cover with aluminum foil. Bake for 40 minutes in a pre-heated 375 degree oven. Remove from pan. Slice and serve.

OCTOBER 16 GEFILTE FISH (JEWISH)

Ingredients:

Broth:

3 onions, peeled

3 carrots, peeled

3 celery stalks

1 qt. water

2 tsp. each of kosher salt & black pepper

1 tsp. sugar

Heads & bones from fish

Gefilte:

2 lbs. fish, bone in (white fish, pike, or carp)

1 onion

3 eggs

3 tbs. matzo meal

¼ cup cold water

2 tsp. kosher salt

Directions:

Fillet the fish but reserve the bones and head. In a large stockpot, add in all of the ingredients for the broth as well as the heads and bones from the fish. Heat over medium-high heat, bring to a boil; then reduce heat and simmer for 2 hours. Strain the broth and place back into pot.

In the meantime, place the filleted fish and onion in a food processor and process until smooth. Add in the eggs, matzo, water, and salt. Pulse until well blended and a paste-like mixture has formed. Moisten hands and shape fish mixture into balls.

Drop balls into stock, cover and simmer on low for 1½ hours. Add water if stock has reduced. Carefully remove fish from stock, place in a bowl and pour remaining stock over the fish. Serve with horseradish.

OCTOBER 17 HARIRA (MOROCCAN RAMADAN SOUP)

Ingredients:

32 oz. organic vegetable stock

2 cups chopped yellow onion

½ cup brown lentils

½ cup crushed tomatoes

½ tsp. salt

¼ tsp. black pepper

½ cup fava beans

1/3 cup finely chopped celery

¼ cup fresh cilantro, chopped

¼ cup chopped fresh parsley

1 tsp. tomato paste

1-15 oz. can garbanzo beans

¼ tsp. powdered saffron   8 lemon wedges

Directions:

Using a large sauce pot, place first 7 ingredients in pot and bring to a boil over high heat, uncovered. When mixture has boiled, cover, reduce heat, and let simmer for 20 minutes. Then, stir in the next 6 ingredients. Increase heat and bring to a boil. Cover, reduce heat and simmer until vegetables are tender. Serve hot with lemon wedges and naan, if desired.

OCTOBER 18 STRING BEAN, ZUCCHINI, AND EGGPLANT STEW (MEDITERRANEAN)

Ingredients:

3 tbs. olive oil

1 bunch scallions, white & green parts, sliced

2 lg. garlic cloves, finely chopped

1-35 oz. can crushed tomatoes

1 tsp. salt

1 tsp. black pepper

1 tsp. oregano

2 cups fresh cut string beans

2 med. zucchini, cubed large

1 lg. eggplant, cubed large

Directions:

In a 5 or 6 qt. sauce pan, heat oil over medium heat. Add in the scallions and garlic. Sauté until scallions are translucent. Next, add in the tomatoes, salt, pepper, and oregano. Simmer on medium-low heat for 5 minutes. Add in the string beans, zucchini, and eggplant then cover and let cook until consistency is that of a thick stew. Serve with crusty bread.

OCTOBER 19 ROASTED PUMPKIN & BLACK BEAN CHILI

Many people only use pumpkins as a fall decoration; however, pumpkin can be used in so many recipes such as this hearty chili.

Ingredients:

4 cups pumpkin, cut into 1" cubes

Extra-virgin olive oil

1 lg. onion, diced

3 garlic cloves, minced

1 cup frozen corn

2-15 oz. cans diced tomatoes with liquid

1 bottle pumpkin beer (seasonal)

2 tbs. chili powder

1 tbs. oregano

½ tsp. cayenne pepper

2-15 oz. cans black beans, rinsed and drained   Salt and pepper

1-15 oz. can pumpkin puree'   Cheese and green onions for garnish*

Directions:

Place pumpkin cubes on a large rimmed baking sheet. Drizzle with oil; season with salt and pepper. Place in a pre-heated 400 degree oven and bake until tender and deep golden. Stir occasionally.

In the meantime, heat about 2 tablespoons, oil in a large sauce pan over medium-high heat. Add in the onion and garlic and cook until golden. Next, add in the corn, beans, and pumpkin puree'. Lower heat to medium and stir. Cook for 2 minutes. Add in the tomatoes, beer, chili powder, oregano, and cayenne. Stir and simmer for 15 minutes. Then add in the roasted pumpkin, season with salt and pepper and simmer over medium-low heat for an additional 30 minutes. Serve hot. *Garnish each bowl with shredded cheddar cheese or pepper jack cheese, and chopped green onions.

OCTOBER 20 KORMA (INDIAN)

Ingredients:

3 tbs. canola oil   1-4 oz. can tomato sauce

1 med. onion diced   1 tbs. salt

1½ tsp. fresh ginger root, minced   2½ tbs. curry powder

6 garlic cloves, minced   1½ cups frozen peas

3 white potatoes, diced   1 green bell pepper, seeded & chopped

6 carrots, diced   1 red bell pepper, seeded & chopped

2 jalapeno peppers, seeded & sliced   1½ cups heavy cream

¼ cup unsalted cashews, ground   3 cups steamed rice

Directions:

Heat oil in a heavy skillet over medium heat. Stir in onion. Cook until translucent. Next, add in the ginger and garlic and cook for 1 minute. Then, add in the next 7 ingredients. Cook for about 10-12 minutes, until potatoes are tender, stirring occasionally.

Finally, add in the last 4 ingredients through the cream. Reduce heat to medium-low. Allow to simmer for 15 minutes for all flavors to blend. Serve over steamed rice and may be accompanied with naan.

OCTOBER 21 **SMOKED BLUEFISH-APPLE HASH**

Ingredients:

1 cup sour cream

2 tbs. horseradish

4 tbs. butter

2 med. sweet potatoes, boiled, cooled & diced

1 sm. yellow onion, finely chopped

1 Granny Smith apple, diced

Salt & pepper, to taste

1/8 tsp. crushed red pepper

½ cup heavy cream

4 oz. smoked bluefish, flaked

1½ tsp. fresh dill weed

1 tsp. fresh chives, sliced

Lemon wedges

Directions:

In a small bowl, mix together the sour cream and horseradish. Chill until ready to use.

Heat a 12" or 14" cast iron skillet over medium-high heat. Melt butter in skillet; add in potatoes and cook until crispy (about 10 minutes), turning occasionally. Next, add in the onions and apples, and cook until tender, stirring occasionally. Season with salt and pepper; add in red pepper flakes, then stir in the cream. Cook for about 5 minutes without stirring. Using a large metal spatula, gently turn the hash. Cook for another 5 minutes, then carefully stir in the fish, dill, and chives. Remove from heat, and squeeze fresh lemon juice over the hash. Serve at once along with the chilled sour cream sauce.

OCTOBER 22 **MEXICAN FLATBREAD PIZZA**

Ingredients:

2-12" pre-made flatbread or pizza crust

2 tbs. canola oil

1 lg. onion, chopped

1-14 oz. can diced tomatoes, drained

3 cups shredded "4 Cheese Mexican"

½ cup sliced green olives

2 tbs. jalapenos, seeded & chopped

Directions:

Place pre-made pizza crust on 2 pizza pans in a pre-heated 400 degree oven for 10 minutes. Heat oil in a large skillet over medium-heat then stir in the onion and cook until slightly golden. Stir in the tomatoes. Cook together for about 8-10 minutes. Remove crust from oven. Divide sauce among the 2 crusts spreading equally.

Sprinkle 1½ cups of cheese over each crust. Spread sliced olives and jalapenos on each.

Place pizzas in a 350 degree oven and cook for about 15 minutes until cheese has melted. Slice into wedges and serve hot.

OCTOBER 23 BAKED FARFALLE WITH VEGETABLES

Ingredients:

8 oz. farfalle, cooked al dente	3 garlic cloves, minced
2 tbs. olive oil	1 tsp. fresh basil, julienned
1 med. eggplant, cubed	1 tsp. dried oregano
1 sm. zucchini, diced	¼ tsp. crushed red pepper
1 med. onion, chopped	1 cup ricotta
2 cups Roma tomatoes, chopped	1½ cups shredded mozzarella

Directions:

Cook pasta according to package directions to al dente and drain. Heat olive oil in a large heavy skillet over medium-high heat. Add in the eggplant, zucchini, and onion and sauté for 7-8 minutes, stirring frequently. Add in the tomatoes and garlic, sautéing for 3-4 minutes, stirring frequently. Stir in the pasta, basil, oregano, and crushed pepper.

Transfer pasta to a 9" X 12" baking dish. Next, stir in the ricotta. Mix well. Sprinkle mozzarella on top and bake in a pre-heated 375 degree oven for 20-25 minutes or until bubbly and crispy on top.

OCTOBER 24 BAKED FLOUNDER WITH TOMATO BASIL MARINADE

Ingredients:

2 green onions, white and green parts, sliced	1 tsp. sea salt
1-15.5 oz. can diced tomatoes, including juice	Juice of 1 lemon
3 tbs. fresh basil leaves, julienned, extra for garnish	2 tbs. olive oil
2 garlic cloves, minced	4-6 oz. flounder fillets
½ tsp. freshly ground black pepper	2 cups steamed rice

Directions:

With the exception of the fish and rice, combine all other ingredients in a medium bowl and let marinate in the refrigerator for 1-2 hours. Pre-heat oven to 375 degrees.

Place fillets on a baking sheet lined with parchment paper and bake for 10 minutes or until no longer translucent. Then top each fillet with the marinated vegetables. Return to oven for 5-7 minutes and serve.

Garnish with additional basil. Accompany with steamed rice.

OCTOBER 25 **KALE SOUP**

Ingredients:

2½-3 tbs. olive oil

1 lg. onion, chopped

5 garlic cloves, minced

1 bunch kale, stems removed, chopped

2-32 oz. containers vegetable stock

1-15 oz. can diced tomatoes

2 lg. white potatoes, peeled and diced

2-15 oz. cans cannellini beans, drained & rinsed

1 tbs. dried oregano

2 tbs. dried parsley

Sea salt & black pepper

½ tsp, crushed red pepper flakes

Seasoned croutons

Directions:

Heat the oil in large sauce pot over medium-high heat. Add in the onion and garlic and cook until tender. Next, add in the kale, stir and cover for 10 minutes on medium-low heat.

Stir in the remaining ingredients through the pepper flakes. Keep heat to medium-low and simmer for about 45 minutes until potatoes are tender. Serve hot and top with croutons.

OCTOBER 26 **BAKED EGGS WITH ACINE PEPE IN TOMATO SAUCE**

Ingredients:

3 tbs. extra virgin olive oil

1 med. onion, chopped

4 med. garlic cloves, minced

½ tsp. sugar

Salt & pepper

2 cups acine pepe pasta, cooked al dente

1-35 oz. can crushed tomatoes	4 lg. eggs
6-8 fresh basil leaves, julienned	1 cup grated Parmigiano-Reggiano cheese
½ tbs. oregano	

Directions:

In a medium sauce pan, heat oil over medium heat, add in onions and garlic and sauté until golden. Add the crushed tomatoes, basil, oregano, sugar, salt and pepper. Stir; cover with lid and simmer for 40 minutes on low heat.

In the meantime, prepare the acine pepe as directed on package, drain, and divide among 4 oiled 10 oz. ramekins. Generously spoon the tomato sauce into each ramekin and mix with the pasta.

Crack an egg on top of each ramekin and generously sprinkle with cheese. Bake in a pre-heated 375 degree oven until egg whites are set but yolks remain soft, 12-15 minutes.

OCTOBER 27 **CASSOULET (FRENCH)**

Ingredients:

¾ cup olive oil, divided	3-19 oz. cans cannellini beans, rinsed & drained
3 med. leeks, cut into ½"pieces	1 qt. water
4 med. carrots, peeled & diced large	4 cups coarse fresh bread crumbs
3 celery stalks, diced large	4 garlic cloves, minced
1 tbs. fresh parsley, chopped	¼ cup parsley, chopped
1/8 tsp. ground cloves	1 tbs. garlic, fine chopped
1 tsp. thyme	Salt & pepper
1 bay leaf	

Directions:

Heat half the oil in a large heavy Dutch oven over medium heat. Add in the leeks, carrots, celery, 1 tbs. parsley, cloves, thyme, bay leaf, and ½ teaspoon each of salt and pepper. Stir and cook until vegetables are tender. Next, stir in the beans and water. Simmer on medium-low, partially covered, for about 30 minutes.

In the meantime, pre-heat oven to 350 degrees. Cut a French baguette into thick slices and place in food processor to make fresh bread crumbs. Transfer crumbs to a large bowl, toss with remaining oil, minced garlic, and a dash of salt and pepper. Mix well. Spread crumb mixture over a baking sheet, place in oven and toast until crisp and golden. Stir when halfway done. Remove from oven, return to bowl, add in ¼ cup parsley and 1 tablespoon chopped garlic and let cool.

Remove bay leaf. Mash some of the beans to thicken the mixture. Sprinkle bread crumbs over cassoulet and serve hot.

OCTOBER 28 **EGGPLANT STIR FRY**

Ingredients:

3 tbs. sesame oil

2 med. eggplants, peeled & cubed

1 zucchini, cubed

1 green, red, & yellow, bell pepper, cut into strips

2 onions, thinly sliced

2 cups grape tomatoes, cut into 3's

Kosher salt

Freshly ground black pepper

¼ tsp. red pepper flakes

2 cups steamed rice

Directions:

Heat oil in a wok or large skillet over high heat and toss in all the ingredients with the exception of the tomatoes stirring frequently. Cook until vegetables are tender. Add in tomatoes and seasonings. Stir and cook for an additional 3-4 minutes. Serve over rice.

OCTOBER 29 **CREAMY SHRIMP AND WILD RICE SOUP**

Ingredients:

2 tbs. olive oil

1 lg. onion, chopped

1 lg. carrot, peeled & diced

2 stalks celery, diced

32 oz. low-sodium vegetable stock

¾ cup wild rice, rinsed & drained

1 tbs. melted butter

2 tbs. flour

2 cups half and half

Sea salt

Freshly ground black pepper

1 lb. medium raw shrimp, peeled & deveined

Parsley sprigs, for garnish

1 pkg. lg. seasoned croutons

Directions:

Heat the oil in a 5 qt. sauce pan over medium-high heat and add in the onion, carrot, and celery cooking until tender, about 5-7 minutes. Add stock and rice; increase heat to high and bring to a boil. Then, reduce heat and cover simmering for about 40 minutes until rice is tender.

Meanwhile, in a bowl, combine melted butter and flour to form a smooth paste. Add ¼ cup cooking liquid to paste and mix well. Stir into the large pot of soup. Cook until thickened and bubbling. Add in the half and half. Season with salt and pepper, then add in the shrimp and cook for 3 additional minutes. Garnish with parsley sprigs and serve with seasoned croutons.

OCTOBER 30 **STUFFED TROUT**

Ingredients:

1 cup olive oil, divided	4 oz. lump crab meat
1 med. onion, chopped	2 tbs. fresh parsley, chopped
½ red bell pepper, chopped	2 tbs. fresh lemon juice
3 garlic cloves, minced	4-8 oz. whole trout, sliced open lengthwise
1½ tsp. dried thyme	Sea salt
1 cup cremini mushrooms, chopped	Black pepper

Directions:

Pre-heat oven to 400 degrees.

Heat 2 tbs. oil in a large non-stick skillet over medium-high heat. Add in the onion, bell pepper, garlic and thyme. Sauté for 4-5 minutes, stirring frequently. Toss in the mushrooms and cook for an additional 4-5 minutes. Remove from heat and transfer to a bowl. Allow to cool. Stir in the crab meat, parsley, and juice when mixture has cooled down.

Pat fish dry with paper towels. Drizzle with olive oil and sprinkle with salt and pepper. Spoon ¼ of the vegetable/crab mixture onto one side of each fish and cover by folding over the other side.

Line a large rimmed baking tray with parchment paper. Arrange fish on the tray and drizzle with remaining oil. Bake for 20 minutes or until desired degree of doneness. Serve hot.

OCTOBER 31 *HAPPY HALLOWEEN!* **PUMPKIN SOUP**

Ingredients:

2 tbs. butter

½ cup chopped onions

2 tbs. flour

1 tbs. curry powder

4 cups vegetable stock

2-15 oz. cans pumpkin puree'

1 tbs. honey

1½ cups evaporated milk

1/8 tsp. nutmeg

Salt & pepper

Directions:

Melt butter in a medium sauce pan over medium heat and add in onions sautéing until translucent. Next, add in the flour and curry and stir until a smooth paste. Pour in vegetable stock and whisk until thickened. Add remaining ingredients, stir and bring to a boil. Reduce heat and let simmer on low heat for 30 minutes.

NOVEMBER 1 **HUEVOS RANCHEROS**

Ingredients:

4 tbs. olive oil

1 lg. onion, diced

2 tbs. chopped cilantro, divided

1-14 oz. can black beans, drained & rinsed

1 cup water

12 corn tortillas

8 eggs

1½ cups tomato sauce

1 cup Monterrey Jack cheese

1 cup cheddar cheese

2 med. tomatoes, diced

Directions:

Heat oil in a medium skillet over medium heat then add onion and cook until golden. Add in 1 tablespoon cilantro, beans, and water. Stir well, bring to a boil. Then, reduce heat and simmer for 5-7 minutes.

In the meantime, drizzle some oil into a large cast iron skillet, and heat over medium heat. Cook each tortilla on each side for about 30 seconds. Arrange 3 tortillas into each of 4 round individual casseroles overlapping so that the entire bottoms are covered. Also, leave approximately a 1" overhang at the edge of each pan. Spoon bean mixture into each casserole but create a well in the center for the eggs. Crack 2 eggs into each well (sunny side up), top with tomato sauce and bake in a pre-heated 375 degree oven for 6-8 minutes. Remove from oven, sprinkle with Monterrey Jack cheese, cheddar cheese, and tomatoes. Return to oven until cheese has melted. Garnish with remaining cilantro and serve immediately.

NOVEMBER 2 **GRILLED SHRIMP IN A BALSAMIC-MOLASSES SAUCE**

Ingredients:

Wooden skewers soaked in water

6 tbs. molasses

3 tbs. balsamic vinegar from Modena

¼ tsp. red pepper flakes

1½ lbs. lg. shrimp, peeled & deveined

2 tbs. fresh rosemary, chopped

Directions:

Soak wooden skewers in water for about 1 hour before using.

In a bowl, combine the molasses, vinegar, and pepper flakes. Thread shrimp onto skewers, and place on a pre-heated 300 degree grill. Grill for 1 minute on each side.

Base with sauce and grill each side for an additional 1 minute. Remove from grill, place on a platter, and garnish with chopped rosemary.

NOVEMBER 3 **SQUASH FRITTATA**

Ingredients:

Olive oil

2 sm. zucchini

2 sm. yellow squash

¼ cup diced onion

8 eggs

¼ cup heavy cream

Sea salt

Black pepper

¼ cup grated Parmigiano-Reggiano cheese

2 tbs. chopped fresh tarragon

Chopped chives, for garnish

Directions:

Heat oil in a non-stick skillet over medium heat then add in the zucchini, squash, and onion, one layer at a time. Brown both sides. Transfer to a platter that has been lined with paper towels.

Meanwhile, in a medium bowl, whisk the eggs, then add in the cream, salt, pepper, cheese, and tarragon. Blend well.

Drizzle additional oil in skillet and return squash to the pan. Pour egg mixture over the squash and allow to cook on stove for 2 minutes over medium heat then transfer to a pre-heated 350 degree oven for about 8-10 minutes or until the top is completely set. Remove from oven, invert onto a large round serving platter and garnish with chopped chives. Serve with grilled slices of bread.

NOVEMBER 4 **SPLIT PEA SOUP**

Ingredients:

¼ cup olive oil

4-5 garlic cloves, finely chopped

3 carrots, peeled and sliced

2 celery stalks, sliced

1 lg. onion, peeled & thinly sliced

1-16 oz. bag green split peas, washed & drained

1½ tbs. oregano

Water

Salt & pepper

Directions:

Heat oil in a 5 qt. saucepan over medium heat then add in the garlic and sauté until golden. Stir constantly. Do not overcook garlic.

Add in the carrots, celery, and onions and 2 cups of water. Cover and simmer for 10 minutes. Remove cover and add in additional ingredients then fill the remainder of the pot with water. Cook on low-medium heat for 3 hours until soup thickens, stirring occasionally to prevent burning on bottom of pot. Serve with croutons, crackers, or crusty bread.

NOVEMBER 5 **AUTUMN SALAD WITH ROASTED VEGETABLES**

Ingredients:

4 med. beets, peeled & lg. diced

¼ cup balsamic vinegar

1 med. butternut squash, peeled & lg. diced

Olive oil, for drizzling

2 tbs. dark brown sugar

6 cups mixed greens, washed & drained

1 med. red onion, thinly sliced

½ cup olive oil

1/3 cup balsamic vinegar

1 tsp. mustard

Salt & pepper

1/3 cup honey roasted pecan halves

1 lg. Granny Smith apple, diced

Directions:

Spread beets on a baking sheet. Drizzle with oil and vinegar. Bake in a pre-heated 375 degree oven until tender. Place squash on another baking sheet. Drizzle with oil and sprinkle with brown sugar. Mix well. Place in oven along with the beets and bake until tender as well. When beets and squash have completed baking, remove from oven and let cool.

In the meantime, transfer salad greens to a large bowl. Add in the apples, onions, beets, and squash. In a small bowl, whisk together the oil, vinegar, mustard, salt, and pepper. Pour over the salad. Sprinkle with pecans. Serve at room temperature.

NOVEMBER 6 **MUSSEL BISQUE PROVENCAL**

Ingredients:

2 tbs. olive oil	1 cup heavy cream
2 onions, chopped	1½ cups half & half
5 garlic cloves, minced	4 cups dry white wine
2 lg. carrots, peeled & diced	3 lbs. fresh mussels, cleaned
Sea salt & black pepper	½ tsp. crushed saffron
1-12 oz. can plum tomatoes, diced	¼ cup fresh parsley, chopped

Directions:

Heat oil in a heavy pot over medium-high heat; add in the onions and garlic and cook for 3 minutes. Add in the carrots, salt, and pepper. Cook for 5 minutes on low. Add in the tomatoes; cook for an additional 2-3 minutes. Next, add in the cream, half & half, and wine. Bring to a boil.

Toss in the mussels, cover, and reduce heat. Cook until mussels have opened. Discard any that have not opened. Stir in the saffron and parsley. Cook for another minute. Serve immediately with hard, crusty, sliced bread on the side.

NOVEMBER 7 **COLLARD GREENS-SPICY HOT**

Ingredients:

2 tbs. olive oil

1 lg. onion, chopped

4 garlic cloves, finely chopped

1 tsp. red pepper flakes

2 celery stalks, diced

2 lg. carrots, peeled & diced

1-15 oz. can black beans, rinsed & drained

1-15 oz. can black-eyed beans, rinsed & drained

1 tsp. chili powder

1 tsp. smoked paprika

¼ tsp. black pepper

1½ tsp. salt

1½ lbs. collard greens, washed & drained

1-32 oz. pkg. vegetable stock

Directions:

Heat oil in a 6 qt. sauce pan over medium-high heat the add in the onion, garlic, and red pepper flakes. Sauté until onions are translucent. Add in celery and carrots.   Sauté for 5-7 minutes. Next add in the beans, chili powder, paprika, pepper and salt. Stir.

Add collard greens and stock to pan and simmer on medium-low heat for 3 hours until greens are soft and tender. Serve hot.

NOVEMBER 8 **BAKED STUFFED YELLOW SQUASH BOATS**

Ingredients:

1½ cups water

1 cup rice

3 med. yellow squash

Olive oil

Kosher salt

Black pepper

½ cup flat leaf parsley, chopped

¼ cup unsalted pecans, chopped

1/3 cup dried currants

1 tsp. fennel seeds

1 tsp. minced ginger

Zest of ½ orange

2 tbs. freshly squeezed orange juice

¼ tsp. crushed red pepper flakes

Directions:

In a medium sauce pan over medium-high heat, bring water and rice to a boil then lower heat, cover, and simmer for 20-25 minutes. Drain and set aside.

In the meantime, pre-heat oven to 400 degrees. Line a rimmed baking sheet with aluminum foil.

Slice each squash in half lengthwise, scoop out the seeds and pulp, and remove the "neck" or top portion. Brush with olive oil and season with salt and pepper. Place on lined baking sheet and place in oven. Reduce heat to 375 degrees and roast until fork tender.

While squash is roasting, prepare the filling. In a large bowl, add about 3 tbs. olive oil, the rice, parsley, pecans, currants, seeds, ginger, zest, juice and pepper flakes. Stir well.

Fill each squash with the filling, return to oven and cook for an additional 20 minutes.

NOVEMBER 9 **ASIAN SPICY SALMON**

Ingredients:

4-4 oz. salmon fillets, skin removed	1 tbs. red curry sauce
1 tbs. sesame oil	½ cup orange juice with pulp
¼ cup red onion, chopped	1 tbs. dark brown sugar

Directions:

Pat salmon dry with paper towels. Heat the oil in a large heavy cast iron skillet over medium-high heat. Add salmon to skillet and sear for 2-3 minutes on each side. Reduce heat to medium and continue to cook until fish becomes opaque. Remove from pan, transfer to an oven-proof platter, and place in a 200 degree oven.

Increase heat under skillet back to medium-high. Stir in the onions and cook until translucent. Stir in the remaining ingredients and simmer until liquid is slightly reduced. Remove salmon from oven; place back into pan and spoon liquid over salmon covering each fillet. Serve hot. May be accompanied with steamed Basmati rice.

NOVEMBER 10 **NEW ENGLAND CLAM CHOWDER**

Ingredients:

2 tbs. butter	1 cup heavy cream
1 med. onion, finely diced	3 lg. potatoes, cubed
2 celery stalks, diced small	Salt and pepper
3 tbs. flour	3 bay leaves

2 cups whole milk

1 tbs. dried parsley

2-10 oz. cans chopped clams

1 tsp. dried thyme

Directions:

Melt butter in a large Dutch oven. Add in the onion and celery and sauté until tender, stirring frequently. While stirring, add in the flour and mix well with the onion and celery. Add the milk, juice from clams (but not the clams), cream, potatoes, salt, pepper, bay leaves, parsley, and thyme. Stir well. Bring to a high simmer. **Do not boil.** Stir frequently and when potatoes are tender, lower heat, add clams, and cook for just 2-3 more minutes. Serve with croutons or oyster crackers.

NOVEMBER 11 **VEGETABLE POT PIE**

Ingredients:

6 tbs. butter

1 cup flour

1 lg. yellow onion, diced

2 cups vegetable stock

10 oz. button mushrooms, sliced

4 tbs. heavy cream

1 cup carrots, diced

1½ tbs. fresh thyme, chopped fine

1 cup butternut squash, diced

1 tsp. salt

1 cup diced Russet potatoes

½ tsp. black pepper

1 cup frozen peas, thawed

1-10" pie crust

1 cup frozen pearl onions, thawed

1 egg yolk, beaten

Directions:

Melt butter over medium heat in a Dutch oven. Add onions and mushrooms into pot and sauté for about 4-5 minutes until mushrooms are tender. Next, add in the carrots, squash, and potatoes and cook for about 5-6 minutes, stirring occasionally. Add in the peas and pearl onions; cook for another 1 or 2 minutes. Sprinkle flour over the vegetables and stir. While stirring, add in the stock, cream, thyme, salt, and pepper. Increase heat to medium-high until mixture thickens and bubbles. **Do not allow to boil.**

Pre-heat oven to 375 degrees. Transfer vegetable mixture to a buttered 10" deep pie plate. Place pie dough on top and trim off any excess. Brush with egg yolk and, using a fork, cut slits in the top to release steam while baking. Bake for about 35-40 minutes or until crust is golden. Serve hot.

NOVEMBER 12 **OATMEAL, CHEESE, AND EGGS**

Who said oatmeal was just for breakfast?

Ingredients:

4 ½ cups milk

1 tsp. salt

1½ cups rolled oats

8 oz. extra sharp white cheddar, shredded

1 tbs. olive oil

4 lg. eggs

Sea salt

Black pepper

Directions:

Heat milk in a medium sauce pan over medium heat and bring to a boil. Add in salt and oats. Reduce heat and let simmer until mixture thickens (about 5 minutes). Stir in the cheese. Keep warm.

In the meantime, heat the oil in a non-stick skillet over medium heat. Crack eggs into pan and season with salt and pepper. Fry eggs but leave yolks a little runny.

Spoon oatmeal into 4 individual bowls. Top each with a fried egg and serve.

NOVEMBER 13 **VEGETABLE GRATIN**

3 slices artisanal sourdough bread

3 garlic cloves

3 tbs. olive oil

1/3 cup freshly grated parmesan cheese

4 lg. carrots, peeled & sliced into ½" thick pieces

2 lg. turnips, peeled & diced lg.

2 lg. yams, peeled & diced lg.

2 med. butternut squash, peeled & diced lg.

2 cups pearl onions, peeled

Salt & pepper

½ tsp. dried thyme

¼ tsp. ground nutmeg

2 tbs. brown sugar

Directions:

Pre-heat oven to 325 degrees. Place bread on a baking sheet and bake until crispy and dry. Remove from oven and rub each side of the bread slices with 1 clove of garlic. Allow to cool then cut into large cubes. Place in a food processor and pulse until coarse crumbs are formed. Transfer crumbs to a bowl, drizzle with 1 tablespoon olive oil, then stir in the cheese. Mix well and set aside.

Mince the remaining cloves of garlic. Heat remaining 2 tablespoons olive oil in a large skillet. Add in the vegetables, salt, pepper, thyme, nutmeg, and garlic. Cook until vegetables start to turn golden brown, stirring occasionally. Add in 1/3 cup of water and the brown sugar. Stir. Cover and simmer until vegetables are fork tender. Increase oven temperature to 400 degrees.

Transfer vegetable mixture to a large casserole dish. Sprinkle with bread crumbs and bake until top turns a deep golden brown. Serve hot.

NOVEMBER 14 SPINACH AND BEAN QUESADILLAS

Ingredients:

1-10 oz. box frozen chopped spinach, defrosted	¼ tsp. crushed red pepper
1-15 oz. can black beans	½ cup roasted red pepper, diced
3 garlic cloves	¼ cup med. salsa
1 tsp. cumin	2 cups shredded "4 Cheese Mexican"
1 tsp. chili powder	Tortillas
½ tsp. salt	Cooking spray

Directions:

Using a blender, add spinach and black beans (liquid included) and pulse until smooth. Add in the garlic, cumin, chili, salt, and red pepper flakes and pulse in blender. Transfer mixture to a bowl. Combine with roasted red pepper, salsa, and 1 cup of cheese.

In the meantime, heat the oil in a large skillet. While oil is heating, spread mixture on one half of a tortilla, sprinkle with cheese, then fold tortilla in half. Place in skillet and cook on each side until golden. Serve hot. Repeat the process.

NOVEMBER 15 SPAGHETTI WITH LEMON AND TOASTED PECANS

Ingredients:

1 cup pecan halves	2 lg. garlic cloves, minced
1/3 cup extra virgin olive oil	1 tsp. black pepper
½ cup grated Parmesan cheese	1 lb. spaghetti
¼ cup fresh lemon juice	1 cup lemon basil, julienned

2 tsp. lemon zest

Directions:

Toast pecans in a small skillet over low heat for about 7-8 minutes. Remove from heat and set aside.

Whisk together the oil, cheese, lemon juice, zest, garlic and pepper in a large bowl. Set aside.

Cook pasta in salted water according to package directions. Drain but reserve ½ cup pasta water. Add pasta to large bowl with oil mixture. Stir well. Garnish with the lemon basil and give a quick toss. If pasta is too dry, add in some of the reserved pasta water a little at a time. Serve immediately.

NOVEMBER 16 **ZUCCHINI CAPRESE PANINI**

Ingredients:

2 med. zucchini, peeled & cut lengthwise	Pinch of black pepper
1½ tbs. olive oil, divided	4 ciabatta rolls
2 garlic cloves, minced	2 med. ripe tomatoes, sliced
1½ tsp. balsamic vinegar from Modena	8 thick slices fresh mozzarella
Pinch of salt	12 lg. fresh basil leaves

Directions:

In a shallow dish, add in half the oil and all of the garlic. Stir well. Place the zucchini slices in dish one at a time and coat well on both sides. Heat a large grill pan and place the zucchini in pan. Grill each side until grill marks show. Transfer back to the shallow dish, drizzle with the vinegar, and sprinkle with salt and pepper.

Slice rolls in half and place on heated grill pan to toast sliced sides only. Remove from pan and brush outer sides with remaining oil. Layer the zucchini, tomatoes, mozzarella and, finally, the basil onto the bottom slices of each roll. Top with top halves and place sandwiches on a Panini press or same grill pan with a press and heat until warm and cheese has melted. *****NOTE: Eggplant could be substituted for the zucchini.**

NOVEMBER 17 **BLACKENED CATFISH SANDWICHES**

Ingredients:

1½ tsp. paprika	4-6 oz. catfish fillets
1 tsp. dried oregano	2 tbs. olive oil
¾ tsp. red pepper flakes	Coleslaw (from the deli)
¾ tsp. Old Bay Seasoning	8 slices thick artisanal bread, toasted

Directions:

Combine first 4 ingredients in a small bowl. Generously, sprinkle both sides of fish with the mixture.

Heat the oil in a large non-stick skillet over medium-high heat. Swirl pan to coat with oil. When pan is very hot, place fillets in pan and cook for 4-5 minutes on each side.

Place 1 fillet on each of 4 bread slices and spoon on coleslaw. Top with second slice of bread and serve. May be accompanied with vegetable chips.

NOVEMBER 18 **NEAR EASTERN CURRY (INDIAN)**

Ingredients:

2 tbs. canola oil	1-15 oz. can chickpeas, drained
1 lg. onion, finely chopped	½ head cauliflower, cut into 1" pieces
3 lg. garlic cloves, minced	1 lg. zucchini, sliced
2 tsp. grated ginger	1 butternut squash, peeled, cut into 1" cubes
3 tbs. curry powder	1-14 oz. can coconut milk
¼ tsp. cayenne pepper	8 oz. fresh string beans
1 tbs. sugar	1 lg. bell pepper, seeded, cut into strips
1 tbs. salt	2 tbs. fresh lime juice
1-15 oz. can diced tomatoes, drained	4 cups steamed rice for serving
1 eggplant, cut into 1" cubes	

Directions:

Heat oil in a large sauce pot over medium-high heat then add the onion and garlic cooking until golden. Add in the next 5 ingredients, stir, and cook for 1 minutes to allow spices to blend.

Add in the next 7 ingredients. Increase heat and bring to an active simmer, then reduce heat and simmer on low for about 2 hours or until vegetables are tender. Add in the string beans and bell pepper and continue to cook until tender. Stir in lime juice, give a quick stir and serve over rice.

NOVEMBER 19 **GOAT CHEESE AND SUN-DRIED TOMATO PIZZA**

Ingredients:

4-8 oz. round naan bread	2 tsp. dried oregano
8 oz. goat cheese, room temperature	Freshly ground black pepper
32 slices of sun-dried tomatoes	1/3 cup small fresh basil leaves

Directions:

Pre-heat the oven to 400 degrees. Place naan on 2 baking sheets lined with parchment paper. Divide cheese into 4 equal parts. Spread cheese evenly over each naan. Evenly arrange 8 sun-dried tomatoes on top of goat cheese. Sprinkle with oregano and black pepper and place in oven for 10 minutes.

Remove from oven and sprinkle with basil leaves. Serve immediately.

NOVEMBER 20 **BEAN CASSEROLE (TEX-MEX)**

Ingredients:

2 tbs. olive oil	1-14.5 oz. can Italian stewed tomatoes
1 lg. onion, chopped	1 jalapeno, seeded & finely chopped
2 cups instant brown rice	1 tsp. garlic powder
2 cups low-sodium vegetable stock, divided	½ tsp. salt
1-15.5 oz. can dark red kidney beans	¼ cup freshly ground black pepper
1-15.5 oz. can garbanzo beans	1 cup med. salsa
1-15.5 oz. can black beans	1 cup canned corn

1-15.5 oz. can black-eye peas   ¼ cup chopped cilantro

Directions:

Heat 2 tablespoons olive oil in a large Dutch oven over medium heat. Add onion and cook until translucent. Next, add all ingredients from rice through black pepper. Stir well and increase heat to bring to a boil, then reduce heat, cover and let simmer for 15-20 minutes. Stir in the salsa, corn, and cilantro. Cover and let simmer for an additional 15 minutes. Serve hot.

NOVEMBER 21 **CARROT-FENNEL SOUP**

Ingredients:

1 fennel bulb, thinly sliced	1 ½ tsp. salt
3 tbs. olive oil	1 tsp. thyme
1½ cups chopped onion	½ tbs. ground ginger
2 garlic cloves, minced	4 cups water
1 lb. carrots, peeled & sliced	1 tbs. toasted fennel seeds, for garnish
1 lg. sweet potato, peeled & sliced	Paprika, for garnish
2 med. apples, peeled, cored, & sliced	

Directions:

Remove the fronds from the fennel bulbs and cut into thin slices. Heat the oil in a large sauce pan over medium heat. Add in the fennel, onion, and garlic, and cook until the fennel and onion are soft. Toss in the carrots, sweet potato, and apples. Add the salt, thyme, and ginger. Stir. Next, add in the water and increase heat to medium-high to bring mixture to a boil. Then cover, lower heat and let simmer until the vegetables are tender, about 30-40 minutes.

In the meantime, place fennel seeds in a small skillet over medium-low heat and toast until slightly golden. Do not burn. Remove from heat and set aside.

When vegetables are fork tender, puree the soup either by using a blender, food processor, or an immersion blender until smooth. Re-heat until hot. Serve in individual soup bowls; garnish with toasted fennel seeds and sprinkle lightly with paprika.

NOVEMBER 22 **PENNE WITH LEMON RICOTTA**

Ingredients:

2 tbs. olive oil

4 garlic cloves, minced

2 sm. yellow squash, diced

½ cup vegetable stock

8 oz. arugula

4 oz. fresh mint leaves

12 oz. penne, cooked to al dente

1½ cups ricotta, room temperature

2 tsp. lemon zest

½ tsp. black pepper

1 tsp. sea salt

Directions:

Cook pasta according to package directions and drain. In the meantime, heat olive oil in a skillet over medium heat. Add in the garlic and cook until lightly golden. Add in the squash and sauté for 5 minutes. Next, add in the stock and heat for another 2 minutes. Toss in the arugula and mint.

Transfer pasta to a large bowl. Stir in the vegetable mixture.

Place ricotta in a bowl and stir in the lemon zest, salt, and pepper. Mix well.

Plate pasta into individual pasta bowls and spoon cheese mixture on top. Serve immediately.

NOVEMBER 23 **MASH PIYAZU/BEAN & ONION PORRIDGE (PERSIAN)**

Ingredients:

1 cup uncooked red kidney beans

Approx. 6 cups water

1 cup lentils

1 cup mung beans

5 whole med. onions, peeled

½ cups olive oil

7 med. onions, sliced

1 lg. garlic clove, minced

¾ cup cracked wheat (not pre-cooked)

¾ cup rice

3 tsp. salt

2 tsp. turmeric

1 tsp. black pepper

Directions:

In a large Dutch oven or stockpot, simmer kidney beans in water for about 45 minutes. Then, add in lentils and mung beans and simmer for an additional 30 minutes. Additional water may be needed. Stir frequently to avoid sticking to bottom of pot.

Peel 5 onions but add them whole to the porridge and simmer for about 40-45 minutes. When soft, remove from pot, mash well, and return to pot.

In a medium skillet, heat olive oil over medium heat and add in sliced onions and garlic. Sauté onions until golden and translucent. Add in remaining ingredients and stir well. Transfer to Dutch oven. Combine well and simmer for an additional 15 minutes. Serve hot with grilled flat bread on the side.

NOVEMBER 24 **SEARED SCALLOPS WITH LEMONY BABY SPINACH**

Ingredients:

5½ tbs. olive oil, divided	Salt & pepper
1 ½ tsp. grated lemon zest	4 cups baby spinach, rinsed & drained
2 tbs. fresh lemon juice	2¼ lbs. lg. sea scallops
1 tbs. chopped fresh dill weed	1 lemon, cut into wedges
¼ cup shallots, minced	

Directions:

Whisk together first 6 ingredients (using only 3 tablespoons oil) in a small bowl. Set aside.

Heat a large cast iron skillet over medium heat. Add in 1½ tablespoons olive oil. Once oil is hot, toss in the spinach and stir as it begins to wilt. Once done, transfer to a medium bowl and pour in the lemon dressing. Mix well and divide amongst 4 dinner plates.

Using the same cast iron skillet, heat 1 tablespoon olive oil over medium-high heat. Pat dry the scallops and add to skillet. Sear for 2 minutes on each side and divide evenly among the 4 plates, placing the scallops on a bed of spinach. Place lemon wedges on each plate and serve.

NOVEMBER 25 BLACK-EYED PEAS, NECTARINE & MANDARIN SALAD

Ingredients:

2-15.5 oz. cans black-eyed peas, drained

2 tsp. ground cumin

1 tsp. ground coriander

1 tsp. orange zest

1½ tbs. champagne vinegar

¼ cup olive oil

1½ tbs. fresh orange juice, not from concentrate

½ cup red onion, very thinly sliced

4 lg. nectarines, pitted & sliced

2 sm. cans mandarin oranges, drained

6 cups baby spinach, washed & drained

Salt & pepper

½ cup crumbled bleu cheese

Directions:

In a large bowl, combine the first 3 ingredients. In a smaller bowl, whisk together the next 4 ingredients. Add the onion into the black-eyed pea mixture. Next, slice each of the nectarines into 8 slices and toss those along with the mandarin segments into the black-eyed pea mixture as well.

Toss in the spinach and stir gently. Season with salt and pepper. Pour dressing over salad and toss thoroughly, but gently. Sprinkle with cheese and serve.

NOVEMBER 26 BAKED STUFFED SHELLS

Ingredients:

¼ cup extra virgin olive oil

1 med. onion, chopped

4 med. garlic cloves, minced

1-35 oz. can crushed tomatoes

16 oz. water

1 tbs. dried oregano

6-8 fresh basil leaves, julienned

1 tsp. sugar

1 cup grated Parmigiano-Reggiano cheese, divided

1 tsp. salt

¼ tsp. crushed red pepper flakes

1-12 oz. box of jumbo shell pasta

1-2 lb. container ricotta cheese

1 lb. shredded mozzarella, plus extra

Salt & pepper, to taste

<u>Directions:</u>

In a medium sauce pan, heat oil over medium heat and add in the onion and garlic. Sauté until golden. Add in the tomatoes and next 7 ingredients. Stir. Cover and simmer on low-medium heat for 1 hour.

Next, prepare pasta as stated on package but be sure not to overcook. The shells must remain firm to hold the filling. Drain and set aside.

In a large bowl, add in the ricotta, mozzarella, ½ cup grated cheese, salt, and pepper. Combine all ingredients.

Pour 2 cups of tomato sauce into a 9" X 12" roasting pan and spread to cover the entire bottom of the pan. Stuff each shell with cheese filling (about 1 tablespoon) and place the stuffed shells in the pan lined with the sauce. When pan is full, spoon more sauce on top and sprinkle with mozzarella and remaining grated cheese.

Bake in a pre-heated 350 degree oven for about 40-45 minutes or until cheese on top has melted and edges of shells begin to lightly crisp. Serve hot.

NOVEMBER 27 **SPICY CURRIED OKRA AND BASMATI RICE (INDIAN)**

<u>Ingredients:</u>

3 tbs. peanut oil	½ tsp. ground coriander
1 yellow onion, chopped	½ tsp. ground ginger
1 lb. fresh okra, sliced	1 tsp. spicy curry paste
½ tsp, turmeric	1½ tsp. salt
½ tsp. ground cumin	2 cups steamed Basmati rice

<u>Directions:</u>

Heat the oil in a large non-stick skillet over medium heat then toss in the onion and cook until translucent. Add in remaining ingredients (except rice). Stir well to combine. Reduce heat to medium-low and cover. Sauté for about 20-25 minutes or until okra is fork tender. Do not overcook. Serve over rice.

NOVEMBER 28 **SALMON LOAF**

Ingredients:

2½ lbs. salmon fillet

1 tsp. black pepper

2 tbs. mayonnaise

1 tbs. garlic powder

2 tbs. Dijon mustard

1 tbs. lemon juice

2 shallots, rough chopped

¼ cup bread crumbs

2 tbs. fresh dill weed, chopped

½ cup green olives stuffed with pimentos, sliced

1 tsp. salt

Directions:

Pre-heat oven to 350 degrees. Place all ingredients with the exception of the bread crumbs into a food processor and pulse until finely chopped. Remove from processor, place in a bowl and, using your hands, mix in bread crumbs and sliced olives.

Spray a loaf pan with spray oil and transfer salmon mixture into loaf pan forming into a loaf. Place pan in oven and bake for 40/45 minutes until mixture is set and top starts to turn golden. Remove from oven and let cool for about 10 minutes before slicing. Serve warm and accompany with a light salad.

NOVEMBER 29 **CRUNCHY ASIAN SHRIMP SLAW IN CABBAGE CUPS**

Ingredients:

For Dressing:

3 tbs. fresh lime juice

½ tsp. red pepper sauce

1 tsp. ground cumin

1/8 tsp. crushed red pepper

2 tsp. honey

For Salad:

10 oz. frozen corn in butter sauce

3 tbs. chopped fresh cilantro

2 cups tri-color coleslaw blend

3 oz. uncooked ramen noodles, coarsely crushed

2 cups shredded baby spinach

2 tbs. toasted sesame seeds

2 cups canned tiny shrimp, drained

6 lg. cabbage leaves, washed & dried

<u>Directions:</u>

For Dressing:

Place all 5 ingredients in a large bowl and whisk together. Set aside.

For Salad:

Cook corn as directed on package. Then add to bowl with dressing. Stir to combine. Allow to cool for 5-10 minutes then add the coleslaw blend, spinach, shrimp, and cilantro. Toss well to evenly coat. Add the crushed ramen to the salad as well as the sesame seeds. Give a quick stir.

Arrange cabbage leaves onto 6 plates and place the salad into the cabbage leaves. Serve immediately.

NOVEMBER 30 **CREAMY CORN CHOWDER**

<u>Ingredients:</u>

3 tbs. butter

2 celery stalks, finely chopped

2 garlic cloves, minced

1 onion, finely chopped

1 lg. red bell pepper, seeded & diced

1 lg. green bell pepper, seeded & diced

1 lg. potato, diced

3 cups organic vegetable stock

4 cups corn kernels, fresh or frozen, thawed

2 tbs. flour

1 cup heavy cream

1 cup half & half

Salt & pepper, to taste

<u>Directions:</u>

In a large sauce pan or Dutch oven, melt butter over medium heat. Add in celery, garlic, onion, red pepper, green pepper, and potato. Sauté until vegetables are soft and onions are translucent.

Next, stir in stock and corn. Bring to a boil, then reduce heat and let simmer for 15 minutes. Increase heat to medium, whisk in flour, cream, and half and half. Let simmer on low-medium heat for about 6-8 minutes then season with salt and pepper. Serve hot.

DECEMBER 1 **MUNG BEAN SOUP**

Ingredients:

5 cups water

2 cups mung beans, washed & drained

2 tbs. olive oil

1 lg. onion, finely chopped

4 cloves garlic, finely chopped

¼ tsp. crushed red pepper flakes

2 lg. carrots, peeled & diced

2 celery stalks, diced

10 oz. frozen spinach

Salt & pepper, to taste

32 oz. organic vegetable stock

Directions:

Place mung beans in a large sauce pan, add water and bring to a boil. Reduce heat to medium and cook until tender. Note: if water boils down, simply add more water.

In the meantime, in a smaller sauce pan, heat oil over medium heat. Add in onion, garlic, and pepper flakes. Sauté until onions are translucent and garlic is golden. Add in carrots, and celery cooking until tender.

Add vegetable mixture to sauce pan with beans; combine well. Next add in the frozen spinach, season with salt and pepper, then, add in the stock.

Reduce heat and simmer for an additional 20-25 minutes. Serve hot.

DECEMBER 2 **SAUTEED KALE WITH PINE NUTS & DRIED CRANBERRIES**

Ingredients:

1 lg. bunch of kale, washed & dried

1/3 cup pine nuts

2 tbs. olive oil

3 cloves garlic, finely chopped

¼ cup dried cranberries

Salt, to taste

Directions:

Remove stems from kale; discard stems, and roughly chop the kale.

Place the pine nuts into a small frying pan and turn on heat to medium. Toast the nuts until lightly golden on each side by giving a quick stir. Do not burn.

Pour olive oil into a large skillet, add garlic, and sauté until golden. Toss in the kale and let wilt for about 6-8 minutes. Turn off heat and toss in the pine nuts and cranberries; stir well. Add salt, to taste.

May be served with toasted flat bread or grilled sliced baguette.

DECEMBER 3 BAKED ITALIAN STYLE STUFFED SQUASH BOATS

Ingredients:

4 med. yellow squash	Salt & pepper
Olive oil	1 egg
1 lg. onion, diced	2 cups Italian style panko
4 garlic cloves, minced	1 cup grated Pecorino-Romano cheese, divided
1 tbs. dried basil	3-4 cups marinara sauce
1 tbs. dried oregano	

Directions:

Cut squash in half lengthwise. Scrape out seeds and pulp. Discard. Scrape out flesh and set aside.

Heat oil in a skillet over medium heat. Add in the onion and garlic cloves and cook until golden. Next, add the flesh of the squash and season with basil, oregano, salt, and pepper. Cook until very soft. Transfer to a bowl; add in the egg, panko, and ½ cup cheese. Mix well.

Stuff each boat with mixture, pour sauce on top and sprinkle with extra cheese. Bake in a pre-heated 375 degree oven until stuffing is golden and crispy on top.

DECEMBER 4 QUNINOA SALAD WITH SHRIMP

Ingredients:

1 cup cooked quinoa, as per pkg. directions	1½ tsp. fresh ginger root, grated
1 tbs. lime juice	2 garlic cloves, finely minced
1½ tbs. oil	½ lb. pre-cooked med. shrimp
½ cup chopped onion	½ cup fresh parsley, chopped
½ cup orange or yellow bell pepper, diced	

Directions

In a bowl combine the quinoa and lime juice. Set aside.

Heat oil in a medium skillet over medium heat and add in the onion and bell pepper. Cook until tender then add in ginger root and garlic. Sauté for 2-3 minutes.

Reduce heat to medium-low and toss in the shrimp. Sauté for an additional 2-3 minutes. Remove from heat and combine the shrimp mixture with the quinoa mixture. Stir well; garnish with parsley and serve.

DECEMBER 5 WHOLE WHEAT LINGUINE, TOMATOES, AND CLAMS

Ingredients:

4 cups grape tomatoes, halved

1/3 cup fresh Italian parsley, chopped

5 cloves garlic, minced

1 tsp. sea salt

½ tsp. freshly ground black pepper

1½ doz. littleneck clams, cleaned

12 oz. whole-wheat linguine

Directions:

Place tomatoes, parsley, garlic, salt, and pepper in a large bowl. Mix well. Set aside at room temperature.

In the meantime, cook the pasta according to package directions to al dente.

In a sauce pan bring 4 cups of water to a boil. Add in the clams and cook for 5-7 minutes until shells are fully open. Drain and discard any unopened shells.

Drain pasta and set on a large platter. Toss in the tomato mixture, and clams. Stir and serve immediately.

DECEMBER 6 ROCKFISH WITH PARSLEY-ONION SALAD

Ingredients:

3 cups fresh parsley, chopped

2 cups very thinly sliced yellow onion

1 tbs. lime juice

1½ tbs. extra virgin olive oil

Salt & pepper, to taste

1½ tbs. olive oil

4-6 oz. rockfish fillets, patted dry

Directions:

In a medium bowl, combine the parsley and onion together. In a small bowl, whisk together the lime juice, olive oil, and salt, and pepper. Pour over parsley and onion combo. Mix well and set aside.

Heat a large ovenproof skillet over high heat. Pour in the olive oil and swirl to coat. Sprinkle fish with salt and pepper, and add fish to pan. Fry until lightly browned on each side, then place pan in a pre-heated 400 degree oven and cook until desired degree of doneness.

Plate each piece of fish on 4 individual plates and spoon salad onto each plate. Serve immediately.

DECEMBER 7 **BAKED BRIE EN CROUTE**

Ingredients:

1-17 oz. pkg. frozen puff pastry sheet, defrosted	8 tbs. dried cranberries
8 tbs. fig jam or any jam of choice	8 tbs. chopped walnuts
8 oz. Brie cheese	1 egg, beaten, for brushing

Directions:

Pre-heat oven to 375 degrees.

Cut each puff pastry sheet into 4 squares for a total of 8. In the center of each square spread 1 tbs. fig jam. Next, place a small round of Brie on top of the jam then, sprinkle 1 tablespoon dried cranberries plus 1 tablespoon chopped walnuts around the Brie.

With a small brush, brush the egg all around the edge of each puff pastry square. Fold up all 4 corners creating pouches and seal at top. Place on a rimmed baking sheet lined with parchment paper. Then brush each pouch with the egg and place in oven. Bake for about 15-20 minutes or until crust is golden and puffy. Serve immediately.

DECEMBER 8 **ROASTED VEGETABLE AND RICOTTA PIZZA**

Ingredients:

1 lb. fresh store bought pizza dough	Spray oil
2 cups Baby Bella mushrooms, sliced	2 cups tomato sauce
1 cup diced zucchini	¼ cup grated Parmesan cheese

1 med. green bell pepper, diced	1 cup shredded mozzarella cheese
1 med. red onion, chopped	½ cup ricotta cheese
2 tbs. olive oil	1 tbs. dried oregano
½ tsp. freshly ground black pepper	

Directions:

Pre-heat oven to 475 degrees. Remove dough from refrigerator. Place in a greased bowl and tightly cover with plastic wrap. Let stand until dough rises to double in bulk (abut 30-45 minutes).

In the meantime, combine next 6 items on a baking sheet and toss well. Place in oven and bake for about 15-20 minutes.

Punch dough down and roll out to a 15" circle. Spray a pizza tray with oil, place dough on tray and spray with oil as well. Spoon sauce on dough but leave a ½" border all around. Sprinkle with Parmesan cheese and mozzarella. Top with roasted vegetables and dollops of the ricotta. Sprinkle with oregano and place in oven until crust is golden. Cut into wedges and serve warm.

DECEMBER 9 SAVORY SHRIMP, SPINACH, & ONION TURNOVERS

Ingredients:

2 tbs. canola oil	2 tbs. fresh thyme
2/3 cup orange bell pepper, diced	½ tsp. salt
2/3 cup yellow onion, diced	½ tsp. crushed red pepper
3 cups baby spinach, washed & drained	1-14 oz. pkg. refrigerated pie dough
2-4 oz. cans baby shrimp, drained	1 egg, beaten

Directions:

Heat oil in a large non-stick skillet over medium heat then add in the bell pepper and onion. Sauté until tender, about 3-4 minutes. Stir in spinach and cook until wilted. Stir in the shrimp, thyme, salt, and pepper, and remove from heat.

Pre-heat oven to 375 degrees.

Cut dough into 4 equal portions. Roll each into a 5" circle. Spoon vegetable and shrimp mixture over half of each circle but make sure to leave a ½" border. Fold other half over and tightly crimp edges. Place turnovers on a parchment lined baking sheet. Brush with egg and place in oven for about 20 minutes or until crust is golden brown.

DECEMBER 10 **SPICY FLOUNDER WITH BELL PEPPERS & ROSEMARY**

Ingredients:

4-6 oz. flounder fillets

2 tsp. garlic powder

½ tsp. sea salt

2 tsp. finely chopped rosemary

¼ tsp. black pepper

½ cup dry white wine

1 tbs. olive oil

1 cup no sodium vegetable stock

1 red bell pepper, cut into thin 2" long strips

4 tsp. flour

1 orange bell pepper, cut into thin 2" long strips

½ tsp. crushed black pepper

½ cup chopped shallots

¼ cup pitted sliced black olives

2 tbs. grated lemon zest

1 ½ cups cooked orzo

Directions:

Pat dry each fillet. Season with salt and pepper. Heat olive oil in a large non-stick skillet over medium-high heat. Add flounder and cook on each side for 2 minutes. Remove from skillet.

Next, stir in the peppers, shallots, zest, garlic powder, and rosemary. Cook until vegetables are tender but still firm. Pour in the wine and stir. Reduce heat to low and simmer until liquid has reduced to half.

Whisk together the stock, flour, and black pepper then add to skillet. Simmer until sauce has thickened. Return flounder to skillet and simmer for 2 minutes. Sprinkle with olives and serve with the orzo.

DECEMBER 11 **CREAMY MUSHROOM SOUP**

Ingredients:

¼ cup butter

1 tbs. chopped fresh thyme

1 cup chopped shitake mushrooms

2 tbs. flour

1 cup Portobello mushrooms

1-14.5 oz. container vegetable stock

2 shallots, chopped

1 cup heavy cream

1 garlic clove, minced

Salt & freshly ground black pepper

<u>Directions:</u>

In a large sauce pan over medium-high heat, melt butter and sauté the mushrooms, shallots, and garlic, until soft. Add in the thyme and sauté for an additional minute.

Next, stir in the flour until smooth. Gradually pour in the stock and stir. Cook until thick and bubbly, stirring continuously. Add in the heavy cream and season with salt and pepper. Reduce heat to low-medium and cook for 3 additional minutes. Serve in individual bowls.

DECEMBER 12 **BAKED PASTA WITH SPINACH AND BUTTERNUT SQUASH**

<u>Ingredients:</u>

6 cups diced butternut squash	5 cups baby spinach, rinsed & drained
Olive oil, for drizzling	2½ cups no sodium vegetable stock
Salt and pepper	2½ tbs. flour
1 lb. penne	½ tsp. crushed red pepper
2 tbs. olive oil	1 cup mascarpone
2 cups chopped onion	½ cup grated Fontina cheese
5 garlic cloves, minced	

<u>Directions:</u>

Pre-heat oven to 375 degrees.

Place squash on a large rimmed baking sheet. Drizzle with olive oil and sprinkle with salt and pepper then toss with hands and place in oven. Bake for about 30 minutes or until squash is tender.

Next, cook the pasta according to package directions, to al dente; drain.

In the meantime, heat olive oil in a large skillet, swirl to coat bottom of pan, toss in the onion and garlic. Cook until onions are translucent. Add in the spinach and continue to cook for 2 more minutes or until spinach has completely wilted.

For the sauce, bring 2 cups of stock to a boil. Whisk together the remaining half cup of stock and flour in a small bowl. Add flour mixture to heated broth and cook until thickened. Add in the crushed red pepper flakes, and the mascarpone.

In a large bowl, combine the squash mixture, pasta, spinach mixture, sauce, and Fontina. Toss well then transfer to a greased 9" X 13" baking dish and place in oven for about 30-35 minutes or until bubbly and browned.

DECEMBER 13 OATMEAL FOR DINNER WITH MUSHROOMS AND ASPARAGUS

Ingredients:

2 tbs. olive oil

8 oz. small Portobello mushrooms, cleaned and sliced

1 bunch baby asparagus, cut into 1" pieces

½ tsp fresh thyme

1 tsp. garlic powder

3½ cups whole milk

1½ cups heavy cream

2 cups rolled oats

1½ tsp. salt

½ tsp. freshly ground black pepper

Directions:

Heat the oil in a medium skillet over medium heat. Add mushrooms to pan and cook until tender. Remove from pan and set aside. Next, add asparagus to same pan. Cook until tender, not soft. Return mushrooms to pan and cook together with asparagus. Add in the thyme and garlic powder. Cook together for I minute more and remove from heat.

Combine milk and cream in a medium sauce pan. Bring to a boil. Stir in the oats and reduce heat. Add in the salt and let simmer on low until thick (about 5 minutes). Spoon oatmeal into individual bowls. Top with mushroom/asparagus mixture and season to taste. Serve hot.

DECEMBER 14 DEEP FRIED CALAMARI AND SHRIMP

Ingredients:

Calamari:

Vegetable oil for frying

1 lb. cleaned squid, cut into ½" thick rings, cut tentacles as well

2 cups all-purpose flour (use any leftover flour for the shrimp)

Salt & pepper

2 lemons, cut into wedges

1 cup marinara sauce

Shrimp:

Vegetable oil for frying

2 lbs. raw shrimp, peeled & deveined

2 eggs, beaten

½ tsp. each salt, garlic powder, & onion powder

2 lemons, cut into wedges

2 cups shrimp cocktail sauce

Directions:

Calamari:

Pour enough oil into a heavy deep sauce pan. Heat oil to 350 degrees. Mix flour with salt and pepper. Toss the squid into the flour to coat well. Add the squid to the oil in small batches; fry well until lightly golden and crispy. Using a kitchen spider or slotted spoon, transfer to a paper lined plate to drain excess oil. Place on a clean platter with lemon wedges. Sprinkle with salt. Place a cup of marinara sauce in the center of the platter for dipping.

Shrimp:

Pour enough oil into a heavy deep sauce pan and heat to 350 degrees. Beat the eggs in a small bowl then pour flour into another small bowl, adding in the salt, garlic powder, and onion powder. Mix well. Toss shrimp into the egg, draining excess then immerse in flour mixture, coating well. Deep fry until golden. Drain on a plate lined with paper towels. Transfer to a clean plate lined with lemon wedges. Place a small bowl of cocktail sauce into the center of the plate for dipping.

DECEMBER 15 **PASTA PUTANESCA**

Ingredients:

2 tbs. olive oil	2 tbs. capers, rinsed & drained
3 garlic cloves, minced	1 tsp. sea salt
2 tbs. anchovy paste	½ tsp. crushed red pepper
1-28 oz. can crushed tomatoes	1 lb. fettuccine, cooked to al dente
1 cup pitted Kalamata olives, chopped	½ cup freshly grated Parmesan cheese
1½ tbs. fresh Italian parsley, chopped	plus extra for serving

Directions:

Heat oil in a large skillet over medium heat then add in the garlic and anchovy paste, stirring constantly for 30 seconds. Add in the tomatoes, olives, parsley, capers, salt, and red pepper. Reduce heat and simmer for 20 minutes.

In the meantime, prepare pasta as directed on package. Drain and add to sauce. Toss together until pasta and sauce are thoroughly combined. Add in the cheese, toss again, and serve. Sprinkle cheese on each individual serving.

DECEMBER 16 **GRILLED TROUT WITH SAUTEED GRAPES**

Ingredients:

3 tbs. olive oil, divided	2 tbs. white balsamic vinegar
2 cups red & white grapes, halved	4-6oz. trout fillets
2 shallots, chopped	1 tsp. dried rosemary
Salt & pepper	1 tbs. chopped chives

Directions:

Heat 2 tablespoons oil in a medium skillet over medium heat then add in the grapes and shallots and season with salt and pepper. Cook for about 5-6 minutes until grapes begin to soften then remove from heat and let stand for 1-2 minutes. Stir in the vinegar and set aside.

Heat an indoor griddle pan over high heat. Brush trout on both sides with the remaining oil and season with salt and pepper. Place trout, 2 at a time, on griddle pan. Grill each side for 2 minutes or until grill marks show. Remove from heat and keep warm. Repeat process with remaining trout. Plate trout on a large serving platter, top with sautéed grapes and garnish with chives. Serve.

DECEMBER 17 **SHRIMP & GRITS**

Ingredients:

Grits:	**Shrimp:**
4 cups vegetable stock or water	2 tbs. butter
½ cup heavy cream	1 med. onion, finely chopped
1 cup quick cooking grits	2 garlic cloves, minced
1 tbs. unsalted butter	1 green bell pepper, chopped
¼ cup freshly grated Parmesan cheese	2 lbs. raw shrimp, peeled & deveined
Salt & pepper, to taste	¼ cup dry white wine

Directions:

Using a 5 quart sauce pan, over medium heat, add in the stock or water and cream and let simmer. Slowly add in the grits and constantly whisk until mixture has thickened. Next add in the butter, cheese, salt, and pepper. Stir well, remove from heat and set aside.

Melt butter in a 10"-12" skillet over medium heat, add in the onion, garlic, and green pepper and sauté until tender. Add in the shrimp and sauté for 1 minute on each side or until pink and no longer translucent. Add in the wine, salt, and pepper. Sauté for 5 additional minutes then remove from heat. Serve grits onto individual plates and spoon shrimp mixture on top.

DECEMBER 18 KUKU SIBZAMINI/POTATO PANCAKES (PERSIAN)

Ingredients:

4 med. potatoes, peeled, boiled, & mashed	½ tsp. black pepper
1 med. onion, finely grated	½ tsp. turmeric
3 eggs	½ tsp. fresh dill weed, chopped
½ tsp. salt	¼ cup canola oil

Directions:

In a medium bowl, combine the mashed potatoes, onions, eggs and seasonings. Mix well then shape into 3"patties.

Heat the oil in a non-stick skillet over medium heat. When oil is hot, place patties in skillet and brown on both sides.

Serve on individual plates with warmed flat bread, plain yoghurt, and a combination of fresh herbs such as basil, mint, and parsley.

DECEMBER 19 FISH SOUVLAKI PITAS WITH DILL SAUCE (GREEK)

Ingredients:

Sauce:

Pitas:

Sauce	Pitas
6 tbs. plain Greek yoghurt	4-6" pitas, cut in half
2 tbs. shredded cucumber	1 cup shredded Romaine lettuce
1 tbs. freshly squeezed lemon juice	½ cup very thinly sliced red onion
5 garlic cloves, minced	1 lg. seedless cucumber, sliced ¼" thick
1½ tbs. fresh dill weed, chopped	3 lg. Roma tomatoes, sliced ¼" thick

Fish:

3 tbs. extra-virgin olive oil, divided	¼ tsp. each salt & pepper

1 tsp. dried Greek oregano   8-4 oz. cod fillets

Directions:

For the sauce, combine the all 5 ingredients together in a small bowl. Refrigerate.

In a small bowl, whisk together the oil, oregano, salt, and pepper. Pour mixture into a baking dish and place fillets in same dish. Marinate 10 minutes on each side.

Heat the oil in a large non-stick skillet over medium-high heat. Place fish in skillet and cook until crispy on each side.

Divide fillets evenly into each pita. Fill each pita with lettuce, onion, cucumber, and tomatoes. Spoon sauce over each and enjoy!

DECEMBER 20 **MEXICAN STUFFED SHELLS**

Ingredients:

2 tsp. oil   1 cup taco sauce

2 jalapenos, finely chopped   1 cup cheddar cheese, grated

1 med. onion, finely chopped   1 cup Monterrey jack cheese, grated

4 garlic cloves, minced   **Toppings:**

2-14 oz. cans light red kidney beans   Sour cream

1 pkg. taco seasoning   Green onions, sliced

4 oz. mascarpone cheese   7 oz. black beans, drained

16 jumbo pasta shells   ¼ cup pitted black olives, halved

1½ cups salsa

Directions:

Heat the oil in a medium skillet over medium-heat then add in the jalapenos, onion, and garlic and sauté for 3-4 minutes. Add in the beans; reduce heat to medium-low, and simmer for 45 minutes. Do not let beans dry out. Add some water should this happen.

Next add taco seasoning to the bean mixture and prepare according to package directions. Stir in the mascarpone cheese and simmer on low until cheese has melted and becomes incorporated into the bean mixture. Set aside.

In the meantime, cook the pasta according to package directions to al dente. Do not overcook. Drain. Arrange shells in a 9" X 13" roasting pan. Stuff each shell with the fried bean mixture. Combine the salsa and taco sauce, pour over each shell then sprinkle the cheddar cheese and Monterrey jack cheese over each. Bake in a pre-heated 350 degree oven for 45 minutes. Remove from oven and top with the sour cream, green onions, black beans, and olives. Serve while hot.

DECEMBER 21 ROASTED VEGETABLE & GARBANZO BEANS WITH COUSCOUS

Ingredients:

1 med. zucchini, cubed small	½ tsp. black pepper
1 red bell pepper, cut into small thin strips	½ tsp. ground cumin
1 yellow bell pepper, cut into small thin strips	¾ cup grape tomatoes, sliced into 1/3's
1 sm. onion, chopped	2 tbs. fresh parsley, chopped
Olive oil, for drizzling	3 tbs. fresh lemon juice
2 cups water	1 tsp. fresh lemon zest
½ tsp. salt	1 tbs. olive oil
2 tsp. olive oil	1-15.5 oz. can garbanzo beans, drained
2 cups uncooked tri-color couscous	1/3 cup crumbled feta cheese

Directions:

Pre-heat oven to 400 degrees. Place cubed zucchini, sliced peppers, and chopped onion into a roasting pan. Drizzle with oil, toss, and place in oven for 40 minutes. Stir every 15 minutes. Cook until tender and slightly browned. Remove from oven and place in a large bowl. Set aside.

Bring water, salt, and oil to a boil in a medium sauce pan over high heat. Add in the couscous. Cover, remove from heat, and set aside.

Add the remaining ingredients to the garbanzo beans to the large bowl with the roasted vegetables. Combine well.

At the end of the 5 minutes, fluff the couscous with a fork. Transfer to the same large bowl and toss well. Sprinkle with feta and serve.

DECEMBER 22 **CANNELLONI WITH ALFREDO SAUCE**

Ingredients:

Cannelloni:	**Alfredo Sauce:**
1-16 oz. box cannelloni	1¼ sticks unsalted butter
2 lbs. ricotta cheese	1 cup flour
¾ cup freshly grated Parmesan, + ¼ cup for sprinkling	6 cups milk
½ cup chopped fresh parsley	1 tsp. salt
½ tsp. salt	½ tsp. white pepper
½ tsp. white pepper	¼ cup grated Parmesan cheese

Directions:

Cannelloni:

Follow directions on package to cook pasta. Cook until tender but yet firm to allow for stuffing. Drain pasta.

In a medium bowl, combine the next 5 ingredients. Fill the pasta with the cheese mixture and place in a baking dish that has been coated with the Alfredo Sauce (see below). Spoon the rest of the sauce over the pasta and sprinkle with the remaining ¼ cup Parmesan cheese. Place in a pre-heated 350 degree oven until bubbly and top turns golden (about 40-45 minutes).

Alfredo Sauce:

Melt butter in a medium sauce pan over medium heat. Add the flour and whisk until a smooth paste forms. Add the milk, salt, and pepper, whisking constantly until a thick creamy sauce has formed. Add in the cheese, stir, and remove from heat.

DECEMBER 23 **NO-FUSS VEGGIE POCKETS**

Ingredients:

1 tsp. olive oil	¼ cup onion, chopped
1 cup zucchini, peeled and diced	1 tbs. dried oregano
1 cup broccoli florets, chopped small	½ cup shredded mozzarella cheese
½ cup mushroom, chopped small	1/3 cup tomato sauce
¼ cup red bell pepper, diced	1 lb. pizza dough

Directions:

In a medium skillet, heat oil over medium heat. Add in the zucchini and broccoli and sauté until fork tender, about 3-4 minutes.

Meanwhile in a medium bowl, combine the mushrooms, peppers, onion, oregano, mozzarella, and sauce. Add in the zucchini and mushroom mixture when done and combine.

Pre-heat oven to 400 degrees.

Divide pizza dough in half and roll out each piece into a 10" square. Then cut in half lengthwise and widthwise to form eight 5" squares.

Divide the vegetable mixture and place in the center of each of the 8 squares. Fold the four corners of each square up over filling and pinch edges together to seal. Place each pocket onto a rimmed baking sheet that has been lined with parchment paper and bake until golden, about 20 minutes. Serve hot.

DECEMBER 24 *CHRISTMAS EVE* SHRIMP SCAMPI

Ingredients:

2 lbs. jumbo raw shrimp, peeled & deveined	1/3 cup dry white vermouth or sherry
Salt & pepper	1½ tbs. fresh lemon juice
3 tbs. unsalted butter	2 tbs. chopped fresh parsley, divided
5 cloves garlic, minced	¼ tsp. crushed red pepper flakes

Directions:

Pat shrimp dry with paper towels and season with salt and pepper. Melt butter in a large skillet over medium heat. Once butter has completely melted, quickly add the shrimp as a single layer so that they will cook evenly. Cook for 1 minute and then add the garlic. Cook for an additional minute. Quickly turn all of the shrimp over and cook for 1-2 more minutes or until pink and opaque. Do not overcook because they will become rubbery. Remove shrimp from skillet and set aside on a serving platter.

Using the same skillet, add the vermouth or sherry and the lemon juice. Bring to a boil. Add 1 tablespoon parsley and crushed red pepper. Pour juice evenly over the shrimp and sprinkle with remaining parsley. Serve immediately. ***NOTE:** You may serve with linguine and garlic and oil on the side if you like or a light salad.

Ingredients:

Sauce:

3 tbs. extra virgin olive oil

1 med. onion, chopped

4 med. garlic cloves, minced

1-35 oz. can crushed tomatoes

16 oz. water

1 tbs. dried oregano

6-8 basil leaves

1 tsp. sugar

¼ cup grated Parmigiano-Reggiano cheese

1 tsp. salt

¼ tsp. crushed red pepper flakes

Crepes:

7 eggs

3 cups flour

3 cups water

1½ tsp. salt

Olive oil

Filling:

3 lbs. ricotta

1½ lb. shredded mozzarella, divided

1 ½ cups grated Parmigiano-Reggiano

Salt & pepper, to taste

Directions:

Sauce:

Heat the oil in a 5 qt. sauce pan over medium heat then add in the onions and garlic. Cook until golden. Add in the crushed tomatoes and remaining ingredients. Stir, cover, and simmer on medium low heat for about 1 hour.

Crepes:

In a large bowl, beat the eggs using a hand mixer. Add in the flour, water, and salt and continue to mix until a smooth batter has formed. Heat a 6" non-stick skillet over a moderately high heat. Brush the skillet with oil and heat pan until hot. Ladle about ¼ cup of the batter into the middle of the pan and swirl to coat entire bottom of pan. Cook for about 1 minute until crepe is firmly set on top and the bottom is golden. When crepe is done, slide onto a large platter. Continue this process until the batter has been completely used. Place wax paper in between layers. *****Note:** The manicotti crepes can be made 1 day in advance. Just cover with plastic wrap and store in refrigerator.

Filling:

Combine the ricotta, 1 lb. of the mozzarella, 1 cup of the grated cheese, salt and pepper into a large bowl and stir well combining all ingredients.

To assemble and fill each crepe, place 1 crepe at a time on a clean work surface (the browned side should face up). Spoon approximately 2-3 tablespoons of the cheese filling into the middle, and then roll up the crepe folding in the sides in order to keep in the filling. Once all the crepes have been filled, spoon about 2 cups of sauce into a 9" X 12" roasting pan and swirl to cover the entire pan with the sauce. Place the manicotti one layer at a time with the seam side facing down. Spoon sauce over tops of each crepe; sprinkle with mozzarella and remaining grated cheese. Do the same with the next layer or use another pan for additional crepes if only 1 layer is desired. Bake in a pre-heated 350 degree oven for 40 minutes or until cheese has melted and edges begin to slightly crisp.

DECEMBER 26 **SPICY ISRAELI COUSCOUS WITH BUTTERNUT SQUASH AND PISTACHIOS**

Ingredients:

5 tbs. olive oil, divided

1 med. shallot, chopped

3 lg. garlic cloves, minced

½ tsp, crushed red pepper flakes

2 cups butternut squash, peeled, & sm. cubed

Kosher salt & black pepper

1 tbs. ground cumin

½ tsp. ground cinnamon

2 cups vegetable stock

½ tsp. salt

2 cups Israeli couscous

¼ cup fresh cilantro, chopped

1/3 cup chopped unsalted pistachios

Directions:

Pre-heat oven to 375 degrees.

Heat 1 tablespoon olive oil in a small skillet over medium heat. Add in the shallots, garlic, and pepper flakes. Cook until golden.

Place squash on a rimmed baking sheet. Drizzle with 2 tablespoons olive oil and sprinkle with salt, pepper, cumin, and cinnamon. Toss then place in oven for 40 minutes, stirring occasionally, until tender and slightly golden. Remove from oven and set aside.

In a medium sauce pan over medium-high heat, bring stock, along with 2 tablespoons oil, and salt to a boil. Add in the couscous and stir. Cover, remove from heat and set aside for 7-8 minutes. Then fluff with a fork.

Combine all ingredients into 1 large bowl. Sprinkle with cilantro and pistachios. Give a quick toss and serve.

DECEMBER 27 **CHIP CRUSTED FISH FILLETS**

Ingredients:

4-6 oz. cod or haddock fillets

2 oz. kettle-style potato chips, crushed

2 tsp. olive oil mayonnaise

½ cup tartar sauce or creamy Caesar dressing

Dash of salt and pepper

Directions:

Pre-heat oven to 400 degrees.

Arrange fillets on a non-stick baking tray. Brush mayonnaise on top of each piece of cod. Sprinkle with a dash of salt and pepper over each. Using your hands, gently press crushed chips on top of each fillet. Place in oven and cook until golden brown (about 10-12 minutes).

Serve hot with your favorite dipping sauce!

DECEMBER 28 **PEPERONATA ON ROSEMARY FOCACCIA**

Ingredients:

¼ cup extra virgin olive oil

Sea salt & black pepper

5 bell peppers (2 red, 1 yellow, 1 orange, 1 green)

½ tsp. crushed red pepper flakes

  seeded & sliced thin vertically

1½ tsp. oregano

2 red onions, sliced very thin and round,

¼ cup toasted pine nuts

  so that each slice forms a circle

3 tbs. capers, rinsed & drained

4 lg. garlic cloves minced

2 tbs. balsamic vinegar

1 tbs. thyme

Rosemary focaccia

Directions:

Heat the oil in a very large heavy skillet over medium heat. Add in the next 6 ingredients. Cool until peppers and onions are tender but not overly soft. Do not brown. Stir frequently. When done, turn off heat, and add in the next 4 ingredients. Stir well to combine and allow flavors to blend.

Transfer to a large platter. Place large pieces of focaccia all around the platter and everyone can help themselves to a serving of bread and peperonata.

DECEMBER 29 ISRAELI COUSCOUS WITH EGGPLANT AND PLUM TOMATOES (MIDDLE EASTERN)

Ingredients:

3 tbs. olive oil

2 shallots, chopped

8 garlic cloves, minced

1 med. eggplant, peeled & diced

1-12 oz. can plum tomatoes with juice, chopped

1 tsp. ground turmeric

1 tsp. red pepper flakes

1 tsp. hot paprika

Kosher salt & black pepper

1¾ cup no sodium vegetable stock

1½ cups Israeli couscous

¼ cup fresh cilantro, chopped

8 fresh basil leaves, julienned

Directions:

Heat oil in a large non-stick skillet over medium heat then add in the shallots, garlic, and eggplant. Cook until eggplants are tender. Next, add in the tomatoes, juice, and next 4 ingredients. Cover, and reduce heat to low. Cook for 20 minutes.

Bring the stock to a boil in a medium sauce pan over medium-high heat. Add in the couscous and stir. Cover and reduce heat to low for 7-8 minutes.

Combine the eggplant mixture with the couscous on a large platter. Sprinkle with cilantro and basil and serve.

DECEMBER 30 FISH KABOBS AND ROASTED TOMATO SALAD

Ingredients:

Fish Kebabs:

¼ cup freshly squeezed lemon juice

2 garlic cloves, finely chopped

¼ cup fresh dill weed, finely chopped

2 lbs. white fish, cut into 1" cubes

2 red bell peppers, cut into 1" pieces

Extra virgin olive oil

Salt and pepper

8 metal skewers

1 pint grape tomatoes

2 yellow squash, cut into ½" slices, skin on

Directions:

Fish Kababs:

In a medium bowl, whisk together the lemon juice, garlic, and dill. Add in the fish. Stir, then cover with plastic wrap and refrigerate for 1 hour.

Next, heat indoor grill pan. Alternately thread skewers with fish, tomatoes, squash, and peppers. Brush with olive oil and season with salt and pepper. Place skewers over medium heat and grill each side for no more than 6-8 minutes.

Ingredients:

Roasted Tomato Salad:

2 lg. beefsteak tomatoes, sliced thickly	1 sm. red onion, chopped
Olive oil for drizzling	4 tbs. olive oil
Salt & pepper	3 tbs. balsamic vinegar
6 cups baby spinach, washed & drained	Sea salt & black pepper
1-8 oz. container crumbled herbed feta cheese	8 slices crusty French sliced baguette

Directions:

Roasted Tomato Salad:

Pre-heat oven to 400 degrees.

Place tomatoes on a rimmed baking sheet, drizzle with oil and sprinkle with salt and pepper. Place in oven until roasted, about 10-15 minutes. In the meantime, place spinach in a large salad bowl and toss with feta and onions. Add in the oil, vinegar, salt and pepper. Mix well. Divide onto 4 dinner plates. Place roasted tomatoes on each along with 2 slices of bread and drizzle all with olive oil. Evenly divide the fish kebabs onto each plate as well.

DECEMBER 31 *NEW YEAR'S EVE* **SALMON WITH DILLED RICE**

Ingredients:

4-4 oz. cuts of salmon

8 pats butter

¾ cup fresh lime juice

2 cups Basmati rice

1 tsp. turmeric

1 bunch fresh dill, finely chopped

1½ tsp. garlic powder

Olive oil

Kosher salt and coarse black pepper

Directions:

Place the salmon into a glass baking dish and pour in the fresh lime juice. Next, sprinkle on the turmeric and garlic powder over each piece. Season with salt and pepper and place 2 thin pats of butter on top of each salmon. Cover tightly with plastic wrap and place in refrigerator 4-6 hours or overnight.

Pre-heat oven to 350 degrees; remove plastic wrap and place baking dish in the oven for about 25-30 minutes, basting occasionally.

In the meantime, steam rice according to directions on package, but 3 minutes before rice is done, add fresh dill and lightly drizzle with olive oil then cover by placing a large paper towel over top and set lid over paper towel to steam properly. Toss with a fork before serving alongside of salmon.

Acknowledgments

When I first came up with the concept of creating a vegetarian cookbook with a new recipe for everyday of the year, many people thought I was crazy to try to spend so much time creating 365 recipes. But there were two individuals in particular who encouraged me to do so and they would be my Aunt Julia Lamparelli and my Uncle Danny Pagliarella. I would like to thank you both for believing in me and encouraging me to continue with my writing. I am truly honored that you are proud of my accomplishments and I love you both. And thanks to all my loyal friends who cheered me on during the writing process.

I would also like to thank my husband for his patience with me in the time it took to write this second cookbook because it took many long and arduous hours to not only research but to create, experiment, and tweak 365 recipes! It was a great idea when I first thought of it but I did not realize what I was getting myself into. Seriously though, I am very pleased with the way it turned out and I hope you will be as pleased with it as well.

Made in the USA
Lexington, KY
13 April 2015